D0734373

The Complete Guide to B2B Marketing

The Complete Guide to B2B Marketing

New Tactics, Tools, and Techniques to
Compete in the Digital Economy

Kim Ann King

Publisher: Paul Boger
Editor-in-Chief: Amy Neidlinger
Acquisitions Editor: Charlotte Maiorana
Operations Specialist: Jodi Kemper
Cover Designer: Chuti Prasertsith
Managing Editor: Kristy Hart
Senior Project Editor: Betsy Gratner
Copy Editor: Cheri Clark
Proofreader: Sarah Kearns
Indexer: Tim Wright
Senior Compositor: Gloria Schurick
Manufacturing Buyer: Dan Uhrig

© 2015 by Kim Ann King
Published by Pearson Education, Inc.
Upper Saddle River, New Jersey 07458

For information about buying this title in bulk quantities, or for special sales opportunities (which may include electronic versions; custom cover designs; and content particular to your business, training goals, marketing focus, or branding interests), please contact our corporate sales department at corpsales@pearsoned.com or (800) 382-3419.

For government sales inquiries, please contact governmentsales@pearsoned.com.

For questions about sales outside the U.S., please contact international@pearsoned.com.

Company and product names mentioned herein are the trademarks or registered trademarks of their respective owners.

All rights reserved. No part of this book may be reproduced, in any form or by any means, without permission in writing from the publisher.

Printed in the United States of America

First Printing April 2015

ISBN-10: 0-13-408452-7
ISBN-13: 978-0-13-408452-7

Pearson Education LTD.
Pearson Education Australia PTY, Limited
Pearson Education Singapore, Pte. Ltd.
Pearson Education Asia, Ltd.
Pearson Education Canada, Ltd.
Pearson Educación de Mexico, S.A. de C.V.
Pearson Education—Japan
Pearson Education Malaysia, Pte. Ltd.

Library of Congress Control Number: 2015930938

In memory of Danny Lewin and Wendy Ziner Ravech

For Bill and Shoo Shoo, with all my love

Contents

Foreword

It's a New Day, and I'm Feeling Good

It's no wonder that these timeless lyrics from the 1965 hit single have resonated through the ages. It isn't just Nina Simone's deep, unparalleled contralto or the muffled appeal of the early recording; there's nothing more seductive than the concept of a new age beginning. This iconic song perfectly embodies the world it was born into—an era that was new, visceral, evolving at lightning speed, and filled with unprecedented ideas. I can only imagine the feeling that the music executives had when Nina's words washed over them for the first time, but I imagine it was a sense of tingling excitement, optimism, and awe. It's a feeling that accompanies most new ages, including the new age of business-to-business marketing that Kim Ann King flawlessly describes and guides us through in the pages of this book.

In the '60s, the advertising world was caught up in a mixture of visual appeal and direct action. There were five marketing channels to master, and sales teams were still answering telephones. The B2C world was filled with slogans and jingles that sold everything from soap to cars, yet B2B marketing was relegated to the dingy world of trade publications and trade shows. Marketers as a whole were thought of as nothing more than a group of people making subjective guesses on their impact to the bottom line, and outside of the B2C world, they were given very little credit for their efforts. The world they marketed in was disconnected, subjective, and static.

Since then, the marketing world has seen generations of progress, movement, and advancements in technology. The bright lights of mass marketing have finally set, and the new day of true one-to-one communication has dawned—one that Kim has meticulously outlined in the next 200-plus pages. This new age rewards the businesses that can build personal relationships at scale, by understanding that an interplay of all marketing mediums is necessary to speak to a *single* prospect with relevant messages at the correct time. By using data-driven strategies to identify, nurture, and convert higher-quality leads in a shorter time, modern businesses can bridge the gap between marketing and sales to form one cohesive revenue department. This is the future of B2B marketing—a future that requires a complete view of the marketing landscape, including the changes in buyer habits and modern strategy that Kim discusses in this book. Her in-depth analysis of modern B2B marketing and buyer trends describes a marketing environment that is anything but flat and outlines an inarguable case for investment in modern tools and techniques.

As you progress through the book, you'll get a deeper look at the modern B2B marketer, including specific use cases, teachings on how to attract more potential prospects into your marketing funnel, tips for turning your prospects into actual closed business, and advice to help you increase the lifetime value of those customers. To go along with this new insight, you'll need to learn a new set of tools. Kim explores how this new world of tools can help scale your marketing, prove the value on your marketing efforts, and manage a much larger marketing effort with less work.

You have begun your journey with this book, but it will not stop here. I implore you to be a diligent student of your craft and use this reading to set a new foundation—one that you can continue to build upon over time. Take Kim's message to heart: Make one cohesive effort to unite your people, processes, and technologies, and continue to strive for operational excellence. Today's new age of marketing sets a higher bar for B2B marketers, and Kim does a wonderful job guiding us through the vastness of new tools, techniques, and best practices to hit the higher mark. Let her words sink in just as Nina's words impacted the music executives on the couch. Hear them for the first time, notice the change in the air, and feel the promise of a new way to drive results.

Mathew Sweezey
Marketing Evangelist, Pardot—a salesforce.com company
Author, *Marketing Automation for Dummies*

Acknowledgments

This book would not have happened had Judah Phillips not introduced me to his publisher at Pearson. Thank you, Judah, for helping to make my dream of publishing a book come true.

I am a huge fan of Mathew Sweezey and honored that he has contributed the foreword; thank you.

I'd like to thank the colleagues who graciously agreed to be interviewed for this book. To Jane Buck, Stefanie Lightman, Alex MacAaron, John Matera, Hans Riemer, and Heidi Unruh; thank you so much for sharing your expertise with the world.

Although I came to the position with decades of experience, I have learned so much more about B2B marketing during my tenure as Chief Marketing Officer of SiteSpect. Thank you, Eric Hansen and Larry Epstein, for taking a chance on someone who was unknown to you—I am so proud of what we've accomplished so far at SiteSpect.

Lastly, thanks go to Jeanne Levine, Charlotte Maiorana, Betsy Gratner, and all the dedicated professionals at Pearson who have guided me through the incredible voyage of publishing my first book; thank you very much for this opportunity.

About the Author

Kim Ann King serves as the Chief Marketing Officer of SiteSpect, Inc. (www.sitespect.com), a leading web and mobile optimization solutions provider. There, she is responsible for brand awareness, demand generation, and organizational enablement initiatives. King is the founder of New Leaf Communications, a boutique marketing consultancy. Over the past three decades, she has built high-tech B2B brands and helped to launch several Internet companies. Her high-impact, cost-effective marketing initiatives have consistently achieved brand recognition, marketplace differentiation, and customer acquisition and loyalty at companies including Bit9, Akamai Technologies, and Open Market. King has authored numerous articles on e-commerce, marketing, and optimization. She holds an M.S. in Communications Management from Simmons College and a B.S. in Public Relations with honors from Boston University.

Follow Kim on Twitter: http://twitter.com/kimannking.

Preface

You are holding in your hands a book 30 years in the making; that's how long I've been practicing marketing. It has only been in the past 5 years that marketing has morphed into an almost unrecognizable profession, due to the recent collision of data, creative, strategy, and technology.

When I started working in 1985, it was easy to craft a career first in financial services marketing and then in academic marketing with a little bit of writing talent and some creativity. Still, it was anything but glamorous. The advent of desktop publishing into corporate America was still a couple of years away, and so I typed out newsletter columns on a typewriter, cut and pasted them into layouts, copied them on a photocopier, and mailed them out in stamped #10 envelopes. I developed photographs with chemicals. It didn't seem inefficient or unproductive at the time, but it sure does now.

Ten years later, something big happened: The World Wide Web was commercialized. In 1995, I joined one of the first e-commerce pioneers, Open Market, and since then, I haven't looked back. It was my first foray into the world of B2B marketing, and I'd found my professional comfort zone. B2B marketing was so different from the consumer world—trying to reach not just one potential buyer, but a whole buying committee—in various companies across multiple industries. This enormous challenge was very appealing.

At Open Market, I worked in public relations, finding customers to speak to the media and at trade shows, writing articles for executives, and writing news releases about new customers, partners, products, and other company milestones. It seemed like a lot of responsibility at the time, but now I look back in fondness at how simple and uncomplicated the work was, particularly when compared to an average work day now. One of my favorite projects at Open Market was promoting the company's involvement in creating the world's first online Girl Scout cookie store, which helped not just to sell a lot of cookies and create awareness for our company, but also to alleviate concerns about the security of e-commerce by associating it with something familiar and wholesome.

That helped us to get a lot of press, but we didn't stop there. In the lead-up to Open Market's IPO in 1996, the company was featured in dozens of publications. One was a photo shoot with *Businessweek* that featured our founder surrounded by half a dozen dogs (owned by our employees, including me), riffing on the meme introduced by the famous Peter Steiner cartoon published in the *New Yorker*: "On the Internet, nobody knows you're a dog."[1]

Open Market went on to a successful IPO in 1996, and I was hooked on the tech start-up world. My next major stop was Akamai Technologies, one of the first content delivery network (CDN) providers. Akamai began as a company that would end the "World Wide Wait" through intelligent Internet content delivery. Before its public launch, the company had attracted a great deal of venture capital and other investments, and wanted to maximize its initial publicity. Akamai turned to cause marketing to enhance its growing visibility. The chosen cause came in the form of NetAid, when the company was approached in the spring of 1999 by Cisco Systems, which had recently created the NetAid initiative with the United Nations Development Programme (UNDP).

I came onboard as the NetAid Program Manager, responsible for promoting and coordinating Akamai's involvement in NetAid via all of its marketing activities. Akamai leveraged NetAid as the reason and mechanism to build out its Internet content delivery server network as fast as it could. It did this in order to carry the content of what was expected to be the biggest Internet multimedia event to date and to create the business case for its ensuing IPO, also slated for October, three weeks after the NetAid concerts. Partly because of all the press attention from NetAid, Akamai's IPO was one of the most successful on the NASDAQ Stock Market in 1999. You can read more about Akamai's sponsorship in Appendix B, "An Examination of the Marketing Communications Tools and Techniques Used by Akamai Technologies During Its Sponsorship of NetAid."

Since then, I've worked with several B2B software companies, helping to launch products, secure new markets, find new customers, and refine messaging.

In 2007, I joined the next wave of marketing innovation when I became the Chief Marketing Officer of SiteSpect, a leading web and mobile optimization solutions provider. Today, a typical day includes planning and executing SiteSpect's global marketing strategy, which means managing the people, processes, and technology behind our website, content strategy and marketing programs, online and offline advertising, lead generation programs, public relations initiatives, social media marketing activities, email marketing, and trade shows and events, among other things. I'm fortunate to work with a company doing cool things for amazing customers and for a CEO who can see and appreciate what's possible in marketing.

The Internet makes possible all the digital marketing initiatives that I love creating. To do this, I log in to about a dozen tools every day, including Google Analytics, Pardot, salesforce.com, Google AdWords, LinkedIn, and our own optimization platform, among others. That started me thinking about the growing role of technology in B2B marketing, which became the inspiration for this book.

It's my hope that you will find this volume to be a useful and comprehensive primer for getting started in B2B marketing, rebooting a career, understanding the impact of technology, or just getting up to speed on the new tools and tactics. It's the book I wish had been written five years ago to help me understand and navigate the quickly shifting forces that are shaping marketing today. I could not find such a book for B2B marketers, and so I have written it as my gift to you. May it accompany you and guide you on a long and productive career.

Kim Ann King
December 28, 2014

Endnote

1. "On the Internet, Nobody Knows You're a Dog," Wikipedia.org, http://en.wikipedia.org/wiki/On_the_Internet,_nobody_knows_you%27re_a_dog.

Introduction

When this book is published, it will have been 20 years since the introduction of the World Wide Web, signaling the start of the commercial Internet and the turning point when businesses started to build websites and market themselves digitally. It seems like another lifetime, even quaint, that a company could even exist without a website, paid search, social media, online video, online wire services, digital content, or automation, but that was the reality of marketing before the Internet. These new tools have changed everything about our jobs and the profession itself. Here are just a few things that I've learned about using the technology that has become so vital in marketing:

- Technology solves nothing without established goals, roles, and procedures. In fact, it'll make everything much worse if you don't already have these things defined.

- Just as graphic design software does not create artistic talent, marketing technology does not create good marketing, but it does make it incredibly easy to automate bad marketing.

- Technology enables you to make lots of mistakes quickly and often in public.

- Technology has led us to focus on *how* we're going to fix things with less regard to *what* we're fixing and *why*. But that's a mistake. Just because you can use a tool to do something doesn't mean you should. Strategy must always come first.

The Internet and subsequent introduction of cloud-based tools have put more pressure on marketing by broadening the amount of work and technical know-how necessary to get the job done. That means the inherent challenges for today's B2B marketers are enormous. Consider the difficulty in balancing all the following responsibilities:

- Automating marketing processes across all programs

- Transforming analytics into actionable tactics

- Keeping data clean in order to segment, target, and personalize

- Experimenting with multiple creative versions to discover audience preference

- Planning, programming, budgeting, staffing, and measuring:

  - Managing both the visual and the verbal corporate and product brand(s) across multiple channels (and devices)

  - Understanding the challenges and best practices of each channel

  - Finding the right mix of traditional and digital advertising

  - Creating enough content to nurture prospects during each phase of the buyer journey

  - Generating enough qualified leads for the sales team

  - Contributing to bottom-line revenue

  - Supporting the needs of internal departments

  - Finding and keeping the right talent and skill set on the team

  - Evolving the staff's skills (and yours) to keep up with new tactics, tools, and techniques

  - Staying on budget in a time of increased financial scrutiny

- Executing flawlessly on all fronts

- Reliably delivering results time and time again

To juggle all of that, marketers from all industries are reporting they're doing work they have never done before. In fact, a 2013 BMA/Forrester survey of B2B marketers found that 97% of the respondents say that "they are doing new types of work, new skills for marketers will be desperately needed going forward, and the pace of relentless change in their worlds is expected to pick up."[1]

I am at the epicenter of this change, both as a B2B marketing practitioner and as a vendor of experimentation software that enables our clients to push the boundaries of what's possible. It's an incredibly interesting, exciting, and scary time to work in our profession.

The bottom line for you is that the marketplace is changing, the way B2B buyers research information is rapidly changing, and your marketing strategies, messages, offers, and channels need to change too—from getting your message out, to generating demand, and enabling the organization.

To help you explore what's possible, this book is divided into three main sections (with a fourth consisting of appendices) focusing on the (1) trends, (2) tools and technologies, and (3) tactics and techniques shaping today's B2B marketing profession in the context of actionable advice on strategies, best practices, and tools you can use.

Here's what you'll learn:

- A number of key trends affecting B2B marketing, including a changing buyer, an evolving buying process, more responsibility for revenue, and the rise of technology.

- Four indispensable technologies that will help you better connect with your buyer, create more relevant experiences, and drive more revenue. These include analytics, experimentation, marketing automation, and targeting and personalization. You might not have gone into marketing to get up close and personal with technology, but you will have to get comfortable with it in order to be successful.

- A broad array of techniques at your disposal in planning, programming, budgeting, staffing, and measuring your marketing efforts. You'll learn tactics and best practices for every step of the conversion funnel.

So let's dive right in, starting with key trends to lend context to the brand-new and ever-changing world of B2B marketing today.

Endnote

1. "B2B CMOs Must Evolve or Move On," Laura Ramos, Forrester Research, https://solutions.forrester.com/bma-survey-findings-ramos.

PART I
Trends

This part of the book provides you with some background context for the rapidly evolving B2B marketplace. With more channels, more tools, more responsibility for revenue, and more decisions to make, it can be overwhelming to know where to start. Let's make sense of it all by outlining some of the key trends that are driving B2B marketing today.

1

The Evolving Marketing Landscape

B2B marketing, also known as business-to-business marketing, is simply businesses selling at scale to buyers in other companies. In doing so, B2B marketers must define their target market, target accounts, and ideal buyer; create products and services to meet the needs of those buyers; and correctly position, price, and promote their products and services in the marketplace.

If only it were as easy and straightforward as it sounds. Marketing supports sales, and in the B2B world, these sales can be large, complex deals that involve multiple buyers, users, and influencers across several departments, including legal, procurement, and others, making the process convoluted and complicated. Meanwhile, marketing is tasked with several key roles within the organization:

- **Strategic Partner**—Guiding the company in making the best decisions to market its products and services

- **Brand Protector**—Monitoring usage and enforcing guidelines

- **Revenue Creator**—Generating leads that turn into net new revenue

- **Service Provider**—Supporting other departments with creative and editorial services

On top of that, today's B2B marketer is dealing with forces that make successful planning and execution even more difficult. To provide context, this chapter examines the following trends shaping marketing today:

- A rapidly changing buyer

- An exponential growth in data, often siloed and out-of-date

- More channels and platforms, splintering reach and confusing strategy

- A growing responsibility for revenue

- The ability to do more with less: an increasing scope of functional responsibility, typically without additional personnel or budget

- The need for speed and agility in creating and deploying campaigns and producing results

- New tools and technologies, evolving more quickly than professionals can adapt

It adds up to a very complex environment in which to market—made all the more so by the pace of change along so many different fronts. Let's look at each of these forces at work.

A Rapidly Changing Buyer

Not so long ago, buyers had fewer choices to make and smaller problems to solve. Today we see that B2B buyers are affected by the same ground-shifting complexities that impact vendors:

- Buyers are trying to fix big problems such as improving revenue, creating efficiencies, and managing more work (which vendors are trying to help them do).

- Buyers have many options in solving their problems (which creates competitive pressure for vendors).

- Buyers can research their options firsthand long before contacting a vendor, and are savvier in understanding their potential choices (which makes it difficult for vendors to differentiate and get heard above the clutter).

- Buyers are increasingly mobile—using smartphones and tablets to research and consume information (which vendors must consider in their marketing mix).

- Buyers' expectations have changed in that they expect to engage in two-way communication with vendors (not just be marketed to) and they expect marketing outreach to be personalized and consistently relevant (approaches to which vendors must adapt).

- Buyers are connected with each other such that it is easy to tap into the wisdom of the crowd as well as be heard via social media (which vendors must monitor and respond to).

Because of this evolving B2B buyer behavior, marketers today have to be more technically adept, be more sensitive to context (for example, understanding the differences between mobile and desktop ads, e-mails, and websites), and offer a truly differentiated product via messaging that resonates with buyers. Marketers must bring a keen emotional understanding of the job of personalizing outreach such that it is appropriate 100% of the time—which is not an easy thing to do. And marketers are expected to listen to the social media conversation at all times in the hopes of gleaning insight into the wants and needs of the marketplace, understanding sentiment about their industry, and using that information to add value.

An Exponential Growth in Data

As buyers research options, they are leaving bits of data about themselves and their activities all over the Internet, which are being fed back to vendors via various tools to inform their marketing decisions. Data is nothing without analysis to understand what it means to buyer behavior and why it's important to the buyer journey; only then can companies harness the power of its data to improve the experience. The question becomes how to use data to recognize preferences across channels and devices. But that's difficult when the amount of data can be overwhelming, because it comprises, at a minimum, the following:

- Personal information such as name and title

- Demographic and firmographic information

- Behavioral information, such as the following:

  - On-site activity—pages visited, content downloaded, on-site search queries, form completions

- Offsite activity—ads clicked, social media activity, event participation

- Campaign activity—e-mails opened, links clicked

When used correctly, this data can be used to improve the relationship between the potential buyer and the company by personalizing communication, digital experiences, and content. But two problems quickly arise with so much data:

1. Information can live in many different places within a company, from the CRM database, to Excel spreadsheets on sales executives' desktops, and even to filing cabinets. That means data is siloed and not shared across the company, with different departments having a different view of prospects and customers, depending on what information they're keeping.

2. Data can quickly become out-of-date (leading to what is known as "decay"), which leads to another problem: data hygiene, in which a database devolves over time to contain unmailable contacts with out-of-date records, incomplete records, duplicate records, or even false records. Clean data, created by ongoing data maintenance, is the key to the successful execution of marketing campaigns.

More Channels and Platforms

On top of massive amounts of data, new channels and platforms are also proliferating rapidly. Although they can be useful for reaching new prospects and customers, their usage can come at a cost: the time needed to learn how to use a new platform, hire someone else to do it, or find an outsourced resource to help. For example, social media encompasses a broad array of possibilities, but what is the appropriate mix—and is it even possible to learn every platform? You might use Twitter and LinkedIn, but should your company also be on Pinterest and Instagram, which weren't even around a few years ago? What about YouTube? And what will be new tomorrow that needs to be added to the mix?

This never-ending channel proliferation takes time, money, and effort to learn and feed with new content, and should be evaluated over time to ensure that chosen channels are still relevant to buyers. This puts enormous pressure on B2B marketers to continually learn, evaluate, and maintain new channels and platforms. It's one thing to be responsible for the company's website; it's entirely another thing to be responsible for the company's website, LinkedIn page, Facebook profile, Twitter page, Google+ profile, YouTube channel, AdWords campaigns, Bing campaigns, LinkedIn ads,

Facebook ads, retargeting campaigns, analytics reporting, experimentation program, automation platform, targeting and personalization efforts, content marketing, and e-mail marketing, among other things. That's a lot to learn, master, keep up with, feed, evaluate, and report on, but if you want to be where your buyers are and create the best experience for them, it's what you have to do.

More Revenue Responsibility

Meanwhile, these new channels are critical in delivering new prospective buyers who could, in turn, deliver net new revenue to the business. As B2B marketers find the channels, tools, and data sources to reach, acquire, convert, engage, close, and retain customers, they are becoming increasingly responsible for a portion of a company's revenue. This is an incredible shift in accountability from the past when marketing could come up with creative campaigns and not worry about the contribution to bottom-line results. Today, we're being called upon to account for a specific percentage of revenue delivered, the return on marketing investment, and customer acquisition costs and lifetime value—all made possible by the real-time, data-driven nature of the Internet.

Doing More with Less

Make no mistake—marketers are being asked to do all of that without added staff or extra budget. Before the advent of the web 20 years ago, B2B marketers mostly relied on just a few channels to connect with buyers: media and analyst relations, direct mail, print advertising, and trade shows. Now, the same-sized team is expected to:

- Create and maintain prospect databases and lists

- Create and keep up-to-date web and mobile sites and apps, landing pages, blogs, and microsites—and make them all search engine-friendly

- Create and maintain social profiles across multiple platforms

- Produce and execute social media marketing campaigns across multiple platforms, including LinkedIn, Twitter, Facebook, Google+, Pinterest, Instagram, SlideShare, and YouTube, among others

- Create vast arrays of content in many formats, including whitepapers, e-books, infographics, webinars, and videos

- Build, monitor, and update online advertising campaigns across multiple platforms

- Create, run, and measure e-mail marketing and lead nurturing campaigns

- Learn content management systems, web analytics tools, testing and targeting tools, marketing automation platforms, pay-per-click advertising, and social advertising platforms such as Google, Bing, LinkedIn, Twitter, Facebook, Bizo (now part of LinkedIn), and others

- Handle traditional offline activities such as media and analyst relations, direct mail, print advertising, and trade shows and events

It seems pretty overwhelming, doesn't it? Although cloud-based technology has made it possible to do all of these things faster, with a smaller staff, and for less cost than traditional methods, there are a couple of inherent traps in doing more with less. First, marketers are not being remunerated commensurate with the vastly higher throughput and successful outcomes that technology enables. Second, although today's executive teams expect marketing to turn to technology to do more with less, there is often no plan for how that technology supports strategy, no plan or support for training, and no plan for what happens when the technology fails to deliver or even be properly integrated. That, in turn, is a recipe for burnout and, ultimately, employee retention issues.

One way to mitigate the pressure of doing more with less is to ensure that everything marketing does, every tool marketing uses, and every result marketing delivers will be in the service of supporting strategy. By putting strategy first, marketers can minimize unnecessary activity, reduce superfluous technologies, and better manage expectations along the way.

Need for Speed and Agility

New technologies enable agility in campaign creation and deployment as well as ease in measuring outcomes, both of which are a welcome respite from the manual methods of the past, which will save you a lot of time when done right. Moreover, agile, data-driven marketing creates relevant experiences for prospective buyers, helping you to acquire them more easily and convert them into customers. But this environment also creates the expectation of instant results, ever more successful results, and a never-ending pressure to learn, improve, and move on to the next campaign. That's just as much of a trap as doing more with less. Doing things faster just because you have the tools to do so is another easy way to burn out. Ensuring thoughtful, creative, effective marketing takes time, and that time is your ally in brainstorming and producing fresh ideas. The key here is balancing expediency and efficiency with strategy and results.

New Tools and Technologies

The marketing technology landscape includes analytics, experimentation, marketing automation, and targeting and personalization, among other tools. But learning these tools, and using them on a daily basis, can max out a marketer's ability to take full advantage of them, even when they're fundamental to the job. As tools and technologies evolve, so must a marketer's ability to learn new features and functionality of the tools they've already deployed, as well as the new tools coming into the marketplace.

To take advantage of this new digital reality, think about how you can use these tools to transform processes, rather than as just another interface to log in to in order to get work done. Move your thinking to a higher level. For example, consider these questions:

- How can you evolve traditional rote tactics into insight-driven marketing via analytics?

- How can you shift from one-and-done programs to continuous marketing optimization via experimentation?

- How can you eliminate inconsistent follow-up by adopting programmatic lead nurturing via marketing automation?

- How can you move from a single, generalized campaign message to targeted, personalized content across platforms, channels, and devices?

You'll get the answers to these questions in the chapters to come. Taken as a whole, these new technologies enable B2B marketers to gain insight into their buyers' behavior, test what content and experiences visitors prefer, automate engaging campaigns to nurture potential buyer interest, and deliver the right message to the right buyer at the right time in the buyer's journey. Let's take a closer look at these technologies before we dive into them in the following chapters.

Analytics

Analytics comprises the wealth of data you've accumulated or sourced about your visitors, prospects, and customers, including web analytics, marketing analytics (campaign ROI as well as revenue attribution), and customer analytics. New to the game is predictive analytics, which takes thousands of buying signals to understand a prospect's propensity to purchase. All of this data adds up to nothing without the right people to process it, translate it, and use it to tell a story about what is happening, why it's happening, and what to do about it.

Experimentation and Optimization

Capturing visitor preferences through experimentation tools and techniques enables companies to optimize the user experience on their website, with a product, and through various channels and platforms used for campaigns, such as e-mail and online advertising. In addition to digital testing, there are also survey methods, focus groups, and other means of experimentation to help you understand what experiences your audiences prefer.

Marketing Automation

Marketing automation enables closer relationships with potential buyers by automating the creation of marketing campaigns and tracking results across several channels, including paid search, social media, events and webinars, and the corporate website, which helps marketers to better understand buyer behavior and content preferences, as well as better track marketing return on investment.

Targeting and Personalization

Creating a more targeted, relevant experience for your prospects and customers will win you higher content consumption rates, a better brand reputation, and, most important, higher conversion rates. Effective targeting and personalization can garner long-term customer loyalty and higher customer lifetime values.

Key Highlights

Marketers able to manage the complexity of digital transformation will be the ones to win, and they'll do that by using the new tools and technologies themselves to understand buyer behavior; keep on top of data, channels, and platforms; and do more with less (and more quickly) to generate revenue. One thing is certain: Nothing is simple anymore. Welcome to the new B2B marketing reality! Let's take a closer look at the tools and technologies available to you today.

PART II

Tools and Technologies

From setting strategy to knowing how to evaluate marketing technologies, a great deal of skill and expertise is required to take advantage of the new tools available to you. We'll look at four specific technologies: analytics, experimentation and optimization, marketing automation, and targeting and personalization. While there are many more tools and technologies available, I consider these to be critical for building a robust technological foundation in marketing today.

2

Strategy and Evaluation

The chapters that follow describe several marketing technologies, how they are used, and best practices. Before we begin, we must ask, "Why has technology become part of the marketing function?" One important reason is that most marketing platforms today are available over the Internet in the form of Software as a Service (SaaS). As such, these cloud-based technologies are considered an operating expense under the marketing budget instead of a capital expense under the IT budget. This simple change in accounting shifts the responsibility from IT to marketing.

Let's be clear about one thing: It's not a question of marketing versus technology; it's a question of marketing *and* technology, which enables strategy to be carried much more efficiently, much more directly, and in a measurable, trackable way. The technology of marketing will not displace or replace the art of marketing, but it will refine it and take it to places it could not get to on its own—and in doing so, has the potential to break down departmental silos and align functional areas around goals and outcomes. That's because, as companies get better at using technology to reach their goals, they tend to re-organize—moving from single contributors in a functional area (such as analytics or experimentation) to small teams dedicated to those functions, then to larger teams serving a broader constituency and solving bigger problems on behalf of the company, to a full-fledged, integrated team with cross-departmental authority and processes baked into the fabric of the company. This kind of evolution creates a culture of analytics, experimentation, automation, and personalization that, when done right, organizes a company's activities around the best interests of its customers.

Strategy First

Marketers experiencing problems should not look to technology to solve them until they fully understand what is happening, why, and all of their potential solutions—because technology solves nothing on its own in the absence of marketing strategy.

For example, let's say you have a problem managing leads. If you just purchase a marketing automation platform because the vendor promised it would make managing leads easy, you'd still have a problem after implementing because you did not create a strategy to fix the problem—you merely bought a tool to automate the problem, probably making things much, much worse.

In this case, you should sit down with the sales team, understand the sales cycle, and agree on the following:

- The ideal buyer profile in order to properly grade leads

- How important specific actions are (such as registering for a webinar or downloading a whitepaper) in order to properly score leads and accurately measure their interest

- What score and grade make a lead qualified enough to pass to sales

- The preferred method to pass leads to sales

- What happens when a lead is not qualified enough and needs to go back to marketing for nurturing, and the preferred method for doing so

- How to report progress as leads move through the pipeline

After you do that and create a lead management strategy, you'll have a much better sense of what you need in a technology solution to help manage it.

How to Evaluate Marketing Tools and Technologies

If you have never purchased technology before, note that there are several tried-and-true steps that most buyers go through before selecting a new tool. These are the same steps your B2B buyers are taking when evaluating purchases.

Phase 1: Awareness

Step 1: Set Goals

You've become aware of a problem, made sure your strategy was solid, and are now looking for a solution to help. Before proceeding any further, define your goals. What needs to be achieved with marketing technology? How will success be measured? The more specific the goal, the better; for example, in the marketing automation example given previously, your goal would be this:

> "Improve our lead management process by accurately scoring and grading leads and automating their progression to sales."

Then, you'd figure out how to measure that goal, for example:

> "Increase lead flow to sales by 25%."

Step 2: Create Specifications

Based on goals, you'll identify the features and functionality needed in a solution. Describe must-have and nice-to-have features in order to compare offerings across multiple vendors. You might not need everything a vendor offers, but the solution you choose should provide you with plenty of room to grow.

Step 3: Identify Available Resources

This is the people part of the equation. Who is needed for evaluating potential solutions and implementing the chosen one? The answers could range from IT manager to webmaster, web developer, or CRM administrator to help onboard the new technology and integrate it with existing systems.

Step 4: Outline Time Frame

Next, figure out the steps in your buying cycle and assign a realistic time frame to each of them (the times that follow are arbitrary to illustrate progression):

- **Awareness**—Create adoption plan within 30 days.

- **Research**—Investigate various approaches and solutions within 60 days.

- **Evaluation**—Compare vendors within 90 days.

- **Decision**—Select vendor within 120 days.

- **Implementation**—Finish onboarding of new vendor within 180 days.

Phase 2: Research

Step 1: Research Potential Solutions
After the problem, strategy, goals, specifications, resources, and time frame are defined, research the solutions that are available and the vendors that offer them. Gather general information about options/approaches and the pros and cons of each. Consider searching on Google, Bing, LinkedIn, Twitter, and Quora. Ask questions, participate in groups, and benefit from the wisdom of the crowd.

Step 2: Distribute an RFP (Request for Proposal)
One way to aggregate information is to go directly to vendors and ask them to complete an RFP. Your company might already have an RFP template that you can customize; if not, base the format on the key features and customer support you require, and socialize your draft within your company for feedback before distributing to vendors.

Step 3: Schedule Product Demos
Make sure you've seen a live demo to understand what the product looks like and how it works, and to help assess ease of use. You might be surprised by the difference in ease between the sales presentation of the product and the product demonstration; and if the demo is difficult for the salesperson, consider how difficult the product will be for you to use in a live environment.

Phase 3: Evaluation

Step 1: Evaluate Vendors
Having established the potential vendor landscape, it's time to narrow down available solutions. At this point, think beyond features and functionality and consider the following questions:

- How easy is the tool to use?

- How helpful is the vendor?

- What kinds of consulting resources and training are available?

- What other kinds of support does the vendor offer?

- What kinds of third-party validation are available? The information contained in analyst reports and buyers' guides can be quite useful.

Step 2: Check References

What do other clients say about them? Ask for several reference customers who work in similar industries or companies. When checking references, ask not just about their usage of the system (features and functionality), but also about how the implementation process went, how easy it was to integrate with other systems, the kinds of support they've received, where they unexpectedly ran into problems, and how the vendor helped mitigate those problems. You might ask for feedback over social media as well.

Phase 4: Deciding and Selecting a Tool

Step 1: Make the Decision

Based on the evaluation process, the right vendor will often become apparent. After deciding on the optimal pricing package and working through the details of the service agreement, the next step is to kick off implementation.

Phase 5: Implementation and Usage

Step 1: Implement the Solution

Technology vendors usually have a defined process for implementation. If a local partner is preferred, decide whether working with a company from the vendor's partner program might be more effective. Having said that, sometimes even the best partners cannot beat the domain expertise of the vendor, so if that is the most important criteria for success, stick with the vendor for implementation. Implementing marketing technology is often much more than deploying a JavaScript tag in the global footer of the website, and you'll want the right partner for the job.

Step 2: Continually Monitor

But don't stop there—assess quarterly whether the chosen technology remains the right decision, and evaluate whether the level of service is sufficient. Invest in continuous training by participating in user groups (usually found on LinkedIn or the vendor's website as user/customer forums) to learn something new and different about using the tool. This is particularly important because marketing tools are constantly evolving, so it's best to stay up-to-date by attending product road map webinars, reading upcoming feature release announcements, and subscribing to blog updates, as well as the vendor's customer newsletter. Marketing technology users have the option of participating in beta programs to test out not-yet-released features. If gaining an inside view of what's coming down the turnpike is important, consider signing up to the beta program.

B2B marketers who have procured technology that's shared with other departments (for example, CRM systems and marketing automation) will often find themselves as the internal support point person for these tools; be aware of this dynamic and communicate the expectation of how you want colleagues to ask for support—should they ask you or go to the vendor? In addition, technology users are a de facto extension of the vendor's QA department in that they experience and report bugs, work out glitches in new product releases, and provide feedback on new features that either improve or worsen the user experience—and B2B marketers are no exception. Make sure you budget time for getting up to speed with new product releases and working out the kinks with the vendor.

Examining Four Technologies That Transform B2B Marketing

As B2B marketing has become more sophisticated, several tools and technologies have stood out as most useful in increasing conversions and revenue. As noted earlier, these include the following:

- *Analytics* to derive actionable insights into buyer behavior

- *Experimentation and optimization* to discover what content and experiences buyers prefer

- *Marketing automation* to programmatically deliver campaigns and track buyer behavior

- *Targeting and personalization* to deliver relevant content to visitors, prospects, and customers across channels, platforms, and devices

One thing to consider with these tools is whether a best-of-breed point solution or an integrated platform is necessary. These tools exist both as standalone solutions and as part of a larger marketing suite with additional functionality, and the right choice depends on what your company's needs, goals, and strategy are. For example, Adobe, Oracle, and Salesforce, among others, offer integrated marketing platforms. Another option is building your own marketing platform instead of buying one, but this is typically an option only for the very largest companies when no other solution is appropriate.

Key Highlights

As technology has shifted to the cloud, marketing has become responsible for owning and operating new tools. Make sure you select the right ones for your needs by fully planning, researching, and evaluating potential solutions. When implementing, budget enough time to get up to speed and stay up-to-date.

3

Analytics

What is analytics? Simply put, analytics is derived from data that enables you to make decisions based on what is important to your company—making money, saving money, or making customers happy. The act of measuring, analyzing, and reporting on this data is analytics, which in and of itself is not new, but the plethora of data sources and the rich diversity of information available is—thanks to the Internet. Because prospect and customer behavior is tracked across the web, devices, and channels, you can use the resulting data to improve marketing performance, increase customer retention, improve conversion rates, and provide a better online experience for your target audiences.

That's why analytics is such big business, expected to more than double in the next five years—from a little more than a billion-dollar market in 2014 to more than a three-billion-dollar market by 2019.[1] Analytics in a B2B context comprises four key areas that we'll investigate in this chapter:

1. Web analytics

2. Marketing analytics

3. Customer analytics

4. Predictive analytics

All told, these four areas give you business intelligence that enables you to make better decisions, predict future behavior, and create better forecasting. For example, Google Analytics and other web analytics tools enable you to measure, analyze, and report on your website activity, answering such questions as how many visitors came to your site, where they came from, how long they stayed, and what they did on the site. Knowing this enables you to create an optimal user experience based on patterns of content consumption, user flow, and traffic sources.

When you combine disparate sources of data, such as web analytics, customer analytics, financial data, and other sources, you start venturing into the realm of "big data," which is the aggregation of all the online and offline information related to a prospect or customer. I tend to think of big data as a lot of little data that's aggregated in a meaningful way to get a clearer picture of prospects and customers. Although this book does not delve specifically into big data, it does look at data-driven marketing. We'll look at the importance of delivering the right message to the right customer at the right time—and when you have data, that kind of personalization happens much more easily.

Prospect and customer data is derived from various sources, such as these:

- The technologies you use (such as testing data from your experimentation tool, web and mobile visitor behavior from your web analytics, and response and engagement data from your marketing automation platform, for example)

- The data sources you import (such as lists and information from data appending and data cleansing services such as Data.com or Netprospex, as well as lead source information from providers such as Dun and Bradstreet)

- Channel data from the online and offline programs you are running, including advertising, retargeting, e-mail, direct mail, social media, and others

- The data you create when you analyze the preceding; for example, marketing ROI, revenue attribution, and pipeline analysis

Data tells you what has happened in the past. Where it gets interesting is when we look at this data and use it to predict behavior in the future. This is known as "predictive analytics," and if you haven't heard of it yet, you will. Companies are starting to use predictive analytics to understand opportunities in prospect and customer accounts and how to predict which ones are the best fit. These are just some of the data-enabled strategies made possible by analytics.

Web Analytics

Your website is the foundation of your digital presence and online marketing efforts. But how do you know whether those efforts are paying off? The first place to check is your web analytics, which gives you the ability to understand how your visitors (prospective customers) find you and behave on your website—giving you insight into what's important to them and helping you better deliver on what matters to them.

It also enables you to understand what's not working on your site—where visitors drop off and what they're not doing that you want them to do, such as viewing important content. So just as much as web analytics measures behavior, it also measures the lack of it, and it's important to look at both what's working and what's not working.

All of that information will help you optimize the look and feel, navigation, content, and layout of your site—helping to improve the online experience (and hopefully maximize conversions, such as registering for a webinar or downloading a whitepaper). Analytics is also important because it's a key place to look for improvements to your site that you can then turn into hypotheses to test. We'll investigate that concept further in Chapter 4, "Experimentation and Optimization."

You might have a free or paid web analytics implementation, depending on your company's acumen with and dedication to a data-driven business. Even with a free service such as Google Analytics, you will be able to track many important metrics per any time frame, as well as compare two time frames against each other in order to better understand historical trend analysis. You can further drill down by combining metrics; for example, the percentage of visitors who came to the website from LinkedIn and ended up bouncing.

Some of the things you can measure specifically in Google Analytics are audience, acquisition, behavior, and conversions. When examining these concepts, it's important to keep your website goals in mind to understand whether these metrics are positive or negative.

Audience

Audience metrics tell you how many people came to your site, where they came from, how long they stayed, and how often they returned. This is important to know because it is the foundational benchmark for the rest of your web analytics data. Audience data includes the following:

- *Number of users* who visited your site. Although traffic can be variable depending on the day of the week, seasonality, or whether you've just launched a new campaign, you'll want to be sure you are not losing your audience over time, so check the long-term trend line. Generally, as you ramp up your marketing efforts, you should expect to see your website traffic grow over time.

- *Number of sessions* in which visitors engaged with your site. What is the average number of sessions over time, and is it increasing or decreasing?

- *Number of page views* visitors looked at and *number of pages per session.* Are these more or less over time, and how do they compare to industry benchmarks? This is a good indicator of interest and engagement.

- *Bounce rate* (the percentage of website visitors who leave after visiting one page). If the bounce rate is already fairly low, you don't need to worry about it, but if it is high and you are taking steps to decrease it and it's not going down, you'll need to figure out why. If you have a high bounce rate because most of your traffic goes to landing pages where they register and then leave, that might be okay—but not if you are trying to build engagement with your audience and want them to view many pages.

- *Demographics,* such as age and gender, as well as *interests.* This might seem more suitable for a B2C (business-to-consumer) context, but even for B2B audiences, you might find out something interesting about visitors who convert versus those who don't, based on their demographics and interests. For example, you can see whether men or women bounce more or less, the difference in their number of sessions and content consumed, and the number of goal completions, among other things. Knowing this enables you to better target your website content.

- *Geography* such as language and location. This is important if you target only an English-speaking audience, for example, or sell in certain locations—you don't want to find the majority of your website visitors coming from regions you don't service.

- *Behavior,* such as *new versus returning visitors*—the percentage of visitors who have never been to your site before versus those who have previously visited. If you are spending a lot of money on new visitor acquisition and have a large percentage of returning visitors, something is wrong. On the flip side, if customer loyalty is important to you and you have a lot of returning visitors, you are right on track. Also, check the *frequency and recency* of visits, and the *average duration of a session*—is each of these metrics growing or not? Did a visitor come just once and then never return or have they visited multiple times? Are they spending more or less time on the site over time?

- *Technology* used, such as browser, operating system, and service provider. It's important that your site is compatible with all browsers and operating systems, and you'll find out which ones are favored by your visitors by looking at this section—and you'll be amazed at how they change over time. Optimize your site for the browsers visiting your site.

- *Mobile analytics,* the percentage of traffic from not just desktops, but also tablets and smartphones, and the actual devices used. If you've been keeping an eye on this over time, you've no doubt seen a rise in mobile devices accessing your site over the past five years or so.

- *Benchmarking* enables you to compare your analytics with aggregated industry data (if you choose to share your data) for channels, locations, and devices. For example, Google Analytics gives you the option to share your data anonymously, which strips out any identifiable information and combines it with other anonymous data from similar industries for benchmarking. It's always helpful to know how you are performing based on your peer group.

You can also use the data from your web analytics to understand how your visitors travel through the site (known as users flow)—starting with any dimension, including these:

- Acquisition variables such as medium, source, source/medium, or traffic type

- Advertising variables such as ad group, campaign, or keyword

- Behavior variables such as landing page visited

- Custom dimensions and variables

- Social networks

- User variables such as browser, browser version, city, country or territory, and others

Pay special attention to this information regardless of which analytics tool you use, because knowing how visitors travel through your site is very powerful. Imagine seeing how visitors from your social networks traveled through your site versus those who came from advertising—and how useful that information would be in planning their journey. Or perhaps you'll discover how different the journey was from a particular mobile device. If you think about all the ways you can analyze these variables to better understand the buyer journey through your site, the better equipped you will be to personalize the experience for them.

Acquisition

Use acquisition metrics to better understand where your site traffic is coming from, what keywords visitors are searching on, and how your campaigns are doing.

For example, Google Analytics gives you metrics for the following:

- **Acquisition** (number of sessions, percentage of new sessions, and number of new users)

- **Behavior** (bounce rate, pages per session, and average session duration)

- **Conversion** (number, percentage, and dollar value of goal completions)

And then it reports on these metrics across the following variables:

- **Channel,** such as organic search, paid search, direct, referral, social, display, e-mail, and others

- **Traffic source, medium, source/medium, and keyword** or other dimension

- **Referral sources and landing pages**

- **All advertising campaigns** (not just Google AdWords), as well as paid and organic keywords

The Acquisition section also delves into these metrics:

- **Google AdWords metrics,** such as campaigns, bid adjustments, keywords, destination URLs, and placements, among other things

- **SEO metrics,** such as queries, landing pages, and geographies

- **Social metrics,** such as sources and pages, conversions, plug-ins, and social users flow

You can find the answers to many questions from your acquisition metrics to help you guide decisions in your marketing mix, such as these:

- How many new users came to your website from which channel?

- Which channel delivered the most sessions?

- How did each of your channels compare with the others for acquisition, behavior, and conversion metrics?

- What was the traffic source with the most conversions?

- What is your website's best source of referrals?

- Which are the best-performing ads and keywords?

- Based on the preceding, how should you change your marketing mix?

Behavior

Behavioral metrics describe what content your visitors consume, what they search for, and information about the functioning of your website:

- **Site content**—These metrics track content consumption of all pages, pages by section, landing pages, and exit pages.

- **Site speed**—You can examine average page load times by browser, country, and page.

- **Site search**—This shows you the number of site searches, what visitors searched for, and what pages they visited.

- **Events**—These are user interactions with content that can be tracked independently from a web page or a screen load.

- **AdSense**—This reports interactions with AdSense advertising, but only if your site supports this feature (not likely if you are B2B company).

- **Experiments**—You can use Google Analytics to run simple A/B tests; we'll talk more about that in the next chapter.

- **In-page analytics**—This feature gives you a visual way to see how visitors engage with your web pages, such as what they are or are not clicking on.

All this information is important for various reasons. For example, you need to know about your site performance because faster websites improve the user experience, resulting in better visitor engagement and conversions, whereas slow websites irritate visitors and present a poor image of your company. Knowing your top content pages will help you prioritize optimization opportunities. And understanding the nature of site searches on your website will tell you whether you are giving your visitors the information they need. For example, you might find that a large percentage of visitors search for pricing but that you do not offer that information on your website. Knowing that, you can decide whether you need to create a pricing page or do something else, such as redirecting those queries to a contact form.

Conversions

Use this information to see how many visitors completed a goal, such as filling out a form, downloading a piece of content, or viewing a specific page, as well as the source and medium from which those visitors came, and your conversion rate. It's important to know your conversions (and cost per conversion) by campaign, search term, geography, target audience, social channel, and mobile channels.

As you analyze goal completions, look at the following:

- **Reverse goal path,** which enables you to see where visitors were on your site before completing a goal

- **Funnel visualization,** which illustrates how many sessions, and which pages, counted toward goal completions

- **Goal flow,** which is just like users flow, except that it is specific to those visitors who converted

One of the ways you can get information to show up correctly in Google Analytics is to append parameters to the end of the URLs you want to track. The most popular parameters are campaign source and medium:

- **Campaign Source**—Should be a specific marketing channel, such as Google, LinkedIn, or Customer Newsletter

- **Campaign Medium**—Should identify what the medium is, such as PPC, e-mail, or display advertising

There is a specific way to format this information. For example, if you want to track links from your LinkedIn PPC campaigns, instead of the link you are tracking simply being www.*sitename*.com/*landingpage*, you would format it as www.*sitename*.com/*landingpage*/

?utm_source=LinkedIn&utm_medium=ppc. This will still click through to www.*sitename*.com/*landingpage*, but it will pass the LinkedIn source and PPC medium information into Google Analytics so that you can see specifically from where you acquired traffic and/or conversions for that link or page.

Web analytics vendors come in all shapes and sizes, from free tools such as Google Analytics or Yahoo Web Analytics, to low-cost tools for SMBs such as KISSmetrics, Qualaroo, and CrazyEgg, and more industrial-strength solutions from providers such as Adobe, IBM, Oracle, SAP, SAS Institute, and Webtrends, among others.

Marketing Analytics

Although web analysis is a great start in figuring out how your online marketing programs are doing, you'll want to take a closer look. There are two main ways to derive marketing analytics:

1. Campaign and program metrics, which measure the effectiveness of your various initiatives across channels (also known as channel analytics)

2. Revenue attribution, which quantifies marketing's contribution to revenue

Campaign and Program Metrics

As you think about all of your various marketing activities, you'll need to report what the results were. Sometimes called vanity metrics, these are meant to provide context to the success of a campaign within a certain channel. And because you can attribute conversions (and ultimately revenue) to them, they're not just soft metrics. If you are undertaking any of the following activities, you'll want to report on their associated metrics in order to show results and trends over time. Here are some of the most common campaigns and metrics; you'll want to report at least quarterly and year-over-year trends. Choose the metrics that are most important to your goals; it's simply not possible to report on all of these.

- **Paid Search**—Number of impressions, clicks, and converted clicks; click-through rate, average cost per click, cost per converted click, and click conversion rate; average cost per thousand impressions, total cost, and average position. Also, report on the percentage of traffic that paid search drove to the site.

- **Trade Shows**—Number of shows (and which ones), leads per show, total number of leads from all shows and average cost per lead for all shows as well as specific cost per lead per show; number of opportunities per show and total number of opportunities from all shows; number of deals and associated revenue per show and total number of deals and associated revenue from all shows.

- **Social Media**—Number of followers, likes, shares, retweets, comments, link clicks, Klout score, and sentiment analysis.

- **Public Relations**—Brand awareness score (number and percentage growth of branded keyword searches ending up on your site), number of articles, number of mentions, percentage of mentions in target publications.

- **Organic Search**—Number of searches, popular search queries, and percentage of organic search traffic to your site.

- **Video Analytics**—Click rate, number of videos watched, average length of engagement, and number of leads captured.

- **E-mail**—Number of subscribers, percentage growth year-over-year, delivery rate, open rate, click-through rate, and unsubscribe rate.

- **Webinars**—Number of registrants, number of attendees, percentage of registrants to attendees, and number of leads and opportunities generated per webinar and for all webinars.

As you plan your marketing programs, think about what your goals are, how you will measure success (what are your benchmarks?), and how you will quantify your programs' impact on the business. The idea is continuous marketing optimization—where can you make adjustments for better metrics over time?

Marketing ROI and Revenue Attribution

Your most important marketing metrics are called key performance indicators (KPIs), and the most important KPIs are almost always related to contribution to revenue. For example:

- Number of leads

- Cost per lead

- Lead-to-customer ratio

- Amount of revenue sourced by marketing

- Percentage of revenue sourced by marketing

- Number of new customers sourced by marketing

Revenue attribution can be done in any number of ways, as we'll investigate in Chapter 13, "Measuring." Because the buyer journey can be so convoluted, and can involve multiple campaigns, offers, additional content, website pages, events, webinars, and other activities, multi-touch attribution has come into favor as the fairest model in attributing revenue to a buyer journey that almost always encompasses many steps.

In terms of ongoing measurement, it makes sense to keep track of your efforts on a regular basis. A marketing analytics report or dashboard might contain the following items, for example:

Number of Net New Leads:

- This month

- This quarter

- Percentage of target attained for the year

Number of Opportunities:

- This month

- This quarter

- Percentage of target attained for the year

Number of Marketing-Sourced Customers:

- This month

- This quarter

- Percentage of revenue target attained for the year

This is a good list for a general performance snapshot, but you are advised to go deeper and report on the lead-to-close ratio as well as the ratios of the steps in the sales cycle. The idea is to create a conversion funnel model for your company based on your data and conversion rates through the funnel. It will look something like this, based on SiriusDecisions' Demand Waterfall model, which many B2B companies have adopted as their conversion funnel model of choice:

- Number of impressions = #

- Number of leads = % of impressions

- Number of marketing-qualified leads (MQLs) = % of leads

- Number of sales-accepted leads (SALs) = % of MQLs

- Number of sales-qualified leads (SQLs) = % of SALs

- Number of sales-qualified opportunities (SQOs) = % of SQLs

- Number of closed deals = % of SQOs

We'll talk through these steps and what they mean in more detail in Chapter 9, "Programming, Part 2: Demand Generation." For now, if you start tracking this data, you will have a sense of historical benchmarks for your company and will become better at predicting future contribution from marketing efforts. The important point here is to measure not just quantity of leads, but also quality and how that quality affects their velocity through the pipeline. According to research from SiriusDecisions based on its Demand Waterfall model, a B2B company needs on average at least 351 leads to generate one new deal. How does your company compare? Consider comparing your results against prior years' efforts as well as current industry averages to understand how you are performing historically and against the competition.

Customer Analytics

Marketing's job is to acquire and retain customers, and analytics is one of your best helpers toward that end. This data also helps you identify your best customers, predict future customers, and show you where there is an opportunity to sell more deeply into an account. It all starts with what you already know about your customers, usually stored within your CRM system as a record for each contact:

- **Descriptive data**—Declarative information captured via forms or filled out by sales reps, company attributes (size, location), and any other demographics or firmographics

- **Activity data**—Information about the products and services they use, billing information, and contracts

- **Engagement data**—Content consumed, pages visited, e-mails, and phone call logs

- **Sentiment**—Survey data, product feature requests, social media sentiment, direct feedback, and Net Promoter Score

With a keen eye on these four types of customer data, you can segment customers just as you do prospects (see Chapter 6, "Targeting and Personalization"). Which of your customers are using just a basic offering and might benefit from increased use of your product? Which industries are you most represented in, and would it make business sense to develop special features just for that vertical? What did your customer register for, and based on that, what other kinds of personalized content should you send?

Data is information, and analytics is the process by which you transform that information into actionable insight—in this case, retention of the account as well as possible up-sell and cross-sell opportunities. So how can you do this? The first place to start is surveying your customer base to assess a general sense of satisfaction. This could be a combination of internal scoring from employees who work with customers and external surveying of the customers themselves. When you look at that information in combination with sentiment analysis from social media or e-mail communications, you can then start to assess how satisfied they are. This kind of customer insight will help you understand what your customers need and where those needs might not be currently met. You'll want to have a process in place to review this information regularly. Another indicator of satisfaction is a customer's Net Promoter Score,[2] which is a loyalty metric based on how likely the customer is to refer you to a friend or colleague. Customers simply respond on a scale of 1 to 10, and based on their answers, are grouped into three categories:

- Promoters (those with scores of 9 or 10) are your brand advocates who are likely to serve as references/referral accounts for prospective customers.

- Passives are more neutral about your company.

- Detractors are outspoken in their dissatisfaction with your company, products, or services.

Other key customer metrics include customer lifetime value (CLV), which is the customer's contribution to revenue over the life of the account, and customer acquisition cost (CAC), which is how much it cost to acquire that customer. When you know those two numbers, you can calculate the return on investment (CLV/CAC) of each account, by industry, and as a whole.

Another way to garner better customer data is through predictive analytics, which incorporates thousands of pieces of data on a contact and account level to assess buying signals—not just in your customers, but also in your prospects. Let's look at that more closely.

Predictive Analytics

Now that you've aggregated your web, marketing, and customer analytics, you can use that information to help score and grade new prospective customer leads, determine potential interest in your products and services, and also understand exactly who is not ready to buy so that you can put them into the appropriate lead nurturing/drip marketing campaign. This activity is accentuated by the quickly growing number of cloud-based predictive analytics solutions for B2B marketers.

Predictive analytics starts with a company's CRM and marketing automation data, draws on a multitude of additional data points used as buying signals, and shows the probability of each prospect and account converting. This can be used for more accurate lead scoring, better insights into customer needs and accounts that might be at risk, and discovery of more profitable market segments.

Imagine if you could predict which channels will convert best and which campaigns will provide the best return. That's where marketing is going: becoming more data-driven and scientific in its approach to finding the best customers for its business and providing them with the best product match. Although we've used historical data to assume what would work in the future, predictive analytics will tell us.

So how can you take advantage of predictive analytics right now? To find new prospects, consider running predictive lead scoring on your database to discover which prospects are most likely to convert. This is particularly useful for companies with large databases of several hundred thousand records or more. Predictive lead scoring will take your database, enhance it with data from hundreds of sources, and compare the results to current customers to find the best matches. Look at offerings from vendors such as Infer, Lattice Engines, and Mintigo, among others.

Putting Analytics into Practice

Just as you do with other marketing programs, you will want to specify goals, strategies, tactics, and expected results for your analytics program, and the people, processes, and technology to support them in order to build a culture of analysis. This means building in the measuring and reporting on results as part of program planning.

For a successful web analytics program, take time to understand your website goals, how you plan to support those goals, and how you will measure success. The more specific you can be, the better prepared you will be to create a road map for success.

For marketing analytics, also think about your goals, metrics, and KPIs for each of your channels. What are the quarterly, year-to-date, and year-over-year trends, and what can you do to improve? Make sure you know the best lead sources that turn into customers, the number of customers by lead source, the amount of revenue by lead source, and how you might optimize the marketing mix based on this information.

In terms of customer analytics, you'll want to keep an eye on customer acquisition cost and lifetime value as well as the metrics you track to understand customer satisfaction.

Based on predictive lead scoring, which leads are most qualified to be passed to sales that would not have normally met the threshold? How are they doing in the pipeline? Based on predictive analytics, how are your programs expected to perform and how should you change the mix and the spend in order to obtain the best results?

Analytics Best Practices

What gets measured gets managed, and if you want to manage your marketing, you'll have to measure the results. Plan what to measure based on your KPIs, and pick only a handful that truly matter. Some other best practices include the following:

> **Don't just measure; do something with the data.** This is perhaps the biggest challenge in analytics—turning all of your sources of data into actionable insights that make a difference to the business. As you are learning about what works and what doesn't on your website, in your marketing channels, and with your customers and future customers, share that information with the business. Suggest what must be changed or kept the same based on your analysis.

> **Start small, but plan to grow over time.** Many companies start with just web analytics, but that naturally leads into channel analytics (marketing analytics), which then leads to channel optimization, which then leads to more information about customers and prospects (customer and predictive analytics), which then results in a strategic, company-wide analysis program that includes competitive analysis, and other marketplace dynamics. That means you might start your career in marketing as a web analyst but end up in the corporate strategy department as the director of business intelligence.

> **Report visually.** When presenting the results of your web, marketing, customer, and predictive analytics, consider reporting visually

via a dashboard or scorecard to help your audience better comprehend the results. The more you can show, instead of tell, the more easily your executive team will grasp the effectiveness of your results.

Focus on results first instead of cost. Although you will need cost information to understand your average cost per acquisition and cost per lead, it's best not to start the conversation with it—lead with the contribution to revenue first, then cost per acquisition and cost per lead, and then total cost. So, when reporting: results first, then cost.

Old data = bad data. Your CRM data decays over time, and you will want to append and cleanse your database regularly. The good news here is that your marketing automation system and CRM is likely integrated with a data verification/validation/updating service, such as Data.com, NetProspex, and others. This gives you an automated way to update prospect and customer profiles with current information. Another way to do this is to have your marketing automation system automatically add hard bounces to a list and synch that list with a campaign in your CRM. If you do that, you can go in on a regular basis and simply delete those records.

Get the right people on your team. As analytics tools and approaches evolve quickly, you'll need the resources to adapt to and adopt the latest technology. I never thought data scientists, data management experts, and analysts could or should be part of a marketing team until the past five years, but now finding those people is critical to your success.

Combine analytics approaches across the conversion funnel for maximum effect. After you have sussed out the four key areas of analytics discussed in this chapter, you'll be able to create rolled-up reports that describe your success in every step of the conversion funnel:

- **Reach**—The size of the audience you've touched, measured by impressions across all channels

- **Acquisition**—The number of visitors who interacted with your corporate brand, measured by clicks and shares

- **Conversion**—The number of visitors who registered for your content on your site or a third-party site or visited you at trade shows

- **Engagement**—The number of prospects receiving e-mail or retargeting ads and clicking

- **Close**—The lead-to-close ratio, which is the number of leads it took to close one deal

- **Retention**—The percentage of customers who renew every year

Key Highlights

There are four key areas of data that you should be intimately familiar with: web analytics, marketing analytics, customer analytics, and predictive analytics. Taken as a whole, this information will give you a clearer picture of your website visitors, converted prospects, customers, and the invisible gold stored in your database in the form of untapped leads. Use this information to understand what's working and not working on your website and in your marketing mix and mine for new opportunities among prospects and customers.

Recommended Reading

- *Building a Digital Analytics Organization: Create Value by Integrating Analytical Processes, Technology, and People into Business Operations*, Judah Phillips, Pearson FT Press, 2013.

- *Digital Marketing Analytics: Making Sense of Consumer Data in a Digital World*, Chuck Hemann and Ken Burbary, Que Publishing, 2013.

- *Marketing and Sales Analytics: Proven Techniques and Powerful Applications from Industry Leaders*, Cesar Brea, FT Press Analytics, 2014.

- *Social Media Metrics: How to Measure and Optimize Your Marketing Investment*, Jim Sterne, John Wiley and Sons, 2010.

- *Web Analytics 2.0: The Art of Online Accountability and Science of Customer Centricity*, Avinash Kaushik, Sybex, 2009.

- *Web Analytics: An Hour a Day*, Avinash Kaushik, Wiley Publishing, 2007.

- *Web Analytics Demystified*, Eric T. Peterson, self-published, 2004.

Endnotes

1. "Web Analytics Market by Solution and Services—Worldwide Forecasts," *Website Magazine*, August 15, 2014, www.websitemagazine.com/content/blogs/analytics/archive/2014/08/15/analytics-market-projected-to-more-than-double-by-2019.aspx#.

2. The Net Promoter Score and System, www.netpromoter.com/why-net-promoter/know/.

4

Experimentation and Optimization

When I began my tenure as SiteSpect's Chief Marketing Officer in 2007, I had never used an experimentation tool, but I'd had plenty of experience with the notion of testing. Having run dozens of direct response campaigns, I was used to the idea of testing different creative treatments to understand which version pulled better, or in other words, garnered the most responses.

The concept of online experimentation is much the same: Which version of tested content, layout, navigation, and website features (among other things) do visitors prefer? If you don't have a way of testing and tracking that information, you are missing out on a key opportunity to improve the online experience, which will help you maximize the value of your website, mobile initiatives, advertising, and e-mail.

Experimentation means testing to learn what works and what doesn't; optimization means continuous experimentation to improve the user experience toward a specific outcome, typically improving usability and increasing conversion rates. Nearly 75% of the companies (both B2B and B2C) surveyed by TrustRadius[1] have conversion rate optimization processes in place, and 60% of companies surveyed by Econsultancy[2] say that A/B testing and multivariate testing are "highly valuable" for improving conversion rates.

The Psychology of Conversion

We want our marketing output to be informative, persuasive, and even inspirational in order to communicate facts, create feelings, impart meaning, and generate action. To do that, we need to get into the minds of our prospective customers and understand what persuades them to take action, such as downloading a whitepaper, registering for a demo, filling out a Contact Us form, and whatever else you are tracking as a goal in your analytics tool.

Although experimentation will help you optimize your website, e-mails, advertising, and other marketing initiatives, it's even more powerful when you understand what motivates people's behavior. Maslow's hierarchy of needs is just as important in B2B marketing as it is in B2C marketing. All people seek to have their basic needs met, be safe, feel loved and respected, and have opportunities for growth, so if you don't know where to start in terms of being persuasive, that's a good general list. In other words, how might your product help your customers gain respect in their job, learn something new, further their career, or contribute to the goals of their company?

Here are several additional things you can do (and test) to make your marketing more persuasive:

1. Focus on your customer's needs and wants in order to differentiate your company, products, and services. The more you can organize an experience around what matters to the visitor, the higher converting your marketing efforts (and your business) will be. If you don't know what matters to your prospective customers, your buyer profile needs work. We'll review buyer profiles in Chapter 7, "Planning," and Chapter 9, "Programming, Part 2: Demand Generation."

2. Design the experience to be consistent with the visitor's values, attitudes, beliefs, and perceptions *or* treat them according to the values, attitudes, beliefs, and perceptions you'd like them to have. This is because people tend to behave either the way they view themselves or the way they believe they are viewed by others (depending on whether they are internally or externally focused). So if you'd like customers to be more high-value, treat them as though they already are.

3. Use the well-known principles of urgency and scarcity to prompt action. Avoiding loss is a primal driver of human behavior, and you can use that to your advantage. Scarcity is all about limited supply; urgency is about limited time or limited access. These principles are often used in the B2C world in terms of time-limited coupons, sales, and clearance codes—consider how your business might adopt similar initiatives.

4. Be clear about what you want visitors to do—do not put several calls to action on one page, e-mail, or ad, because more choice can often inhibit decision making. Give visitors a clear path and *one* call to action. Test your information architecture and navigation to ensure that the next steps are apparent and easy (and limit the number of steps a visitor has to go through to accomplish something).

5. Promote social proof in the form of positive client testimonials, vendor reviews, and case studies, which are all helpful in creating a strong preference in the mind of the visitor as well as easing anxiety in doing business with your company.

6. Make it easy to do business with your company by eliminating anything that gets in the way of what you want visitors to do; for example, streamlining visual clutter or a convoluted user experience.

7. Be credible in order to alleviate any visitor fear, uncertainty, or doubt about your company. Display credentials, awards, security icons, and other information to create trust.

Building the Testing Team

Before the availability of testing technology, experimenting with the marketing mix was not easily accomplished because of the number of departments and people involved, for example, developers, designers, marketers, copywriters, analysts, and executive stakeholders. Now, companies are building their own experimentation teams in charge of marketing optimization.

So who gets to be on the testing team? We'll talk more in Chapter 12, "Staffing," about the need for digital talent, and the experimentation function is the perfect place for such folks. Look for people with experience in analysis, who are comfortable with technology, and who have an inquisitive mindset. Because online testing in the B2B world is still fairly new, it's not easy to find experienced optimizers, but web analysts looking to make a contribution to the bottom line are often the perfect place to look.

Different Vendor Approaches to Experimentation

Most experimentation platforms employ client-side JavaScript page tags to swap in test content and track responses. It's fairly straightforward to place a tag in the global footer of your website, but the presence of the tag can make pages load more slowly and create what is known as a "flicker" effect as the original page is loaded and then swapped out with new test content. An alternative approach is to use a tag-free testing solution that enables you to experiment without making changes to your website. It's important to decide which approach works best for your needs, because one of the biggest barriers to experimentation success can be the limitations of the chosen testing tool. Because they can't easily test features and functionality, tag-based tools can limit the number and kinds of tests that can be run.

How to Evaluate an Experimentation Platform

Optimizing your marketing initiatives can get complicated, and you'll want to be sure the experimentation platform you choose can do everything you need. As well as the steps and questions posed in Chapter 2, "Strategy and Evaluation," here are some additional key questions to help you evaluate the experimentation platform you are considering:

- Does it offer both A/B and multivariate testing capabilities?
- Does it offer targeting and personalization?
- Can it test any type of content?
- Can it test mobile web and apps?
- Can it test features and functionality?
- How does it integrate with other technology?
- What are the deployment options?

Types of Experimentation

The optimization platform you choose should allow you to conduct both A/B testing and multivariate testing:

- **A/B testing** is a head-to-head comparison in which one or more new versions of something (a whole page or single element, such as a headline in an ad, a subject line in an e-mail, or an image on a page) are tested against the original version, which is called the control. For example, a new version of a call to action (such as a Download

Now button) might compete against the original call-to-action button to see which one visitors click on more often.

- **Multivariate testing** experiments with multiple elements and multiple variations of those elements being tested. For example, think of a page with a headline, a subhead, copy, an image, a form, and a call to action—those are six individual elements that can be tested. If you test three variations of each of these six elements, you are performing multivariate testing, the results of which will illustrate which combination of these elements visitors preferred, as well as which specific element(s) influenced visitor behavior (and which didn't).

You'll want to decide whether you need to (and are able to) test all the different combinations of elements and variations (full factorial array), or whether testing a subset (fractional factorial array) is sufficient. If you have the time and the traffic volume and your tool supports it, results from full factorial testing will give you the most directionally correct guidance.

Targeting Capabilities

As you'll learn in Chapter 6, "Targeting and Personalization," your testing tool should enable you to target content to audience segments within your test campaigns in order to create personalized experiences. You should be able to target any number of ways, including via on-site user behavior; recency, frequency, and monetary value; day-parting; referral URL; language and geography; and technology (such as mobile device or browser), among other criteria. Also, you should be able to use your own CRM data to define specific criteria for targeting and personalization.

Content Types

Make sure your testing tool can test more than just HTML. Most optimizers start with testing static HTML content, but as you get more experienced, you'll want to be able to experiment with content created in other markup languages, stylesheets, scripting languages, and dynamic content, as well as audio and video. Take an inventory of the types of content on your website and make sure your experimentation platform can support all of them.

Mobile Web and Apps

Even for B2B audiences, your prospects and customers are using mobile devices to search and browse, and you'll want to be able to experiment with your mobile web content and apps in order to optimize them. Consider testing and targeting different device types, keyboard support, operating systems, and browsers.

Features and Functionality

Experimentation is more than just testing content; you also want to be able to test how your site works. Your testing tool needs to support feature testing and segmentation, whole site designs, and optimization of on-site search, as well as changes in process flow. That's not easy to do with tag-based testing tools, but alternatives exist (such as the experimentation platform offered by my employer, SiteSpect) to give you more opportunities to test and optimize your site's functionality.

Technology Integration

At a minimum, your testing tool should integrate with your web analytics so that you can analyze your test results within your analytics platform, but also look for additional integrations with other third-party tools you use in order to gain as complete a picture of performance as possible.

Deployment Options

With tag-based vendors, you install a tag on your website and log in to a website to operate the tool (just like marketing automation and analytics). Tag-free SiteSpect offers both cloud-based and on-premise installation options.

Other Factors to Consider

Testing tools come in a wide range of pricing models, capabilities, reporting functionality, implementation models, and ease of use. If you are new to testing, you'll most likely start by using a free tool such as Google Experiments (found within Google Analytics), move up to a low-cost tag-based tool such as Optimizely or Visual Website Optimizer, and then settle on an industrial-strength experimentation platform, such as those provided by Adobe, Maxymiser, and SiteSpect, among others.

Defining Experimentation Goals

Experimentation is a process that, like analytics and marketing automation, uses technology to achieve its goals. And to do that, you have to understand what you are trying to accomplish. As with any other marketing initiative, define the goals you want to achieve with testing, strategies to help you achieve those goals, tactics to deliver on your strategies, and metrics to measure the success or failure of your experimentation efforts. We'll talk more about testing plans a little later, but for now, a very simple plan could be one like this:

- **Goals**—Improve site conversion rates 14.3%, from 3.5% to 4.0%.

- **Strategies**—Experiment on most-visited pages and landing pages.

- **Tactics**—Optimize forms and calls to action.

- **Expected Results**—An increase in the number of whitepaper downloads.

Where to Start: Process and Program

Your optimization program will have several process steps, from sourcing ideas, to vetting those ideas, planning and creating test campaigns, analyzing the results, and acting on them (see Figure 4.1).

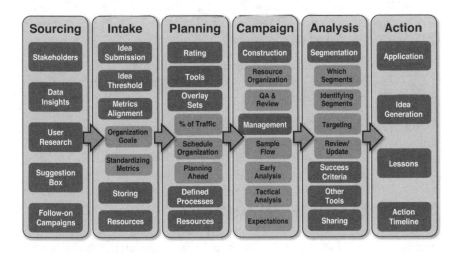

Figure 4.1 The Optimization Process.
Source: SiteSpect, Inc.

Step 1: Idea Sourcing

The first question becomes, where do you get ideas on what to test in order to support your goals?

Anyone with an interest in the testing program will have ideas on what to test. That includes key stakeholders, such as executive sponsors of the testing program, owners of test ideas, and your staff, so you'll want to solicit their feedback, suggestions, and ideas that can be tested by the experimentation team. Another place to look for ideas is your analytics; for example, what is your web analytics data saying about how visitors travel through your website? Where do they get stuck? What is important to your goals that the data shows isn't working? You want to ask "what happened?" in order to analyze the data and perceive opportunities for improvement whereby you formulate new hypotheses to test. For example, you might hypothesize that "changing the descriptive headline of the landing page to include a call to action will increase downloads." Now you have something to test. A hypothesis is simply a "what-if" assumption that you want to test that is both quantifiable and related to your goals in order to measure success. For example:

- What if we changed the page layout from two-column to one-column? We hypothesize that this will lower the bounce rate by X%.

- What if we removed drop-down menus from the main navigation? This will streamline user flow, increasing conversions by X%.

- What if we moved the Register Now button to the middle of the page, above the fold? Doing so will capture more eyeballs, leading to X# more form completions.

- What if we changed the e-mail subject line to include a deadline? That will create a sense of urgency, facilitating X% more opens and X% more click-throughs.

You should also look at feedback from other tools such as visitor surveys and customer experience management systems to learn what's working and not working for inspiration on ideas to test and the hypotheses that support them. Also consider employing user research in the experimentation process, such as UserTesting.com, usability reviews, and focus groups to gain valuable feedback on elements that need improvement.

You might also consider suggestions from employees, as well as the data and results from previous tests you've run, which are an invaluable source of follow-on ideas. Don't overlook your intuition; although it should not be the basis on which you make decisions, it should inspire ideas that you can test. You'll be surprised by how much you are right (and wrong) about something you believe in, and you'll know that only if you test your ideas.

Step 2: Idea Intake

The next step is to create a process for submitting and evaluating ideas. First, how would you like ideas submitted to the experimentation team (for example, e-mail or an online portal)? Perhaps you could create a running list of test idea submissions on the company's intranet. However you decide is the best way, make sure you communicate the process and your expectations.

You will also need to create a vetting process in order to decide what constitutes a good test idea. Then, work with test idea owners to figure out what metrics are important, how they will be reported, and where they will be stored. Creating shared metrics is a common challenge across several programs and channels in marketing and it applies to experimentation as well.

Step 3: Prioritization and Planning

After you know how you will receive and evaluate test ideas, it's time to rate and rank them. One quick way to do this is to graph them based on level of effort versus their expected impact—those with low effort but high impact will be quick wins, but it's still worth undertaking tests that require a high level of effort if they are expected to have a high impact. It's best to avoid any tests that will have a low impact, regardless of whether they're easy or hard to undertake.

At this step in the process, you'll want to have chosen an experimentation tool or at the very least have testing functionality included in your other tools. For example, you can often use features within e-mail service providers or marketing automation platforms to test e-mail campaigns. In addition, advertising networks give you the option of testing as many ad variations as you like—you are limited only by your imagination for text ads and the ability to produce creative treatments for display ads. For website and mobile optimization, look to the testing functionality contained in your analytics platform or marketing suite or choose a standalone experimentation platform.

Another important item to plan is whether you will run test campaigns that overlay with other campaigns in order to understand how that affects traffic (and also what percentage of traffic you want directed to the campaign). This is important in gaining statistical significance, which is the level of confidence in the results of a test. You'll want to run a test to at least 95% confidence (meaning there's a 5% chance of a false positive), and depending on your volume of traffic, it might take you a few weeks to get there. Just be aware of anything that's happening in the meantime, such as campaigns, holidays, or corporate events, which might affect test results.

But it's not enough to know what's happening while you are running the test; you'll also want to be planning ahead for new campaigns. If there are any other standardized processes your company regularly uses, think about how you can apply them to your experimentation program in order to maintain a consistent flow of test ideas and plan.

Lastly, you'll decide what resources are needed to run the test—who will build it, run it, report the results, and what creative treatments and variations are needed. Now you have everything you need in order to create a bulletproof test plan. Make sure your test plan describes these elements:

- Goals: what you want to achieve

- Strategies: how you hope to achieve those goals

- Tactics: what you will do

- Test elements: what's being tested—the control(s) and variations

- Hypothesis: expectations of the test

- Success metrics: how you define success or failure

- Risks: what might require stopping the test

- Required resources: who's doing what and what resources they need

- Who the test requester/test idea owner is

- Results: what happened

- A plan to communicate those results

- Deadlines

The idea is to create a concise, helpful document that will aid in the creation and implementation of the test.

Step 4: Test Campaign Creation and Execution

So now you are ready to build test campaigns, and to do that, you must create the right test design. Good test design encompasses several important considerations. For example, you should do the following:

- Decide whether you need an A/B or a multivariate test. Are you testing just one thing or multiple things? This is important because you want to avoid improper factoring, such as changing an image's size, placement, format, and content in an A/B test when it should be a multivariate test, which will help you understand what change actually mattered.

- Pick the appropriate test array (full or fractional factorial array)— your testing tool should have this built into the functionality.

- Make sure you run the test long enough and have enough traffic to get a statistically valid sample size. Run your test for at least a couple of weeks to smooth out any bias, even if you reach statistical significance before that.

- Target your test to a relevant audience.

Now that you've worked through the test plan, design, and timeline, it's a good idea to double-check the required resources and expectations for execution and analysis. You will need a plan to manage and maintain your current test campaigns.

Step 5: Analysis and Reporting

One of the best ways to gain insight into test results is by segmenting those results. If you already know what segments are important to your business, you'll know which ones are useful for targeting tests. (If not, see Chapter 6.) While analyzing test results, you might even discover significant new segments you hadn't thought of before.

You can segment a test by either ad hoc or post hoc methods. To run ad hoc segmentation, your testing tool identifies visitors from a target segment (such as "visitors referred from LinkedIn") in real time and assigns them to the test.

With post hoc segmentation, you will analyze the results of segmented test participants and compare those results across the control and test groups. Discovering what worked and what didn't for different segments of an audience can be a thrilling experience, because what you learn from the test results in one channel, such as your website, can be tested in other channels, such as your e-mail marketing and advertising.

Before you do that, however, you must clearly define the success criteria of your test. What does optimization success mean for you, your department, and your company? Does it mean:

- A huge increase in conversion rate or revenue?

- An incremental increase in engagement metrics?

- Fewer calls or e-mails to support?

- A specific percentage increase in e-mail opens or click-throughs?

- An increase in ad impressions, click-throughs, or conversions?

There is no right or wrong, but it is important to define success. Not all the ideas that you test will be clear winners, but that does not mean the test is a failure. Testing shows you not only what works, but also what doesn't, and because of that, it's an important way to mitigate risk. At SiteSpect, we like to say that the only test that is a failure is one in which you do not learn something new.

As the results come in, you'll want to share the full test results with colleagues, stakeholders, and sponsors—and perhaps even the entire company, depending on your culture.

Step 6: Taking Action

After you have the results, it's time to take action. As with analytics, one of the worst things you can do in experimentation is to learn something new (and potentially important) and then not apply it. Your results can then be used to generate additional ideas and opportunities for testing. The ultimate goal is to build a culture of optimization within your organization, one that incorporates data from analytics and testing into the overall business decision-making process.

In fact, using the actionable intelligence gathered from a testing program and applying it to each area of your organization where it matters drives a culture of optimization that will help your understanding of these areas:

- Your prospect's and customer's digital body language
- Your success (or failure) in meeting your target audiences' needs
- Your conversion funnel's strengths and weaknesses
- Areas of the site, ads, and e-mail that are working and not working

These lessons learned are helpful in driving new insights and ideas for additional test plans.

Experimentation Best Practices

When you start testing, you should *have a goal in mind,* usually to improve a key performance indicator, the metric of your most important goal. For many B2B companies, typically the most important goal is conversion around lead generation, such as registering for a whitepaper, which means that forms are usually the most important conversion point. Testing their length, verbiage, placement, design, and call to action are key. You might not think that the difference of one word would make a difference, but it can.

Testing should be applied to your *entire conversion funnel*—the content and campaigns that bring visitors to your web and mobile site (or app) as well as the site itself, since it's the center of all of your marketing activities and the place where you communicate your key features, advantages, benefits, and differentiators directly to prospects and customers. Consider testing the following activities:

- **Reach**—PPC ads, banner ads, social media, and offline media

- **Acquisition**—Landing pages, product pages, navigation, and on-site search

- **Conversion**—Forms, form fields, and calls to action related to your KPIs

- **Engagement**—Copy, images, content, and all elements of e-mail

- **Retention**—Receipts, thank-you pages, and additional offers

Also, you'll want to decide what to test in each channel. Here are a few ideas:

- **Website**—Navigation, conversion path, layout, images (content, placement, size, format), fonts (styles, size, color), copy (voice, tone, length), buttons (size, color, style, call to action, placement), and forms (length, specific fields, design, placement)

- **E-mails**—Sender, subject line, format (HTML versus text), layout, headlines, copy, images, call to action, and signatures

- **Advertising**—Format (display versus text), layout, headline, copy, call to action, and landing page URL

Use your analytics to *discover optimization opportunities* and develop a continuous approach to building a successful testing program. Along the way, you'll ask four key questions:

1. What's working?

2. What's not working?

3. What should we do more of (or less of)?

4. What must we change right now?

The answers to those questions will help you get a clearer picture of what to test as well as hypotheses. Beyond your KPIs, consider what other metrics you need from each step in the conversion funnel to measure the success of your testing program. But don't stop there! Experimentation is a continuous activity. Ideally, you'll use test results to inspire future testing ideas (in addition to your analytics data, key stakeholders, and user research).

Key Highlights

You can test anything, and you should, because experimentation is a proven technique to improve the user experience across many channels. Use the principles of conversion psychology to create a continuous, scalable experimentation program that optimizes your website, e-mails, ads, and anything else that can be tested.

After you have a handle on your analytics, you can use that data to inform your testing program, along with other sources. To build that program, you need the right people on the team, the right testing tool, and defined goals, strategies, and tactics. You'll create bulletproof test plans, which will help you with all the steps in the experimentation process:

- Idea sourcing and intake

- Creating hypotheses

- Planning and prioritization

- Creating, executing, analyzing, and reporting on test campaigns

- Optimizing based on results

Think of experimentation as a mind-set and you'll be on your way to creating a culture of optimization that will serve your marketing efforts well into the future.

Recommended Reading

- *Conversion Optimization: The Art and Science of Converting Prospects to Customers*, Khalid Saleh and Ayat Shukairy, O'Reilly Media, Inc., 2011.

- *Convert! Designing Web Sites to Increase Traffic and Conversion*, Ben Hunt, Wiley Publishing Inc., 2011.

- *Experiment! Website Conversion Rate Optimization with A/B and Multivariate Testing*, Colin McFarland, New Riders, 2013.

- *You Should Test That!*, Chris Goward, John Wiley and Sons, 2013.

- *Website Optimization: An Hour a Day*, Rich Page, John Wiley and Sons, Inc., 2012.

Online Resources

- www.marketingexperiments.com

- www.whichtestwon.com

- www.conversionxl.com

Endnotes

1. "Buyers Guide to Conversion Rate Optimization Software," Trust Radius, https://www.trustradius.com/guides/conversion-rate-optimization/2014/introduction.

2. "Conversion Rate Optimization Report 2014," Econsultancy, https://econsultancy.com/reports/conversion-rate-optimization-report.

5

Marketing Automation

If you are not yet using marketing automation, it's likely that you soon will be. According to data from Pepper Global as published in *Advertising Age*,[1] 53% of B2B marketers are currently using marketing automation, 17% are considering it, and 30% are not using it yet.

According to that same study, the most popular marketing automation platforms are these:

- Marketo, used by 29% of respondents

- Eloqua/Oracle, used by 21% of respondents

- Hubspot, used by 11% of respondents

- Pardot[2]/Salesforce.com, used by 11% of respondents

- Act-On, used by 6% of respondents

Marketing automation is simply automated processes via technology that help you identify, nurture, and convert prospective customers. With the rising popularity of marketing automation in the past decade, B2B marketers are now benefiting from a closed-loop, automated demand creation and management system. For example, marketing automation can tell you the following on a prospect-level basis:

- What keyword someone searched on

- What lead source they came from (Google, LinkedIn, Twitter, etc.)

- What pages they visited

- What e-mails they opened or didn't open

- What links they clicked

- What content they consumed—either downloaded or clicked

- What lists they belong to

- What events or webinars they've registered for and/or attended

- Whether they've bounced or unsubscribed

- Whether they're a good fit for your business (grade)

- Whether their activity signals a readiness to engage with sales (score)

Because of this information, marketing automation makes it much easier to build relationships with prospects, personalize content for them, and understand their behavior. Your marketing automation platform will help you discover and understand your individual prospect and customer behavior across several channels, including paid search, social, events, and your website, among other things. Because of this, marketing automation enables agility in responding to buyer behavior, which triggers relevant content, segmentation (and therefore better targeting), and more customization of messages and how those messages are delivered. It gives you a centralized, trackable way to manage your marketing messages across channels and send those messages directly to your prospects and customers. And it helps you measure results—the impact that your marketing has. More than anything, marketing automation helps you improve productivity and do so much more than you could have previously imagined—all while helping to capture leads, nurture them, and close them.

Barriers to Success

One might ask, "With all the benefits that marketing automation conveys, why isn't everyone using it?" The first barrier comes down to budget in that some companies just won't foot the bill for what is still considered a little new and different. Although the percentage of budget typically allocated to marketing automation is small, typically 1% to 10% of the overall budget, it's still large enough of a chunk to have to justify, explain, and defend. As with other types of technology, sometimes it takes an executive advocate to seed the idea, find the funding, and design the strategy—and without such support, it can be difficult to get started or find success.

After that, it comes down to people. It can be difficult (although it's becoming easier) to find skilled personnel who:

- Are comfortable with technology

- Can think through the mechanics of complex campaign creation

- Can write and design e-mails and landing pages or work with writers and designers to make that happen

- Cue everything up in a programmatic way in the system

- Execute flawlessly

- Report on results

Another reason marketing automation fails is a lack of strategy, which can quickly kill success with any technology. What matters most is to have a defined strategy with established goals and expected outcomes in order to make the most of technology, including marketing automation platforms.

Marketing automation success can also suffer from a lack of content, because if a company has not taken the time to create compelling content or design a content marketing strategy, marketing automation will be automating essentially nothing.

How to Evaluate a Marketing Automation Platform

So what's the baseline functionality you should look for in a marketing automation platform? In addition to being easy to use, make sure the system you choose gives you the following:

- *Campaign Creation and Management*
  - Automated campaigns
  - Segmented lists
  - Capability to host content

- Landing pages

- Forms

- *E-mail Marketing*

- *Analytics and Reporting*

- *Lead Management*

  - Scoring and grading

  - Anonymous visitor identification

  - Lead activity insight

  - Bi-synchronous integration with CRM

- *Infrastructure*

  - Database

  - Website integration

  - User management

  - E-mail deliverability

  - Testing

  - Automation functionality

Let's look at this functionality in depth.

Campaign Creation and Management

The marketing automation platform you choose should give you the ability to created automated campaigns and easily manage them. In addition, it should enable you to create lists based on your key audience segments, host a content library, and produce forms and landing pages quickly.

Automated Campaigns

There are several ways to think of campaigns:

- As a naming convention for how records first entered your marketing automation system when you imported leads from other sources; for example:

- Prospect newsletter subscribers

- Past trade shows

- Leads from CRM

- Contacts from CRM

- Opportunities from CRM

- Current customers

- As a naming convention for the sources of campaigns, programs, and activities that are currently generating leads into your marketing automation system, either from a form (sources could include PPC, organic search, publisher e-mail blasts, and webinars, among others) or via a list upload (third-party content syndication or trade show leads).

- As the actual automated campaigns that are nurturing leads within your marketing automation platform (drip marketing campaigns).

In any event, the ability to create campaigns based on lead source is important for reporting on ROI, and the ability to run automated campaigns is important for lead nurturing. Your campaign will consist of several pieces, and the attention to detail in their creation should not be overlooked. These campaign pieces include the following:

- Outreach e-mail(s)

- Autoresponder e-mail

- Thank-you page with or without offer content, depending on whether the offer was included with the autoresponder e-mail

- Landing page—copy and images

- Form for lead capture

- Offer content

- Plan for triggered actions—who gets notified, who is added to a list, and what happens when someone submits a form or clicks a link in the e-mail

Segmented Lists

We'll review segmentation in more detail in Chapter 6, "Targeting and Personalization." Here we address the importance of creating segmented lists in your marketing automation system. Lists are simply groups of recipients, segmented by source, interest, or some other attribute in common with other recipients. Think of lists as a specific, filtered view of your database, because a prospect can be on one or more lists without having one or more records. The more specific your lists are, the better targeted your e-mail marketing and lead nurture campaigns can be.

Regarding the list-building capabilities of your marketing automation vendor, it should be easy to add, delete, and move prospects from static lists as well as create dynamic lists based on specific criteria. Lists make it easy to manage subscription memberships from within your marketing automation system as well as your CRM—for example, the capability to add a new customer to the customer newsletter list with just a few clicks.

So how do you go about segmenting your database into lists that you can use in your marketing automation platform? Use the same criteria as you do with other targeted campaigns. Here are a few ideas:

- Sales stage, such as the following:
  - Leads
  - Marketing-qualified leads
  - Sales-accepted leads
  - Opportunities
  - Customers
  - Lost opportunities
- Title or seniority
- Department or functional area
- Industry
- Account name
- Company size
- Event
- Webinar

- Source

- Product interest

- Website activity

- Score and/or grade

You can even segment by active versus non-active prospects based on whether or not they opened an e-mail or clicked on a link within an e-mail. Another usage for lists is to segment records that have first names and those that do not; the lists with first names receive e-mails with a first name variable tag, whereas the lists without first names receive e-mails with a generic greeting. That way, your prospects will never receive a "Dear %%First_Name%%" e-mail again.

Capability to Host Content

Your marketing automation platform should host all of your content files for easy tracking within the system. You should be able to upload PDFed whitepapers, e-books, and datasheets. Note that some vendors are unable to host video but connect with video hosting providers, such as Wistia. If you are promoting hosted content on a third-party site, be sure to use a custom redirect for tracking and reporting the source correctly.

Landing Pages and Forms

Marketing automation should easily enable you to build landing pages and forms. A landing page is simply a streamlined page on your website designed specifically for one call to action, such as to register for an event, a webinar, or a whitepaper.

Your marketing automation vendor should give you the option of using your current landing-page design or creating landing pages from scratch; either way, they will be hosted on the marketing automation platform, and the data from the forms will be passed into the CRM.

The forms themselves should also be easy to build and integrate into the landing page. Think about what kinds of information (and what's the minimum amount required) you need to collect from a prospect in order to understand whether they're a potential customer. The longer the form, the fewer form completions you'll garner, and the more inaccurate that information might be, but it also might be the easiest way to collect that information if you don't want to append your database records. But there's a way around this, called progressive profiling. The idea is to ask for a minimal amount of information up front in order to maximize the number of form completions, and then ask for one more piece of information when a prospect returns to a website in order to flesh out what's known about them.

For each form, you'll need to think about and address what happens after your prospect fills out the form; for example:

- Assign the lead to a sales rep

- Notify the assigned sales rep

- Trigger a thank-you e-mail

- Redirect the prospect to a thank-you page

Fortunately, these decisions are usually built into the process of creating the form, so they're not easy to overlook.

E-mail Marketing

This is truly the bread and butter of marketing automation—the ability to create and send e-mails, either one-to-one, to a list, or from an automated campaign. There are many dynamics of a successful e-mail marketing program that we'll review in Chapter 9, "Programming, Part 2: Demand Generation." To help you execute e-mail marketing, you'll want to look for a marketing automation platform that offers the capability to carry out these tasks:

- Easily create, design, and edit HTML and text e-mails

- Analyze e-mails for browser compatibility and spam potential

- Create e-mail templates for reuse

- Schedule delivery

- A/B test content to see what recipients prefer

- Create e-mail preference centers so that prospects and customers can manage their list subscriptions or unsubscribe altogether

Analytics and Reporting

Because marketing automation platforms can track prospect behavior and store data, they are the go-to resources for measuring marketing performance. This kind of closed-loop reporting increases visibility and accountability across the entire sales cycle. With marketing automation, first-touch source attribution (see Chapter 3, "Analytics," and Chapter 13,

"Measuring") becomes much easier and marketing can more easily track how their activities influenced deal revenue.

To do this, your marketing automation platform should connect not only with your web analytics provider but also with your other channels. For example, you should be able to report on campaign performance, content consumption, events, form and landing-page data, organic and paid search, conversions, on-site search, social media, webinars, chat, and, of course, e-mail marketing.

In terms of e-mail analytics, you'll want to track the following, at a minimum:

- Total number of e-mails sent.

- Total number of e-mails delivered.

- Delivery rate. (Aim for 90% at a bare minimum; there's no reason your delivery rate can't be 98% or higher when you keep your lists clean.)

- Total bounces.

- Kinds of bounces (vacation replies versus inactive e-mails, for example).

- Open rates.

- Number of unique clicks (and who they are).

- Click-through rates.

- Opt-outs.

- Spam reports.

Because the analytics in your marketing automation platform encompasses several channels, you can report on more than just e-mail, for example:

- Advertising performance

- Keyword popularity

- Social media activity

- Content consumption

- Event engagement

- Webinar registrations and attendance

You also should be able to report on each stage of the prospect life cycle to understand how prospects are moving through the conversion funnel and to get a better sense of the buyer journey. Because your platform will be able to track everything, you'll be able to report on everything in the pipeline:

- Number of net new leads

- Number of opportunities in the pipeline

- Pipeline velocity—days that it took for leads to progress through the pipeline

- Lead-to-close ratio and any other stage-to-stage ratios to understand what percentage of leads make it through the pipeline

- Campaign results and ROI from each channel

Lead Management

Your marketing automation platform will help you understand the quality of leads in your pipeline via scoring and grading, track prospect activity, and also report on which companies have visited your website.

Scoring and Grading

One of the ways to ensure you are passing the most appropriate leads to your sales team is to score and grade them. A score is a measure of prospect activity; a grade is a measure of whether they're a good fit as a customer for your company based on their demographic information. Think of scoring as a measure of your prospect's interest in your company and grading as a measure of your interest in the prospect.

Marketing automation enables you to automatically score, grade, and segment your prospects such that you follow up with only the ones that are the best pattern match to your ideal buyer profile. Scoring and grading is an important step in qualifying prospects for sales follow-up, while less-qualified leads stay in marketing for nurturing.

Lead scoring is very easy; you decide how much each prospect action counts, based on a point value. For every action a prospect takes, they are automatically scored and that score is aggregated. For example, viewing the pricing page, downloading a whitepaper, or attending a webinar each adds points to a prospect's score. You can set the score for each activity. Let's say your prospect signed up for a webinar worth 50 points, but then did not attend, which subtracts 25 points. They now have only 25 points, whereas a prospect who registered for a webinar worth 50 points and then attended for 50 points now has a score of 100 points.

Pay attention to the most important buying signals on your website, and consider the following behavior worthy of higher point values when scoring leads:

- Landing on your website via a search phrase that signals buying intent; for example: "XYZ vendor comparison"

- Viewing the pricing page

- Requesting a demo

Work with your sales team to decide which actions are more important than others in qualifying prospects. Sales reps should prioritize follow-up based on score and grade, which makes sense because they want to deal only with leads that are likely to turn into new business. You can set up automation rules so that leads that don't meet the minimum score threshold stay in marketing until their scores increase.

Lead grading is also important in qualifying leads, but is not based on behavior. Grades are derived from how well a prospect matches your ideal customer profile based on industry, company size, location, and job title, for example. You can set up automation rules to grade your prospect database as well as adjust grades based on the quality of the pattern match; for example, moving a half grade up or down. Grading works only if you have the information; you might not have enough complete data to accurately grade the database, and will have to either (1) not grade, (2) append the information, and/or (3) do progressive profiling, in order to accurately grade leads.

Anonymous Visitor Identification

Your website might get thousands, hundreds of thousands, or millions of visits every month, and chances are that most of those visits will be from anonymous traffic. The percentage of visitors you can actually identify is related to your conversion rate. So if your conversion rate is somewhere between 2% and 5%, that's how much of your audience is known to you.

The good news is that when you implement marketing automation software, it will conduct anonymous visitor tracking to help identify who is coming to your website. It does this by recording the IP address of the visitor, conducting a reverse DNS lookup to identify a hostname, and then also performing a WHOIS lookup for the IP address to see who owns it in order to further identify the organization and where it is located. This can be particularly helpful to the sales team to know that accounts they are targeting are active on the website, regardless of whether a contact at that account has ever downloaded anything.

Lead Activity Insight

Your marketing automation software will track and record the behavior of both anonymous visitors and known prospects. What's interesting is when an anonymous visitor finally registers and all of his or her previous activity becomes associated with the contact record. You'll have a fully formed picture of a brand-new prospect, including history on the following data:

- Keywords searched on

- Ads clicked

- Pages visited

- Website links clicked

- Files downloaded

- E-mails received, opened, and links clicked

- Webinars registered for and/or attended

- Events registered for and/or attended

- Forms filled out

- Content consumed (such as videos, whitepapers, e-books)

- Site searches completed

One of the things to be aware of is that tracking all of this activity history consumes data storage space in your CRM, and over time you will likely need to increase the size of your CRM database to accommodate all of this new information.

Bi-synchronous Integration with CRM

Some B2B marketers use their marketing automation platform as their CRM, but most often, you'll already have a CRM in place beforehand. You'll want to make sure that leads coming into either system get synchronized with the other system in order to keep everything up-to-date. Having said that, for list uploads, it can be easier to import them into both systems manually so that they can be added to a specific list in the marketing automation platform. If that's not important, just upload in one place and let the synchronization happen. Either way, you'll want to make sure you have lead routing rules in place in one of the two systems—for example, your CRM's automatic lead assignment rule based on geography to assign leads.

Infrastructure

Some of the technical aspects of your marketing automation platform are also important to consider; these include management of your database, integration with your website, email deliverability, and automation functionality, among other things. Let's take a look.

Database

When you procure your marketing automation platform, you will likely do so based on the size of your database of mailable prospects. This is an important reason to keep your database clean—up to one-third of B2B contacts can become obsolete over the course of a year, and if you aren't cleaning up your system on a regular basis, you probably have many out-of-date e-mail addresses. That's a challenge, because it can affect not only your e-mail sending reputation, but also your productivity—you don't want to be e-mailing a bunch of prospects who are no longer in a position to do business with your company nor do you want to be paying for them by including obsolete contacts in your database.

Website Integration

There are a few things to consider here:

- **Tracking Code**—Inserting a line of JavaScript into the footer of every page or global include to track and report on which pages and content your anonymous visitors and known prospects visit

- **Tracker Domain**—Creating a tracker subdomain (CNAME) so that your marketing automation-generated URLs appear that they are from your company; for example: info.*companyname*.com or go.*companyname*.com or www2.*companyname*.com

- **Custom Fonts**—Granting permission so that your marketing automation platform can use any custom fonts used on your website on your new forms and landing pages

Also, because your landing pages will be built and hosted within your marketing automation platform, you might want to use a testing tool to swap the content onto your regular domain so that your prospects see www.*company*.com/*landingpage* instead of info.*company*.com/*landingpage* (or whatever tracker subdomain you choose).

User Management

Make sure you choose a platform that enables you to customize permissions based on user roles to manage what other users can see and what they can change within the platform. Only administrators should have access to account settings. Don't underestimate the time it will take to set up new users, help them create their signatures (or create them yourself), and educate them on how the platform works. You'll have granted them user permissions based on their role, and because of that, they likely won't have all the privileges that you do as an administrator or marketing user. But they should still be able to send trackable e-mails, see results, view known prospects and unknown visitors, and receive lead activity alerts, among other things.

Based on company policy, standard operating procedures, or philosophy, decide how much flexibility other users should have. Should they be able to send e-mails to a list of thousands, or is that something only marketing should be able to do? Either way, agree to the accessible functionality and then hold a kick-off meeting with the team for initial training. Point them to the various training resources your marketing automation platform vendor provides, including tips, hacks, and best practices. (And keep reminding them—often when another department cannot accomplish something with a system or platform officially "owned" by another department, the owner department becomes the de facto help desk for that platform, which is usually an unforeseen and unintended consequence of adopting technology in the first place. Decide ahead of time how you want to handle that situation.)

E-mail Deliverability

You'll need to verify your marketing automation platform in order to send e-mails via your own domain, and to do this, you'll likely have to work with your IT department, which will help authenticate e-mails through Sender Policy Framework (SPF) and DomainKeys Identified Mail (DKIM). ISPs and corporate spam filters check for authentication, so you'll want to make sure this step is complete before using the platform for sending e-mail.

Something I learned from working with Pardot is that if you are doing e-mail marketing in earnest for the first time, you will want to "warm up" your IP address by sending several smaller blasts before larger ones. The idea is to send fewer than 5,000 e-mails per day for the first week to your most accurate lists to build your sender reputation.

Testing

As you read in Chapter 4, "Experimentation and Optimization," it's as important to test your e-mail marketing as it is to test your web and mobile sites and apps. Make sure your vendor supports this kind of testing on e-mails, forms, landing pages, and any other activities you'll be conducting. It's fun to see the kinds of subject lines, offers, sender identification, and calls to action that move the needle in behavior, and this kind of testing should be easy to accomplish within a marketing automation platform.

Automation Functionality

Lastly, before you select a platform, understand the breadth and depth of the automation functionality available to you. At a minimum, the platform should:

- Create dynamic lists based on selected criteria

- Trigger autoresponders and thank-you pages

- Trigger actions based on activity on pages, forms, files, e-mails, and links, such as add to CRM campaign, add to a specific list, or adjust lead score

- Trigger notifications based on activity

- Be able to create automated lead nurturing/drip marketing programs

Implementation

Before you get started in implementing a marketing automation platform, make sure you have the appropriate resources. At the very least, you will need the help of your webmaster/web developer(s), IT department, sales operations/CRM administrator, and marketing and creative teams to help you with setting up the technical and creative infrastructure.

The setting-up activity includes, but is not limited to, the following:

- Website integration.

- Database creation—including importing prospects, customers, and previous unsubscribes, as well as creating segmented lists.

- Campaign creation to associate prospect sources.

- Content library creation, including uploading files, and creating forms and landing pages.

- Automation rules, page action triggers, and form completion actions.

- Drip program(s) creation.

- Grading and scoring rules.

- E-mail template creation.

- Lead assignment process.

- Integration with CRM, social media, webinar hosting platforms, site search, and other marketing tools. (Many marketing automation systems use out-of-the-box connectors that make it extremely easy to integrate.)

- Custom redirects to track clicks outside of your website.

- Dynamic content rules and creation.

- User management.

It's a lot to consider, but those are the basic elements of what needs to be done to implement marketing automation software, which is much easier if you don't have a lot of infrastructure in place just yet.

Measuring Effectiveness

When measuring the effectiveness of their marketing automation efforts, B2B marketers typically look at five things first:

1. Lead volume
2. Cost
3. Conversion rate
4. Lead velocity
5. Revenue generated

In other words, how many leads did you generate, how much did those leads cost, at what percentage did they convert, how quickly did they move through the pipeline, and how much deal revenue did they generate? When you have that information, you can understand your cost per lead (spend/ number of leads), which is the start to understanding your lead-generation ROI. We'll talk more about this in Chapter 13.

Marketing automation also helps you track your engagement metrics, such as open rates, click-through rates, and website visits generated, although most B2B marketers are finding that these are becoming a little less important as they become more and more accountable for generating real pipeline opportunities and actual revenue.

Marketing Automation Best Practices

Here is some hard-won advice, as well as best practices, to get you started on the right track.

Practice Database Hygiene

The implementation process itself is one of the most important factors determining marketing automation success, because it's your first and best opportunity to make sure that everything is right, and that means you should clean up your CRM database *before* implementing marketing automation. Your marketing automation software will synchronize with your CRM, and if you have a lot of duplicates or bad records, you'll have a big problem that will need to be cleaned up in both systems. Let's say someone has come to your site and registered for an e-book, and you've converted the lead to a contact. Without marketing automation, when they come back to your site, they typically register again with an e-mail address, which means the same contact could be in your database (as both a lead and a contact) with multiple e-mail addresses and other contact information. This is unfortunate, because marketing automation platforms match on e-mail addresses, but that doesn't mean they know which e-mail is the best one—that's your job.

In addition to deduping, convert all leads to contacts as appropriate, associate those contacts with their known accounts, and standardize all the account names. For example, GE might be in your database as GE, Ge, G E, Gen Elec, General Elec, Gen Electric, or General Electric—but they are all the same account and need to be deduped, merged, and standardized.

Other issues with data quality include not only different spellings of a company's name, but also the following situations:

- Different e-mail addresses for the same contact

- Typos generated when the data was entered

- Missing data (no first name, last name, company name, or e-mail address—this is particularly difficult for marketing automation systems, which typically match on e-mail address)

- Intentionally wrong information, such as a prospect registering as Abcd Efghijk

- Different mailing addresses

You must merge, purge, delete, and convert contact records; do whatever is necessary so that the database records you are importing into your marketing automation software are as pristine as possible.

Validate/Verify Your Data

One of the ways you can manage bad data before you upload your CRM contacts into the marketing automation platform is to run them through an e-mail appending/verification service. That way, you can identify, update, or delete the bad e-mails before you ever upload them. At the same time, you can append important information that might be missing that will enable you to segment the database into targeted lists, such as company size, industry, and title.

Cleaning up your e-mail lists means you will be able to lower your bounce rate when you run your first e-mail campaign, which is important. One of the mistakes B2B marketers make when they are first starting out in marketing automation is to run an e-mail campaign to the entire database to see who bounces or unsubscribes, and then use the resulting e-mail addresses as the master database—but that's not a recommended best practice.

Here's why: If your database has a higher than 10% bounce rate, you could face future issues with e-mail deliverability such that legitimate e-mail addresses could begin to bounce. Your e-mail sending reputation for your e-mail domain will degrade and possibly result in blacklisting of the IP used to send e-mail—so, make sure you clean up your records and verify your remaining e-mails through a third party before importing them into your marketing automation platform.

There are many e-mail appending/verification services that can help you clean up your CRM, and it's a good idea to use that service even if you aren't considering marketing automation, just to keep your CRM in order. People move, they change jobs, and companies open new offices all the time—leading to questionable data quality. The only way to deal with this situation is to keep up with it. Data.com and FreshAddress are two well-known data appending/cleaning services to check out; there are many others.

Align Your Sales Team

Marketing automation affects the processes and agreements you have with your sales team, so you need to have a conversation about the upcoming marketing automation implementation and how you expect the new platform will change previously standardized processes. For example:

- Will it change the way leads are assigned?
- Will it change the volume of leads assigned?

- Will or should automated drip marketing take the places of sales outreach for inbound leads? If so, when and how?

- How will marketing partner with sales to create customized lead nurturing programs and personalized outreach campaigns?

- What else can your departments do together to maximize the success of the marketing automation program?

You'll have many more questions than these to answer, and the discussion will be different for every company. The bottom line is to make sure you do your homework before implementing marketing automation, because your sales team will pepper you with questions, and they will expect answers, even if you don't have them yet.

Don't Overreact

Avoiding overreacting is particularly important now that your sales team has visibility into who is visiting your website. Make sure they (or anyone else) are not sending e-mails that say something like this:

> I see that you came to our website from an e-mail sent by our marketing staff last week and just downloaded the XYZ Whitepaper. In fact, it looks like you've visited a lot of our pages in the past week—are you interested in receiving pricing on our product?

As the unfortunate recipient of many e-mails like this after I've simply downloaded a whitepaper, I find this approach intrusive. Just because you have the knowledge of someone's on-site behavior does not mean it's always appropriate to use that knowledge to act; sometimes, just observing behavior over a period of time can often yield more complete insights.

Be Transparent

Make sure website visitors know what they are getting themselves into when they register for something on your website; don't automatically add them to your newsletter list if they did not ask to subscribe. Similarly, ensure that you are following the best practices for the countries in which you do business. For example, if you use cookies and you have European visitors, make sure that your cookie use policy is somewhere on your website. Also, in August of 2014, Canada enacted the Canadian Anti-Spam Law (CASL), which makes it unlawful to e-mail or social message anyone who did not expressly opt in (as opposed to the U.S.'s opt-out CAN SPAM law). Many marketers joke that the U.S. CAN SPAM law means that you *can spam* as long as you provide a mechanism to the recipient for opting out, a physical mailing address, and a subject line that correctly describes the content of the e-mail—but many recipients do not know these details and might accuse you of spamming just because they received an unwanted e-mail.

Be Careful

Your e-mail campaigns and landing pages should be written and designed outside of your marketing automation platform. That's because after you have something cued up in the system, it's extremely easy to make it public, whether it's ready or not. I say this from experience; I was just about to e-mail an event landing-page URL to a key client who was speaking at the event when I thought to myself, "I'll just check to make sure the auto-triggered thank-you e-mail is all set." There was no reason for me to think the thank-you e-mail wasn't all set; I was just being super cautious. And good thing too—the e-mail was half-written, with placeholder text and typos galore. But there it was—cued up as an autoresponder to a live landing page!

Strengthen Review Processes

Following that scenario, we put into place much more stringent review processes such that nothing would ever get cued up again that hadn't gone through a rigorous and systematic editing and QA process. That might sound like status quo, but you'd be surprised by how much can happen with all the moving parts in marketing automation, all the different people touching the system, and all the content being generated—something is bound to be overlooked. For example, I recently looked at another company's live landing pages created by a marketing automation platform and noticed that they weren't rendering correctly; it happens all the time.

Put Strategy First

As mentioned in Chapter 1, "The Evolving Marketing Landscape," technology does not solve problems; strategy solves problems. Technology only serves to worsen the problems you already have—and it's just as easy to automate bad marketing as it is to automate excellent marketing. After you have the right strategy in place, examine your people and processes. Do you have the right staff? Are the right goals, roles, and procedures in place, and are they properly communicated? Only when you answer these questions should you look to technology to help you.

Continually Educate Yourself

As with most other marketing tools, you'll never stop learning about marketing automation usage and best practices. Don't underestimate how much time it will take to learn what you need in order to maximize your investment in the new system—and then commit to taking that time to educate yourself, regardless of how difficult it is.

For example, in the two months I spent implementing Pardot at SiteSpect, I spent five to ten hours a week attending webinars, reading the vendor knowledgebase and user forums, and participating in user groups. In addition, I spent another five to ten hours working in the software—understanding features, uploading lists, creating e-mail templates, creating connectors with other tools, building drip marketing campaigns, configuring settings, adding users, and so on. Twenty hours a week is a lot of extra time on top of a normal work week, but it's worth it. What you will learn will keep your marketing skills fresh and pave the way toward accomplishing much more success in much less time moving forward. But don't just invest time in the beginning—continue to research functionality, best practices, and upcoming features, and you'll stay on top of your game when it comes to this and any marketing technology.

Key Highlights

Marketing automation is starting to become more pervasive in the B2B world, and chances are, if you are not using it yet, you soon will be. Make sure you inventory your company's needs and look for the platform that offers the functionality that best meets your needs, from automated campaign creation to e-mail marketing to landing-page creation, anonymous visitor ID, and more. Don't overlook the importance of education in getting up to speed on this (or any) new platform and setting expectations with other departments on its usage. Think through what you want to accomplish and why before setting out to automate, and remember: strategy first!

Recommended Reading

- *Digital Marketing Depot's B2B Marketing Automation Platforms 2014: A Buyer's Guide*, http://downloads.digitalmarketingdepot.com/rs/thirddoormedia/images/MIR_1303_MarketAuto.pdf.

- *Marketing Automation Buyer's Guide*, Pardot, www.pardot.com/whitepapers/marketing-automation-buyers-guide-2/.

- *Marketing Automation for Dummies*, Mathew Sweezey, John Wiley and Sons, 2014.

- *The Definitive Guide to Marketing Automation*, Marketo, www.marketo.com/definitive-guides/marketing-automation/.

Endnotes

1. *Advertising Age*, "B2B Marketing Fact Pack," Crain Communication, May 19, 2014, Marketing Fact Pack, http://gaia.adage.com/images/bin/pdf/B2Bfactpackweb.pdf.

2. I currently use Pardot at SiteSpect and have been very satisfied with both the functionality and the ease of use of the platform, as well as the entire process, from procurement to implementation to usage. Other vendors can learn a lot from Pardot about how to organize a business around servicing the customer.

6

Targeting and Personalization

Creating relevant experiences for prospects and customers can lead to higher content consumption rates, a better perception of the vendor that results in enhanced brand reputation, and, most important, higher conversion rates. This is accomplished primarily through targeting and personalization.

B2B targeting is mostly done to personalize content on websites, in e-mail campaigns, and across advertising networks. The amount of personalization you can undertake is limited only by the data you have—the more information you have and the more accurate it is, the more personalized an experience can be. But before you can personalize, you must target; before you target, you must segment; and before you segment, you must have data (see Figure 6.1).

Figure 6.1 Steps in Personalization.

The idea is to be able to segment and target based on the data you know about a prospect, such as the person's activity history, search history, location, web activity, demographics, and other information. In this way, you'll be able to deliver the right message to the right prospect at the right time in the right channel for a truly personalized experience.

About That Data

So what do you know about your prospects that will help you target them and create a better experience for them? If you are like most B2B companies, you are likely already using forms to capture some information, such as name, title, company, e-mail address, phone number, and perhaps some geographic information such as country or state. That's a start. With just that information, you can create campaigns for everyone within a certain zip code or area code, from a certain company, or with a particular title, for example.

Whatever data you have should be segmented into meaningful groups that share similar characteristics—the idea is to segment as finely as possible in order to best target your audience. Although targeting prospective customers has always been important in B2B marketing, functionality within experimentation tools, marketing automation platforms, and advertising networks make it more powerful than ever.

When done correctly, targeting and personalization garner long-term loyalty and therefore higher customer lifetime values. When done incorrectly, they create cynicism and exasperation. For example, something as simple as personalizing e-mail can go wrong when the e-mail is addressed to "FNAME," "%%First_Name%%," "firstname," or some other variable tag that doesn't get dynamically generated, in this case because the contact record does not contain a first name in that field. Another example is when the e-mail is addressed to someone else, such as a "Dear Mark" e-mail that recently arrived in my inbox.

Segmentation Strategies

Let's look at some of the ways to segment an audience. Ideally, these segmentation strategies will be based on characteristics from your buyer profile (discussed in Chapter 7, "Planning"). These characteristics describe the ideal buyer for whom you are personalizing, and help shape the messages and content on your website as well as the campaigns driving traffic to your website—and the more targeted and personalized the content, the more engaging and relevant it will be.

The idea is to target content based on these segments and experiment to see what works and what doesn't in order to create the optimal experience. This is typically performed via an experimentation platform, a marketing automation platform, or an advertising network, and analyzed via those tools' reporting interfaces or analytics tools to understand the impact that targeting and personalization produced.

Some ways to segment your audience data include these criteria:

- **Job Title**—Group the titles of buyers, users, and influencers separately so that they receive only the information that is useful to them.

- **Functional Area**—Segment by department; for example, Marketing, Accounting, Human Resources, and so on.

- **Seniority**—Group the titles of buyers, users, and influencers by level, such as Vice President, Director, Manager, or Specialist, in order to further refine content by level of expertise.

- **Company Size**—Group companies by size; for example, SMB, mid-market, or Fortune 500.

- **SIC or NAICS Codes**—Use these to segment by vertical industry. Targeting via multiple criteria such as job title, company size, and industry is considered a best practice in reaching the ideal buyer.

- **Product Interests**—Segment by declared interest in products, solutions, use cases, or services.

- **Geographic Location**—Segment by sales territory, states, countries, or geographic regions.

- **Language**—Target by preferred language. For example, if most of the prospect base is in France, there's no point in sending e-mails written in English or producing web pages in anything but French, right?

- **Sales Stage**—Consider segmenting and personalizing content based on where prospects are in the sales stage; for example, from lead to marketing-qualified lead all the way to closed business. You should have content that's different for bottom-of-the-funnel prospects than for anonymous visitors, for example.

- **Activity History**—Combine sales stage with activity history for identified leads for a very powerful combination in customizing the online experience, for example:

  - Previous pages visited

  - Current actions on the website

  - Specific offer or content consumed

  - Tradeshow/event history

- **Product Context**—Know whether prospects are using competitive products, products built in-house, or no solution at all as a helpful way of segmenting an audience.

Website Targeting and Personalization

Because your company's website is integral to the B2B buying process, it's critical that the content on it is relevant for multiple audiences. To do that, companies use site personalization to gear content toward specific prospects according to segmentation criteria such as title, industry, department, function, company size, and geography.

It's important to know whether you are engaging with your target audience on your website, so more important than the volume of traffic to your site is the actual demographic makeup of that traffic. Are the titles, industries, functional areas, company sizes, and level of seniority of your buyers, users, and their influencers you are targeting engaging with content on your website? You can investigate this by examining your analytics as well as the visitor activity history in your marketing automation platform.

Additionally, use the dimensions and segments from your web analytics tool, such as search terms, day-parting, geography, and traffic sources, to analyze traffic. Your experimentation platform should be able to help you target and optimize for each visitor segment based on a number of criteria, such as these:

- User behavior, such as new versus returning visitors

- Recency, frequency, and monetary value

- Location, such as country, region/state, and marketing area (known as Metropolitan Statistical Area, or MSA)

- Mobile device and capabilities, such as touchscreen versus keyboard

- Browser and operating system

- Contextual information, such as referring site, search engine, search terms, paid versus organic, and specific landing page

- Day- and time-parting (day of week, time of day, or even time zone, for example)

- Language

- Externally defined criteria, such as from CRM, user databases, or third-party data sources

For example, if you know that a visitor is arriving from Germany using a smartphone after a Google search, you can personalize the experience with the appropriate language, format, and content.

Marketing automation also enables you to personalize the website experience through the use of dynamic content, which is simply HTML content on the site, forms, landing pages, and/or e-mail messages that changes based on who is viewing it. Dynamic content is served when visitors match the criteria you set up in the marketing automation platform, such as industry, title, or score or grade. For example, if you are targeting e-commerce companies, and a potential customer from that industry visits your website, you can set up dynamic content to show only e-commerce case studies, testimonials, usage stats, and customer logos. In this way, only content that is relevant to that particular visitor is displayed.

Progressive profiling was mentioned in Chapter 5, "Marketing Automation," and it's also a form of dynamic content that can be used to personalize the website experience. Pretty much anything can be personalized using dynamic content, including forms, landing pages, thank-you pages, and more.

Targeting Previous Website Visitors

Let's say you'd like to target specific groups of prospects—for example, visitors who have come to your website before but have not filled out a form or prospects in your CRM database. One way to do this is through retargeted advertising, and there are several ways to accomplish this. The first way is to cookie visitors to your website and then use that cookie to serve up retargeted ads across the web and social networks via services such as AdRoll,

ReTargeter, Bizo, and others. You can also use some of these services to retarget prospects in your CRM with ads; this is known as CRM retargeting.

If you are using Google AdWords, you have the option of creating remarketing campaigns for those visitors who have previously visited your website. As with other forms of targeting and personalization, you can use any combination of segments to create a remarketing audience. Google remarketing comes with some predefined segments, but you can also use dimensions and segments from your own analytics. For example, you might want to remarket to visitors who:

- Visited the website five times

- Counted toward a goal completion (such as registering for a webinar or downloading a whitepaper)

- Visited the website once in the past 30 days

These segments are completely customizable, and which ones you choose to remarket to will depend on the goals of your website and marketing programs that drove visitors to the website. For example, if it's important to drive returning traffic to your website, you might decide to remarket to visitors who looked at your content but did not register, in an effort to re-engage them. The only limit is that the audience size must be at least 100 unique cookies for Google to target the segment on its Display Network.

E-mail Personalization

Your e-mail marketing program is a likely beneficiary of personalization, perhaps even more so than the company website. For example, every time you use a variable tag, such as in the salutation "Dear %%first_name%%," you are personalizing the experience based on what you know about the recipient. So how else can you personalize e-mails? At a minimum, you could personalize the following:

- Subject line

- Layout

- Copy/Content

- Images

- Sender

And based on the segment you are targeting, you could experiment with many variations, such as these:

- Copy variations based on title, industry, or company size

- Subject line variations based on recent history, product interest, and content consumption

- Layout based on mobile versus desktop browser

- Event invitations based on location or interest

The combination of segments and the elements of what you are personalizing (e-mail, website, or ads) is truly limitless. The more finely you can segment your lists (starting with the criteria listed under "Segmentation Strategies" earlier in this chapter) and better use dynamic content, the more relevant you can make the message.

Advertising Targeting and Personalization

Making sure your ads are displayed to the correct prospects is key in successful advertising, and it happens because of targeting. There are many ways to accomplish this; let's take Google AdWords as an example. When you set up your text ad campaigns on the Google Search Network, you have the option to target by these factors:

- **Keywords and keyword phrases** that are relevant to your company's offerings. When potential buyers search for those keywords on Google, your ad will be triggered.

- **Geography and language** so that you can target your ads to specific countries, regions, or cities.

- **Mobile devices** so that your ads are displayed based on device type, time of day, and location.

Another option in search advertising targeting is a service such as ReTargeter Search, which enables you to target ads based on search behavior such that your ads are displayed only to people who are already looking for information on your company and products or your competitors.

If you are using the Google Display Network, you have even more options:

- **Contextual targeting** so that your ad is placed on appropriate partner sites based on your keywords and the partner's content

- **Topical targeting** so that your ad appears on multiple pages about a specific topic

- **Placement targeting** in which you specifically choose the site(s) on which your ad appears

- **Audience targeting** in which you remarket or show your ads to specific audiences in the Display Network

Another option in display advertising targeting is to use a network such as Bizo, which uses business demographics to target audience segments such as job function, job title, industry, company size, and more with display ads across its network.

Targeted Advertising on Social Networks

Social networks enable advertising targeting within their own platforms; for example, Facebook offers a wide array of criteria to segment the audience and also offers a feature called Custom Audiences to help companies advertise to potential customers similar to their own. Facebook advertising targeting includes location, age, gender, languages, interests, behaviors, and connections.

LinkedIn segments by business-oriented criteria such as job title, function, seniority, industry, and company size. Twitter targets by geography, device, gender, language, interest, and username. Like Facebook, Twitter enables targeting specific segments and calls them Tailored Audiences, which are based on visits to your website, e-mail addresses, mobile phone numbers or ad IDs, or Twitter IDs (such as user IDs or actual usernames).

Networks such as Bizo and ReTargeter also enable targeted advertising on social networks such as Twitter, Facebook, and LinkedIn, focusing on not just segment information but also data from marketing automation, which might include such criteria as interests and additional demographics, including geography.

Targeting and Personalization Best Practices

There is a fine line between targeted and creepy. For example, although retargeting can be a helpful adjunct to lead nurturing campaigns, there is something odd about being served a vendor ad in a non-contextual setting. Think about *specifying ad placement* to ensure that there is not any unintended dissonance—the idea of context is increasingly becoming an important part of personalization.

One of the difficulties in having all of that data is *keeping it clean*, and one of the challenges in keeping data clean is that it can reside in many different places within a company. For example, data can live within a CRM system, a billing system, an inventory system, a marketing automation system (that won't synchronize with the same record in the CRM if the e-mail address differs), the customer service/case management system, sales reps' desktops in Excel files, centralized lists on the company server or intranet, and on and on it goes. The problem is that all of this information could be important, but it's not centralized nor is it guaranteed to be up-to-date.

Moving toward a *single view of prospects and customers* can help mitigate this issue—centralizing and integrating systems and databases, cleansing and appending data, and continually monitoring for issues. This is extremely important because people do not have much patience for activities based on data gone wrong. For example, I often visit other company websites and download whitepapers and e-books, and I am already a client of some of those companies. So when a salesperson reaches out to me to measure my interest as a prospect, it looks like they haven't done their homework.

Key Highlights

The use of data and analytics to segment, target, and personalize your website, e-mail, and advertising is a critical differentiator in B2B marketing. Use what you know, append what you don't, clean when you can—and most of all, don't be creepy. A little knowledge goes a long way, and your job as a marketer is to use that information to create a relevant experience.

PART III

Tactics and Techniques

You now have a solid idea of the environment in which you are marketing and some of the tools available to help. The chapters that follow will give you a soup-to-nuts account of everything else that contributes to a world-class marketing program. These chapters cover the following activities:

- **Planning**—Assessing the situation and creating appropriate goals and strategies.

- **Programming**—Creating initiatives for each stage of the conversion funnel in order to support the goals and strategies of the marketing plan. These include the following:

  - Brand awareness

  - Demand generation

  - Organizational enablement

- **Budgeting**—Figuring out how much to spend.

- **Staffing**—Hiring the right team and managing for the right outcomes.

- **Measuring**—Understanding results, return on investment, and the best sources of customers.

7

Planning

You've learned about recent trends affecting B2B marketing and some of the technologies available to help; now let's look at the process of marketing planning, which culminates in the creation of an annual marketing plan. The planning process is critical for defining goals, target markets, competitive differentiators, positioning and messaging, promotional plans, staffing, and budgeting. Your plan must align with the corporate strategy and goals (usually to generate revenue, cost savings, and loyal customers).

Think of plans as the road map for what you hope to accomplish and how you are going to get there, giving you the opportunity to assess where you are, how you did, what has changed, and how you need to change in response.

Whom to Involve in Planning

Unfortunately, marketing planning is often accomplished in a vacuum, to the detriment of the planning process. That's because if you don't engage all of your audiences, you won't get all the answers you need. Not only should you look at your own assessment of the situation, but you also should have conversations with additional internal and external audiences to bolster your understanding of the marketplace, what the company is trying to achieve, and the best and most appropriate ways marketing can contribute. Sometimes what is obvious to other people might not be obvious to you, and you won't know what they know unless you also regularly converse with at least some of the following people:

- Customers

- Prospects

- Sales team

- Executive team

- Investors

- Board of directors

- Industry analysts

- Peers in Finance, Human Resources, IT, and other departments

Research what they think are the company's strengths that will help sales, and weaknesses that will hurt sales. What do they see as external opportunities to improve sales and threats looming on the horizon that you might not have considered? Where is the company succeeding or falling short in their eyes? You might be surprised at some of the answers you get.

The Marketing Planning Cycle

It is important to do an audit before planning so that you can set your expectations of what is necessary, most important, or not urgent at all. In addition to speaking with other professionals, assess the results of your previous marketing programs. As you can see in Figure 7.1, planning starts with data, which gets analyzed to derive insight to create goals that help plan strategies, which are applied through tactics that get executed and generate results, which are measured, creating more data to start all over again.

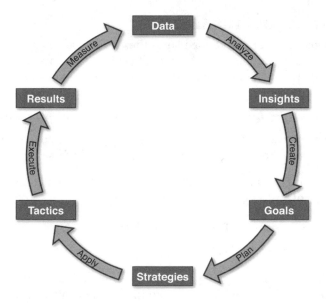

Figure 7.1 The Marketing Planning Cycle.

If you are not sure where to get that data, look at Chapter 3, "Analytics," and Chapter 13, "Measuring." It's necessary to go through each step of the planning cycle in order to create the most successful marketing plan, which includes the following:

- **Situation Analysis**—A description of your company and offerings, competitors, customers, and the marketplace

- **Goals**—What the plan intends to achieve

- **Strategies**—How you will reach your goals

- **Programs/Tactics**—Specific actions you'll take to support those strategies

- **Budget**—How much you are planning to spend

- **Staff**—Who is on the team and what they are responsible for

- **Measurement**—Expected results and an assessment of previous activities

This chapter addresses the first three items of the marketing plan; the following chapters will give you insight into the rest of the plan.

Analyzing the Situation

The first part of your marketing plan is the creation of a situation analysis, which helps set the context for the rest of the plan. There are several steps in analyzing the situation, which are outlined in the following sections.

Step One: Understand and Align with Corporate Goals

Just like every other functional area, Marketing must support the objectives of the company. Some of the important ones include these:

- Reach an annual revenue target through the acquisition and retention of customers

- Increase earnings per share by a certain percentage

- Grow by acquiring other companies

- Attract venture capital in order to be ultimately acquired by another company or in order to stage an initial public offering and become a public company

- Save money through cost-cutting programs

Unless you know what the company goals are, it is difficult to plan the appropriate marketing programs.

Step Two: Describe Your Target Markets, Accounts, and Buyers

Next, you'll seek to understand the marketplace in which you operate, and in order to do so, you need to answer three key questions:

1. What kinds of markets do you serve? Where have you had more success and where are adjacent or similar spaces where you might expect success?

2. What kinds of companies do you serve? Who are your largest and most profitable customers?

3. What kind of buyers do you serve and how do they make purchase decisions? What kinds of problems do you solve for them?

The idea is to better understand (and therefore be able to target) your customers by knowing this information:

- What industries they are in, as classified by the North American Industrial Classification System, also known as NAICS code, or their legacy SIC (Standard Industrial Classification) code

- Where they are located geographically

- Demographic or firmographic information

- The particular size of companies you are targeting—number of employees (Fortune 500, Mid-market, SMBs), amount of revenue, or some other metric relevant to your segmentation strategies, such as number of website page visits per month

- The specific companies you are targeting

- What titles your buyers, users, and influencers have

- What problems they're trying to solve

- How they behave—what sites they visit, what shows they attend, what content they've consumed on your website

- What their path to purchase decision looks like, also known as the buyer journey (comprising awareness, research, evaluation, and decision)

- What their barriers to purchase are (such as lack of budget, lack of expertise, lack of time, or lack of stakeholder support)

- How they will evaluate your products (such as price, features and functionality, level of service, or ease of use)

For example, let's say your business serves customers with more than $100 million in revenue in the financial services, insurance, and real estate sector in North America. Your typical buyers are at the director level in the accounting department and are seeking to solve the problem of late receivables. That's a solid start in targeting your buyer, because when you have a good idea of who your customers are and the problems they are struggling with, you can create marketing strategies that include the creation of content assets that describe how your product helps as well as the campaigns to deliver that content.

Step Three: SWOT Analysis

Now that you have a handle on your target market, accounts, and buyers, you need to look at the strengths, weaknesses, opportunities, and threats regarding your company and competitors. Use this opportunity not only to take a hard look at your own business, but also to review your competitors, their products and services, and their pricing. Who are your biggest competitors? How about up-and-comers? What is unique and different about them?

For yourself and for each competitor, ideally you'll create something called a SWOT analysis, which stands for strengths, weaknesses, opportunities, and threats. The end product of a SWOT analysis is simply a 2×2 grid that describes the following:

- **Internal strengths** (on which you should capitalize). These are the things that make your company valuable, help sales, and are critical to your success.

- **Internal weaknesses** (that you should minimize or eliminate). These describe where you need to develop.

- **External opportunities** (that you should use to your advantage). These describe what can hurt sales, and might include a developing marketplace need, a hole in the competitive set, or a new trend.

- **External threats** (that you should try to mitigate). These might comprise upcoming or unforeseen competitors, regulation, or potential natural disasters, for example.

At the end of the exercise, you'll have something that looks like this hypothetical company's SWOT analysis:

Strengths:	Weaknesses:
Seasoned company leadership Multiple product portfolio Predictable revenue model Brand awareness	Quality control issues Lack of external partnerships Difficulty in hiring
Opportunities:	**Threats:**
Adjacent marketspaces New, favorable tax laws Mobile adoption	Newer, cheaper competitors Overseas product development A maturing buyer

What's important about a SWOT analysis is what you do with it; you want to use this information to fix problems, take advantage of strengths and opportunities, and minimize external risks.

Step Four: PPPPlease Plan

With that market knowledge firmly established, you'll want to look at your product portfolio, how it meets market needs, and your go-to-market strategy. This is the part of the plan where you address what's known as the Four Ps[1] of Marketing:

1. **Product**—Describe your product, how it solves your customers' problems, and other benefits it conveys (saving the customer money, helping the customer make money, or the fact that it comes with great service, for example).

2. **Price**—Report your product's total cost of ownership and return on investment, as well as how it compares to the competition. Describing price as a valuable investment rather than as a cost is a helpful tactic here.

3. **Place**—Explain the channels by which you sell your products; for example, direct sales, indirect sales via channel partners, or online via e-commerce.

4. **Promotion**—Detail the marketing programs and tactics you'll undertake. We'll talk more about these programming activities in Chapters 8 through 10.

Step Five: Positioning, Messaging, and Naming

Next, you'll undertake positioning, messaging, and naming, which shape the perception of your brand. A good position is unique, differentiated, and defensible. There are a number of ways to position your company, such as by the following factors:

- Product features

- Product benefits

- Type of product (product class)

- Use cases

- Customers

- Competitive claims

Typically, you'll end up with a line chart using an X-Y axis to map the features and benefits of your company against its competitors. That way, you'll understand how you compare to the competition and discover areas in which they lack but you might excel—that's your position. All the features and benefits in the world don't matter if they don't matter to your customer. Your differentiators are the benefits you offer your customers that no other vendor can match.

You can also use this exercise to create competitive overview charts to help you understand where you excel versus your competitors. Here's a hypothetical example from an event software company based on benefits and features:

Benefits	Features	Our Company	Competitor A	Competitor B
Increase attendance	Event registra-tion pages	Yes	No	Maybe
Increase revenue	Add-on workshop modules	Yes	Yes	No

At the end of the day, your position will likely boil down to first/best/only/ cheaper/faster/better. If you are pioneering a new category or a new way of solving a problem, your position is first and sometimes only. If you offer the most comprehensive product or service (depending on how your customer defines it, validated by a third party), your position qualifies as best. Perhaps you are the sole vendor of certain functionality or benefits, in which case your position is only. Or your solution is simply less expensive, works more quickly, or is better in one or two functional areas.

To communicate your position to the marketplace, you'll devise a product description based on the following formula, first described by Jack Trout and Al Ries in their seminal book, *Positioning: The Battle for Your Mind*:

> For *(describe the target audience + their problem)*, *(your company/ product)* is the *(positioning description)* that *(does what)*.

For example:

> For corporate event planners who need to increase attendance and revenue, Hypothetical Event Software Company offers the only solution that enables event registration pages and add-on workshop modules.

If you are not sure about your position, consider perusing industry analyst reports on your industry to understand how they position your company and the competition (for example, Gartner's Magic Quadrant reports or The Forrester Wave reports).

Messaging

In addition to sorting out your position in the marketplace, you'll need to describe the top features, advantages, benefits (also known as a FAB set), and differentiators of your products and services. The end product becomes your messaging matrix:

- **Features**—What it does

- **Advantages**—How those features help

- **Benefits**—The end result from those features and advantages

- **Differentiators**—How it's different from alternatives—usually categorized by product, price, or service

Here's what the beginning of a messaging matrix from our hypothetical event software company might look like:

Features	Advantages	Benefits	Differentiators
Event registration pages	Easy to use	Saves customers' time and increases their event attendance	Thousands of out-of-the-box landing page templates
Add-on workshop modules	Free	Saves customers' money and helps them create more revenue	Built-in connector to CRM and marketing automation systems

Between the positioning statement, FAB set, and differentiators, you now have enough information to formulate a unique selling proposition (USP), which answers the question "Why should I buy this from you?" Also known as your company's value proposition, the USP typically follows this format, based on the work of Ries and Trout:

> For *(describe your buyers)* who need to solve *(describe the problem)*, *(your company name)* offers *(product description and advantages)*. Unlike other alternatives, *(name of product)* *(describe your competitive differentiators and their benefits)*.

Using the example of our hypothetical event software company, its USP might look like this:

> For corporate event planners who need to increase event attendance and revenue, Hypothetical Event Software Company offers EventX, the only solution that enables easy-to-use event registration pages and free add-on workshop modules. Unlike other solutions, EventX software features thousands of templates and a built-in CRM connection, saving you time and money.

You'll find that when you have your positioning and messaging nailed down, creating campaigns, headlines, calls-to-action, sales collateral, website copy, advertising copy, imagery, and other marketing materials becomes much easier and more powerful. For example, when I worked at desktop security provider Bit9, one of the key benefits was peace of mind through the software's elimination of security threats; we represented that through the imagery of a meditating businessman. We called him "Zen Guy," someone whom frazzled IT managers could aspire to become with the use of Bit9's software.[2]

Product Naming

You might also be involved in helping name your product lines. I've been involved in about 15 product launches, all the way from naming to marketing execution. There is an excellent guide available to help you brainstorm product names; although it was written for a B2C audience, I have found the techniques invaluable through the years. It's called "Building the Perfect Beast: The Igor Naming Guide—How to Name Companies and Products," and it's available for download here: www.igorinternational.com/process/naming-guide-product-company-names.php

If you have a complicated product portfolio, it will make sense to create a naming/brand hierarchy architecture so that you can easily communicate which products relate to each other.

Creating Marketing Goals

You've completed the situation analysis. You know your corporate goals; target markets, accounts, and buyers; SWOT analysis; Four Ps; positioning, messaging, and naming architecture. Now it's time to define your marketing goals—the strategic results you want to achieve. In other words, are you seeking to:

- Generate more revenue from current customers?

- Attract new customers to expand the customer and revenue base?

- Cultivate reference customers?

- Develop market share?

- Improve company visibility and credibility?

- Influence buyer audiences?

- Attract future investors?

This list is just a sampling of what your marketing goal(s) could be. You can have one, several, or many goals, depending on the complexity of your company, customers, product line, marketplace, and financial situation. If you are not sure what the marketing goals should be, it's likely because the corporate objectives are not clear, in which case, you should ask what those goals are—for example, "What's our net new revenue goal for next year?" and "What other objectives should marketing support?"

Defining Marketing Strategies

After you've analyzed the situation and defined your goals, you can outline the specific marketing strategies that describe how you will compete. Lots of people make the mistake of defining strategy as outbound marketing versus inbound marketing, but those phrases categorize marketing tactics. The last thing to decide before you define your marketing strategy is how you will approach/segment your marketing; for example:

- If you have just one product and a set of buyers with the same problem, you will be engaged in *mass marketing*.

- If you cover different audiences with different products, you'll be doing *segmented marketing*.

- If you are targeting only specific companies or industries, that's *account-based marketing* or *industry marketing*, respectively.

To create your strategy, think about how your approach, positioning, programs, and goals work together in order to give a high-level overview of exactly what you are trying to achieve. That's your strategy. It looks a lot like a condensed version of your marketing plan, doesn't it? Here are some examples of hypothetical marketing strategies:

- We plan to mass-market via product differentiation (first/best/only/faster/better) with a multi-touch, multi-offer, multi-channel approach in order to generate engagement.

- We'll be undertaking an account-based marketing strategy with a service differentiation (high-touch professional services) communicated via thought leadership to create awareness.

- We're going to generate revenue through targeted, segmented marketing with a price differentiation (cheaper) via full-funnel advertising.

The sky is the limit in terms of how you create your strategy from approaches, positioning, differentiators, tactics, and goals. Because your strategy can include just about everything in your plan, many professionals consider their plan to be their strategy, and I think that's smart. It's also another reason why planning is so important!

The rest of your plan should then outline the campaigns and programs that support the goals and strategies you set, the marketing organization, budget, and expected results. When you are finished with the entire planning process, you will have created a marketing plan that answers questions such as these:

- What are your company's goals?

- Who is your customer?

- Who is your competition?

- What is your offering(s)?

- What is your product's position and key messages?

- How does your offering solve the customer's problem(s)?

- What are your marketing goals?

- How will you market your company? In which channels?

- How will you accomplish the plan? What are the tactics you will undertake?

- Who does what?

- When will you engage in marketing activities?

- How will you measure success?

- How much will it cost?

Refer to Appendix A, "Marketing Plan Outline," to see all the sections in a typical marketing plan.

Key Highlights

Marketing planning starts with the data resulting from your previous programs, is aligned with your company goals, and maps out the company's target markets, accounts, and buyers. It describes the company's products, competitors, and strengths/weaknesses/opportunities/threats, as well as maps out the positioning and messaging. The marketing plan will also define the objectives, strategies, programs, budget, staff, and expected results. Don't just plan internally; involve external audiences to get the most complete picture of the marketing landscape.

Recommending Reading

- *Marketing Management*, Philip Kotler and Kevin Keller, Prentice Hall, 2011.

Online Resources

- American Marketing Association, www.ama.org

- Business Marketing Association, www.marketing.org

- MarketingProfs, www.marketingprofs.com

- Marketing Sherpa, www.marketingsherpa.com

Endnotes

1. *Basic Marketing: A Managerial Approach.* Jerome E. McCarthy, Homewood, IL: Irwin, 1964.

2. The Zen Guy campaign was created by B Direct Marketing Communications (www.bdirectmktg.com); read more about them in Alex MacAaron's interview in Chapter 14, "Conversations with B2B Marketing Experts."

8

Programming, Part 1: Brand Awareness

It's time to plan the kinds of activities that will connect your company with your audience at each step of the conversion funnel, as illustrated in Figure 8.1.

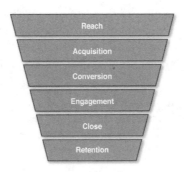

Figure 8.1 Typical B2B Conversion Funnel.

Here's what each of the steps in the typical B2B conversion funnel means:

- **Reach**—Brand awareness initiatives that reach your audience through media and analyst relations as well as social media and public relations programs

- **Acquisition and Conversion**—Demand generation activities, such as advertising, content marketing, and events, which drive traffic (acquisition) and generate leads (conversion)

- **Engagement**—Lead nurturing activities designed to move prospects toward close

- **Close**—Sales enablement activities to help the sales team close the deal

- **Retention**—Loyalty programs for customers

This chapter deals with reach and describes how you can create visibility and credibility for your company.

It's often said that "you're judged by the company you keep," and toward that end, buyers want to know they are dealing with reputable companies. At the same time, as your prospective customers go on the journey of solving their problems, you'll want to make sure you are publicizing and promoting your brand so that your buyers can find you. Thus, maintaining your good name, making more prospective customers aware of you, and engaging with the marketplace are all critical to success. Brand awareness programs that reach your audience help improve the marketplace's awareness of your brand (visibility) as well as its reputation (credibility), and they are typically accomplished via media and analyst relations, public relations programs, and social media activities.

Unless someone has filled out a form on your website (which is typically 5% of website visitors), visited you at a tradeshow, or made some sort of inquiry, the person is not yet a lead and is therefore not in the funnel. These "not in the funnel" prospects are the ones you are targeting through brand awareness.

Consider creating brand awareness mini-plans for each stage of the sales cycle that include goals, strategies, tactics, and metrics. Following are some typical brand awareness planning elements to jump-start your own ideas or to generate further discussion:

Brand Awareness Goals:

- Extend your visibility

- Enhance your credibility

- Propagate your differentiated messaging

- Help customers find you

- Educate potential customers

- Aid in the acquisition of new customers

- Directly communicate with prospects and customers

- Establish your company as a thought leader in the industry

- Form relationships with key audiences

- Test out new ideas with key markets

- Understand what's being said about you in the marketplace

- Influence the influencers

Brand Awareness Strategies:

- **Media Relations**—Conduct continuous outreach to the media, including thought leadership campaigns, product announcements, and pitches around editorial calendars.

- **Analyst Relations**—Keep key analysts informed of your corporate and product activities and news, even if you are not a client, particularly if you sell to companies that read their research—analysts are a key influencer of your prospects.

- **Public Relations Programs**—Promote the thought leadership of your company by developing an awards submission program, a byline submission program, a speaking opportunity submission program, an executive speakers bureau, an industry sponsorship program, and a customer advocacy program.

- **Social Media**—Create and execute a thoughtful, relevant social media program that includes social promotion, participation, and listening so that you maximize the usage of this channel to your company's best advantage.

Brand Awareness Tactics:

- **Media and Analyst Relations**
  - Promote executives for media interviews
  - Write news releases and other press materials

- Pitch news to media outlets and coordinate interviews

- Reach out to media around potential editorial calendar opportunities

- Engage with key influential bloggers

- Coordinate inbound requests for briefings

- Support company and product/services news and launches

- Scan for competitive and industry news

- Scan industry blogs for commenting opportunities

- Write and maintain the news kit (current news releases, corporate backgrounder, executive bios, and typically an analyst presentation)

- Create and update infrastructure (such as news kit, speaking opportunities calendar, byline opportunities, editorial calendars, awards calendar, and lists of trade and business media, industry analysts, bloggers, and other relevant audiences, such as financial analysts)

- Monitor, report, post, and promote news coverage

- Brief analysts regularly on company and product news

- **Public Relations Programs**

  - Identify potential awards and apply for them

  - Write and place bylines in relevant media outlets

  - Create and maintain an annual speaking calendar

  - Develop and submit speaking abstracts

  - Book speakers and publicize speaking opportunities

  - Create presentations and prepare speakers

  - Continually train corporate and product spokespeople

  - Identify industry associations and join as a member

  - Publicize industry association membership and become involved in meetings

  - Identify best customers and develop as press references

- Identify thought leadership topics

- Contract writers or research and write in-house

- Develop abstracts and key messages as scaffolding for speaking opportunities, blog posts, and issues response

- **Social Media**

  - Create company pages on LinkedIn, Facebook, Twitter, and Google+, among others

  - Socialize company news and industry trends on these networks

  - Run content marketing and engagement programs

  - Monitor and report number of likes, followers, retweets, and so on

Let's take a closer look at the four key brand awareness strategies and tactics identified previously.

Media Relations

Media relations is all about continuous outreach to the media, creating a two-way relationship to publicize your company and its products, services, executives, news, and opinions. We're more responsible than ever to write well, communicate effectively, monitor what is being said about us, and understand how to operate in an ever-more-complex environment.

Developing News Releases

News released online is the main vehicle we use to communicate with the press and the marketplace. Think about what kind of news your company has that might be of interest to its various audiences; for example:

- **Customer news,** including wins, extensions, up-sells, testimonials, overall growth of the customer base, and success with your products and services

- **Company news,** such as financials, new investments, new investors, mergers or acquisitions or other change of status, new office space, new executives, and awards

- **Program news,** such as a new partner program, discount program, or beta release program

- **Product news,** including new products, new features, new versions, new uses, and awards or notable mentions such as a positive inclusion in a noted analyst report

- **Upcoming events,** including webinars, trade show participation, user conferences, and other noteworthy participation in industry events

- **Thought leadership news,** such as executive content on industry trends or a response to an industry issue

- **Content news** that announces new e-books, whitepapers, case studies, data sheets, webinars, videos, blog posts, and so on

There are several major wire services to choose from, including Business-Wire, PRNewswire, and MarketWired. In terms of distribution, choose the media outlets wisely in order to target the right audience. Options for targeting include geographic, industry, and demographic options. Wire services have embraced new channels and now syndicate news releases with social sharing links, employing responsive design so that they render correctly across multiple devices. You can also add pictures (such as your company logo, home-page screenshot, product screenshot, or other relevant image), videos, and links to create a multimedia presentation of your news that typically garners more impressions than just plain copy. In addition, you can tag your release with keyword phrases for SEO value. But the best news is that wire services come with reporting and analytics so you can see what the reach of your news release was, including impressions, traffic and search data, and social shares.

In addition to distributing news releases over a wire service, you will post it to your website in the news section, on the home page, and via an RSS newsfeed. Publish this content simultaneous to its distribution on the wire. You'll also want to socialize the news over any particular social media outlets your company regularly engages with, such as Twitter, Facebook, LinkedIn, and Google+. These posts should link back to the news section of your website, and you should also consider posting longer form content on your blog for important news.

On Writing Well

There's a popular social media meme attributed to Pulitzer Prize-winning syndicated journalist William Raspberry that declares, "Good English, well spoken and well written, will open more doors than a college degree. Bad English will slam doors you didn't even know existed." I could not agree more. You can't realistically consider a career in B2B marketing, particularly in PR, unless you can write well and often. As someone who will be responsible for communicating the company's vision, mission, and message, you'll be required to engage in the kind of deep, strategic thinking that doesn't often occur with, say, a status update—so be prepared to write long missives on what's important to your company, its customers, and the industry. Most bylined articles, for example, are 500 to 1,500 words. You'll also be responsible for creating and maintaining the corporate news kit, which typically includes current news releases and recent articles, corporate backgrounder, executive biographies, and a standard company presentation.

In terms of crafting the perfect news release, here are some helpful tips:

- If you have multiple pieces of news that either don't relate to each other or are related but are beefy enough to stand on their own, separate them into different news releases.

- Ensure that the news release topic matters to prospects and customers, and write the release in the way these audiences search, using search keywords and phrases that are likely already on your website.

- Include your contact information:
  - Name
  - Title
  - E-mail address
  - Phone number(s)
  - Social media links, such as Twitter handle

- Do not issue a news release if you (or whoever handles media relations) or your spokesperson is going to be out of the office. There is nothing more frustrating for journalists than trying to arrange an interview around hot news when no one is available—and it signals poor planning on your end, bruising the professional reputation of your company with the media.

- Write a compelling headline that is clear and to the point. Business-Wire recommends that the headline be between 2 and 22 words for proper indexing—noting that search engines often limit titles to 67 *characters*, so put the most important information first.

- Think about how the news release looks. Use text formatting as well as bulleting and numbering to make the news release easy to read.

- Public companies will include their stock symbol, exchange, and International Securities Identifier Number (ISIN).

Writing well takes tremendous pressure off the review process; if you are a meticulous writer, chances are your manager (or whoever proofs your work) does not need to scrutinize your work nearly as carefully, creating extra cycles for his or her own work. Being more lightweight in your need for oversight at work should never be underestimated in its value to your manager.

Refer to the *Associated Press Stylebook* as well as Strunk and White's *The Elements of Style* for specific guidance on writing.

Pitching News

Writing and distributing a news release is just half of the job when it comes to creating news; the second half is to pitch it to the media. Most reporters receive dozens, perhaps even hundreds, of pitches every week. They might be overwhelmed with the volume, but there are things you can do to help your pitch stand out:

- **Give it a great subject line**—This is true for all e-mails to help create interest. Relate the subject line to the body of the mail (in other words, don't promote one thing and deliver another; that's spam).

- **Think visually**—What can you offer to help make the story more visually appealing? Include screenshots, head shots, and graphics when you can. This is also helpful from the reader's perspective—most people appreciate visuals to reinforce a message and underscore the key points.

- **Keep it short**—If you need more than a couple of paragraphs to tell the story, you need to work on making your messaging more concise.

When you are reaching out to the media, sometimes you'll be pitching your news releases, sometimes you'll be trying to line up interviews for executives, and sometimes you'll be coordinating around particular editorial calendar opportunities. An editorial calendar is a year-long look at the expected topics to be covered by a particular media outlet in order to attract advertisers—so the place to look for it is actually in the media kit (advertising kit) of the trade publication. These can be found online. Pitch your company approximately three months in advance of a monthly publication's scheduled coverage of a particular topic in order to be considered for inclusion.

Other Media Relations Responsibilities

Not only will you be pitching news, but you also will be catching news insofar as you will respond to media inquiries that come directly to you or through the website. These inbound requests for briefings can be quite salient, and if a journalist whom you don't already know inquires about a briefing, the responsible thing to do is to vet the request to see whether it's a good fit for your company.

Also, understanding what is being said about your company, products, customers, competitors, and industry is critical in shaping your messaging. To know what your key stakeholder audiences are saying, you must monitor the marketplace conversation. You can do this with the following:

- Alert notifications such as Google Alerts

- Services such as Meltwater News and BurrellesLuce

- RSS newsfeeds

- LinkedIn Groups and Answers

- Online searches

- Social media monitoring tools

- Online communities and groups

You'll be surprised where your company gets mentioned that you might not have known about, and these mentions represent valuable opportunities to promote extra editorial coverage via your website or social outlets.

It's also important to scan important blogs and social media outlets for potential opportunities for comment. Commenting can be a bit of an art, but the basic rules of engagement are as given here:

- Have something valuable to say.

- Identify your employer up front and why you are qualified to comment.

- Make your comment in the form of neutral, helpful, and insightful observations.

- Give a call to action for more information if appropriate (such as pointers to a different blog post or content on your website—but only if it's educational and not promotional).

Too often we see comments from marketers flogging their latest article or e-book that has nothing to do with the topic at hand, and you want to stay away from this behavior.

Lastly, consider how you will create and keep up-to-date the media relations infrastructure. This includes not only creating and maintaining the news kit, but also staying on top of an annual schedule of deadlines for editorial coverage for all of your important trade media, business media, and other editorial outlets, as well as creating and maintaining a calendar of awards programs and deadlines, speaking opportunities, and the lists of trade and business media, industry analyst, bloggers, and other important audiences for your company, such as financial analysts, investors, or board of directors, for example.

Identifying and Training Your Spokespeople (and Those Who Aren't)

Having well-spoken executives to tell the company and product story is a terrific asset in your media relations program. Ideally, if that's not you, you will have identified who will be speaking on behalf of the company and worked with them on the company's key messages.

In addition, you'll want to make sure you have a media policy somewhere public in the company (typically the Employee Handbook) that specifies exactly who should and should not speak to the media and how your company defines media. (Does it include bloggers, your CFO's girlfriend who freelances for the local newspaper, or book authors, for example?) You'll also want to discuss with your HR department how your company will handle infractions to the media policy. I once worked for a public company that had a very strict media policy, and when someone spoke to the *Wall Street Journal* without prior approval from the company, he was ultimately fired for violating company policy.

Briefing the Media

Just like dealing with any other human being, working with reporters requires patience, nuance, appreciation, compassion, good timing, and being able to add value. How can you help them meet their deadlines without annoying them? How can you help them flesh out a story while also promoting your own angle? These are skills developed over time, but it helps if you come to the job with the ability to read people, to be quick on your feet, and to be unfailingly engaging.

When you've lined up an interview, be prepared to talk about not just the news at hand, but also the following:

- **Company**—Year founded and years in business, location of headquarters and key regional offices, and background of the executive team.

- **Product**—Product description, scope of product line, positioning, key features, advantages, benefits, and differentiators.

- **Financials**—Revenue and year-over-year growth, number of customers and year-over-year growth. Note that if you work for a private company, you are under no obligation to divulge this information or the number of employees. When pressed, you can simply say, "As a private company, we do not disclose this information." The reason for doing so is that if these numbers ever take a turn for the worse, the negative trend line will be news in and of itself—even if you don't want it to be. Having said that, if you are a private company that has taken venture capital money, your investors will want you to discuss the amount and the source, and if you are a public company, you are legally obligated to report financial results.

- **Customers**—Company size, type, and industry; for example, Fortune 500 online retail businesses. This is where you talk about your target markets, accounts, and buyers and the problems you solve for them.

- **Partners**—The partner ecosystem and who your partners are.

- **Competitors**—Competitors and alternative solutions. Consider discussing them as a category instead of mentioning them by name—there's no reason to give free press to the competition.

- **Pricing**—The cost of your products and services. If your pricing is customized, give an entry point or a typical range.

- **Plans**—Plans such as product line expansion, geographic growth, and new employee hiring.

- **Special sauce**—Awards, recognition, testimonials, and years of expertise.

Everyone who speaks to the press on behalf of your company should be briefed on the messaging matrix and should be able to speak to it at any time. If you don't have a media relations agency that can train your spokespeople, consider running the training yourself. Role-play with your spokespeople in order to assess their ability to be interviewed and stick to the key messages; it will give them good practice and help you identify their strengths and weaknesses.

Knowing the Ground Rules for Attribution

Everything you say to a reporter should be able to be shared with the public, even if you think you are speaking in confidence. *In other words, there is no such thing as "off the record."* But sometimes journalists will ask for background information or will say they intend to quote you indirectly. Here are the differences between these approaches:

- **On the record** are comments you make before, during, and after an interview. Anything said in the presence of a journalist is on the record and can be attributed directly to you; for example: "We grew 317% this past year," King noted.

  Interviews begin with hello and end with goodbye—everything you say in between can and will be used against you. If you don't want to see it published, don't say it.

- **Indirect quotes** are remarks that may be used in substance (but not verbatim) and attributed to a specific source without quotes. For example: King said that she was satisfied with the company's quarterly growth rate of 93%.

- **Background information** is information that is attributed to a non-specific source within the company, such as: "Company X executives today said that...."

- **Not for attribution** works much like background information in that it is also not attributed to a specific source, but that source is usually external to the company. "Sources close to the company say that it is expected to announce a significant new partner next quarter."

- **Off the record** is information that is not for public dissemination, but that is deemed necessary for a reporter to understand the full context of a complicated story. I advise that you *never* make off-the-record comments, even if you are just making a casual remark about your opinions or want to seem helpful.

Getting Help

Get help when you need it. That means building out your team and choosing an agency wisely—media relations is an intensive process, and an agency or a network of freelancers should be part of the team. Choosing your PR firm is one of the most important decisions you'll make in helping you get the media and analyst coverage you deserve. By the same token, it's important to have the right people in-house to manage the agency.

It is important not only to write well, but also to be verbally fluent in order to add a professional level of erudition and gravitas to your story. You want to look for people who are forthright, expressive, honest, and driven. PR just isn't a great place for introverts or people who don't like to roll up their sleeves.

Analyst Relations

An important adjunct to your media relations effort in order to reach your audience will be cultivating analyst awareness, particularly if you are a technology vendor. This can take several forms, such as these:

- Conducting an informational vendor briefing in which you are making the analyst aware of your latest news

- Subscribing to analyst research in which you are getting up-to-date on key trends

- Using advisory sessions to get analyst feedback on plans and strategies

I have found each of these approaches extremely useful for marketing purposes. Done well, a solid analyst relations program will help you educate an audience that is influencing your prospects and customers, since they are likely reading analyst research as part of their buying process.

About Vendor Briefings

Sometimes you'll have news you want to make specific analysts aware of, or it might be that they don't even know about your company, and they should if they cover your industry. In these cases, you'll use the format of the vendor briefing to bring the analysts up to speed on you, your company, and your products and services.

Consider this a short, informational meeting wherein you are imparting information to the analysts; if you don't have a paid relationship with the analyst firm for which they work, you have no business asking for the analyst's feedback. (That's what advisory sessions are for.) So it's pretty much a one-way conversation unless they have questions. But vendor briefings are a great way to get your message across; analyst firms are an influential communication channel to your prospective customer audience.

Analyst Research

If you need to get up to speed quickly on your industry and competitors, subscribing to analyst research is a very efficient means of doing so. You'll learn what your prospects and customers are reading from analyst firms so that when you engage with analysts, you will be better able to target your messaging for relevancy and value. Analysts can also be very helpful in educating the media about a particular industry, market forces, barriers to entry, and the complexity of a marketplace. In the interest of credible neutrality, they will not promote your company, but they will be able to explain how you fit into the ecosystem in which you operate. So consider using analysts as allies in educating the media in support of your news. In addition, analyst research report reprints or webinars are effective for lead generation and nurturing.

Advisory Sessions

When you are a client of an analyst firm, you will participate in advisory sessions (they can be called different things at different firms), in which analysts give insightful analysis and feedback on your product offerings and their positioning in the marketplace. It can be extremely worthwhile whenever analysts review the following:

- Product features and benefits

- Target markets, accounts, and buyers

- Product positioning and messaging

- Marketing materials and launch collateral

- Marketing strategy

To better prepare for analyst advisory sessions, consider these best practices:

- **Use the meeting as an exchange of information.**

  You're the expert on your company and products, and the analysts are the experts on the industry and trends. Share your insights and solicit theirs. Think dialogue, not monologue.

- **Handle "off the record" or confidential information wisely.**

  Analysts will generally respect requests for confidentiality; however, you must be very specific about which information is public and which is not. State this at the outset of the meeting and note that this is true only for analysts, not for reporters. If you are talking about something sensitive, consider negotiating an NDA, or nondisclosure agreement.

- **Come prepared with an agenda, but be flexible.**

  Know what you want to talk about and what kind of information and feedback you'd like to receive. Understand that each analyst will have his or her own angle and perspective, so each analyst meeting will be different.

- **Solicit opinions on strategy.**

  Analysts serve nicely as a sounding board for strategy. Create a balance between what you are asking them and what you are telling them.

- **Balance what and how much information to give.**

  You can feel free to share more information with analysts than with the media, but recognize that there are still some basic rules to follow. Discuss strategies and what is already baked, but never commit specifically to plans that are still tentative.

Goals for an Analyst Advisory Session

Each session will have a different purpose, but some key objectives tend to remain the same; for example:

- Create visibility and credibility for your company and products with the prospective customers who subscribe to analyst research

- Cultivate analysts as media references

- Create a relationship with the analyst and have a two-way conversation

- Deliver your key messages

- Inquire about future research and the possibility of being included

Analyst Advice from the Analysts

Some of the best advice for managing analyst relations comes directly from the analyst firms themselves. Gartner has published "Optimizing Your Relationships with Gartner Analysts," which you can find here: www.gartner.com/imagesrv/pdf/optimizing_relationships.pdf.

You can also read an analyst relations playbook from Forrester by registering here: https://www.forrester.com/Unleash+Maximum+Business+Value+From+Industry+Analyst+Relations/fulltext/-/E-RES90961.

Both guides contain helpful information in navigating their firms and in dealing with analysts in general.

Public Relations Programs

In addition to a robust media and analyst relations program, there are other public relations activities that you'll need to develop as part of your overall brand awareness strategy:

- Awards submission

- Byline submission

- Speaking opportunities/speakers bureau

- Industry sponsorship

- Customer advocacy program

- Thought leadership

Awards Submission

Social proof is an important credibility factor when it comes to proving your value, and awards are an excellent way to establish social proof. Winning an award means you are better, you've done something differently worth noting, or you are remarkable in some other way. In any event, awards are helpful in establishing leadership and useful for publicity purposes.

The best way to tackle an awards program is to take the following steps:

1. Create a calendar that identifies all the possible relevant awards.

2. Establish the deadlines for submitting applications.

3. Create and submit those applications by the deadline.

4. Track their success or failure.

This is an incredibly time-consuming organizational task best suited to people who love focusing on details.

Byline Submission

Also known as contributed articles, bylines are an easy way to communicate your message, create buzz for your company, and establish links back to your site. Come up with an interesting angle that is related to the line of business you're in, but is not company- or product-related, because that would be too promotional for the media. For example, you could write about the following:

- Best practices

- Top tips

- Must-haves in a solution

- Advice when tackling a specific problem

- Problems facing a specific industry and how to solve them

The structure of a byline submission program is much like awards: You must identify all the byline opportunities first. Drawing from your media list, identify the top ten or twenty publications that cover your space and research whether they accept contributed articles. Of the top ten publications in your space, perhaps seven take contributed articles, and after pitching all seven, you might have three accepted opportunities for byline submission. Follow the publication's word limit guidelines (typically between 500 and 1,500 words, but it can vary) and deadline, and include other elements of the submission, such as a high-resolution photo of the author and a one-line biography (that links to your company's website, of course). Lastly, keep track of when you submitted the byline and when it is expected to be published, and make sure you promote and socialize it when it is published.

Speaking Opportunities/Speakers Bureau

Another detail-oriented task in the PR arsenal is garnering speaking opportunities. Here, you'll be assessing your most important trade shows, understanding when their call-for-speakers deadlines are, creating interesting abstracts from which you'll be comfortable creating and delivering a presentation (or identifying someone else who can), submitting the abstract, tracking progress, and ultimately speaking at a handful of events.

More and more, industry conferences don't want to hear from vendors but do want to hear from customers, so if your company wants to speak at a conference, consider doing the following:

- Identifying your company's vendors that need customer speakers like you at shows that also serve your company's prospective customer audience

- Pitching your own customers for speaking opportunities at shows

- Creating your own event

Remember to publicize, socialize, and promote all of your speaking opportunities.

Industry Sponsorship

Another key activity for creating brand awareness is joining industry associations, sponsoring their events or research, and creating events for members of the community. By becoming an active, trusted partner, you can create relationships for your company that might eventually make it easier to sell into specific accounts, get referrals, or build your e-mail list.

Customer Advocacy

Why not use your happiest and best customers to help you spread the word about your products and services? In doing so, you'll be shining a spotlight on their skills and increasing your engagement with them. A client reference/customer advocacy program can comprise several types of activities; for example:

- Acting as sales references for new prospects

- Speaking at industry events or your own field events

- Answering social media queries, such as those on Quora or Twitter

- Creating user reviews on third-party sites

- Agreeing to be surveyed or interviewed by analyst firms for their research

- Participating in news releases and case studies

- Contributing quotes to be used in marketing materials and on the website

- Participating in client advocacy boards for product feedback

- Organizing user group meetings

One of the best times to engage a client for participation in an advocacy program is when they are renewing their service, have interacted with support, or have had any other significant positive interaction with the company. For example, Pardot surveys its clients after support calls and, based on the feedback, asks the client whether they will serve as a reference, and if so, how often. I know because that's exactly what happened to me after an interaction with the help desk. I had submitted a particularly glowing review and my customer success advocate almost immediately e-mailed me back—that's a good example of a successful customer "ask."

After you have compiled your customer advocates, you'll want to group them into segments just like any other key audience—perhaps by industry, title, type of service they use, or specific expertise in one area of your product. Remember that customers love to get attention just like everyone else, so the more you can reward and recognize them, the better. Don't forget to thank them with a gift anytime they do something for your company—such as sending a gift basket, edibles, or company swag (but check into their gift policies first; some companies do not allow employees to receive gifts from vendors).

Your advocacy program doesn't have to include just customers who sing your praises to the marketplace—be sure to tap your best partners, prospects, employees, investors, board members, analysts, and others who know and believe in your key benefits and differentiators.

Thought Leadership

We'll talk more about content marketing as it relates to demand generation in the next chapter, but here let's recognize that content is also important in reaching audiences who are not yet leads. Consider creating an editorial calendar of brand awareness/thought leadership content development to support all the programs mentioned in this chapter.

Some of the best B2B programs programmatically create thought leadership content to advance the brand and help the company get found online. You might take one theme per quarter and develop content in different formats to support different channels. Consider generating the following thought leadership content formats and adding your specific search terms and keyword phrases for extra SEO power:

- News releases

- Newsletters

- Videos

- Podcasts

- Webinars

- Newsroom content and media kits

- Blog posts

- Interviews

- Bylined articles

- Whitepapers

- E-books

Social Media

The usage of social media has exploded in recent years. In fact, according to a study from the Content Marketing Institute,[1] 87% of B2B marketers use social media platforms in their content marketing efforts. These platforms give you an effective way to promote your company, participate in the marketplace conversation, and listen to what prospects, customers, competitors, and influencers are saying. Don't underestimate social media as a means to also be found by your buyers. That's because they're using social media as search engines to find the specific content in the specific format they need (for example, videos on YouTube, blog posts delivered via e-mail or RSS feeds, or presentations on SlideShare).

There are three main ways in which companies use social media:

1. Promotion

2. Participation

3. Listening

Let's take a look at each of these activities.

Social Media Promotion

This is perhaps the most common usage of social media—using your various corporate channels as a loudspeaker and amplifier for your company message. Use your status updates on your company and individual profile pages to communicate news, events, webinars, new content, interesting articles, and blog posts—whatever might be useful to your buyer and will get them to come back to your website.

It's a lot of work coming up with posts on a daily or weekly basis, and this should be handled by someone who not only is a competent writer with a good sense of corporate voice, but also has a handle on corporate goals and strategies and is mature enough to be trusted to handle this effort. Don't bungle your posts by inappropriately tying them into disasters or other inappropriate subjects.

Having said that, just because you're a B2B company doesn't mean you can't take advantage of consumer holidays to promote your message, so consider tying your posts to the holidays. Figure 8.2 shows a particularly effective example of a tweet from John Matera of RedTail Solutions, promoting the company's presence at a trade show, while also tying in seasonality in a clever twist:

> **RedTail EDI** @RedTailEDI · Oct 14
> Try new Pumpkin Spice EDI @RedTailEDI
> booth 1415 #GPUGSummit #GPUG
> #NAVUG

Figure 8.2 Seasonal Tweet.
Source: RedTail Solutions.

Imagine all the fun you could have with that! Consider playing off New Year's, Valentine's Day, the Fourth of July, Labor Day, Halloween, Thanksgiving, and year-end holidays, or winter, spring, summer, and fall. For example:

- New year, new plans! Learn 12 ways to conquer *XYZ* in our latest e-book.

- Ready to fall in love with some new ideas? Read this whitepaper now.

- Celebrate your independence and learn more about *ABC* in this webinar.

- You've worked hard, and now it's time for a break—kick back and come to our event on *XYZ*.

- Don't get spooked by the latest regulation changes; claim your free guide now.

- We're thankful you're a fan; please join us for breakfast in your city.

Another facet of social media promotion is using other organizations' channels to promote your message, such as announcing the availability of new content in a LinkedIn group. This takes some finesse so that it does not look like spam but does look like a valuable contribution. Typically you'd start by divulging your association with your company, tying in the group's focus, and stating your offer in a neutral way. For example:

DO:

Hi everyone, Kim Ann King here from SiteSpect. As we're all trying to become better B2B marketers and are facing some common challenges, I wanted to let you know of a recent blog post I wrote on 3 Ways to Maximize Lead Generation in 2015. You can find it here: *<hyperlink>*. I hope you find the post helpful, and I welcome your feedback.

DON'T:

You won't believe the incredible secrets that B2B marketers divulge in this new blog post by award-winning marketer Kim Ann King! These long-lost techniques will give you an ROI of more than 1,000%! Read it now or you'll be sorry you didn't—it'll be the only way for you to be successful next year! Peace out.

Social Media Participation

In addition to promoting your own messages (properly), you want to be participating in the marketplace conversation, either by owning and running your own groups and blogs or by commenting on others (as well as articles in the media). You could be responding to a discussion thread or creating your own posts in other organizations' groups (on LinkedIn, Yahoo!, Facebook pages, etc.). Be balanced, informed, and related to what your company does, but not promotional. If you just like to hear yourself talk and you leave throwaway comments on any open group, you are doing your company a disservice.

Social Media Listening

One way to understand what your prospects and customers are talking about is to monitor the conversation in social media. Set up alerts for all of your:

- Branded keywords
- Trademarked words and phrases
- Industry keywords and phrases
- Competitors and their products
- Top hashtags in your industry

What is everyone saying about you and your company's industry? As you track mentions, consider analyzing the sentiment contained in them—are social media users positive or negative about your company, competitors, and industry?

Challenges and Pitfalls

Imagine how much more reach you can achieve by having employees help publish your message. Whether it's someone's network on Twitter, Facebook, LinkedIn, Google+, or even Pinterest, Instagram, or Flickr, every post extends your reach. This is known as social amplification and it can be very helpful in getting your company's message out. Just like other Internet channels, social media can make anyone a publisher.

But not everyone understands the legal and financial risk inherent in being the voice of a company, particularly if you work for a public company. For that reason, it's very important to have a Social Media Usage Policy. For example, are employees allowed to tweet on their own or should they use only marketing-supplied content?

Some of the information you should address in the usage policy includes the following:

- **Proper Usage of Social Media Channels**

  Define the standards, expectations, and consequences of social media usage in your company. For example: How much company information is allowed to be promoted? Where's the line on dissemination of intellectual property?

  Competitors are looking at your employees' social media activity just as you should be monitoring your competitors—and they can glean valuable information about your corporate activities if you are not careful. Given that, how much are your employees allowed to say on behalf of your company, and what is marketing's role in policing that?

  What is your company's stance on non-work-related usage of social media that could potentially damage the company? Do you care if employees post inappropriate content unrelated to work?

- **Handling Complaints**

  What are your policies and standard response times in responding to customer complaints? Do you have a defined process and an identified owner to monitor the social media universe and manage customer concerns?

- **Handling Reputation Infringement**

  What do you do about social media users who try to damage your company in some way, either fairly or unfairly? Do you ignore them or try to mitigate risk (and potentially make the situation worse)?

Who will do that if someone impersonates you, your executives, or your company, and what is the remediation strategy if someone says something damaging?

- **Unauthorized Usage**

  What is your policy on copyright infringement? For example, is it okay for third parties to share the gated, copyrighted content posted on your website on SlideShare? If not, have a process in place to monitor and report violations. Consider running a quarterly check across all channels to ensure that your company's copyrighted content has not been distributed by unauthorized parties. It's fairly easy to file a DMCA (Digital Millennium Copyright Act) takedown notice on most social sites.

- **Account Oversight**

  Make sure you have several official owners of all of your corporate social media accounts, because some of them can be linked to personal profiles and if you have only one person in charge and that person suddenly leaves or is on bad terms, you might have a hard time gaining control of your accounts back from that person. Stipulate in the policy who owns which social media channels.

In addition, you'll want to make sure you have made the guidelines of your company's Social Media Usage Policy clear to your staff through training, communication, and ongoing direction, just as you would with the Media Policy. If you don't already have a formal approval process in place, make it happen so that you are aware of all the social media activity in your company. One of the most difficult things to get right in social media is relevancy and quality—making sure that the things you are saying in social media relate to the goals of your business and marketing strategy—and your approval process should ensure that happens.

Preferred Platforms

According to the Content Marketing Institute,[2] these are the top five social networks used by B2B marketers:

1. LinkedIn (used by 91% of B2B marketers)
2. Twitter (used by 85% of B2B marketers)
3. Facebook (used by 81% of B2B marketers)
4. YouTube (used by 73% of B2B marketers)
5. Google+ (used by 55% of B2B marketers)

LinkedIn

This is the number-one platform for B2B marketers, and the key to success is to take full advantage of it:

- Build a company page to underscore your reputation and brand visibility.

- Post updates to the company page to deliver your messages in your members' news streams.

- Post personal profile updates to bolster the company updates.

- Publish to the LinkedIn Publishing Platform within your own status update (think about repurposing your blog posts) to gain additional credibility and thought leadership.

- Join groups related to your company's line of business and add value by commenting on posts as well as creating posts of your own.

- Create and run groups for your company, industry, events, topics, or associations in order to create a community around what's important to your efforts.

Twitter

The most popular microblogging platform, Twitter enables you to promote your company message in 140 or fewer characters. That's not a lot of words for your message, link, and hashtags, so keep them short, to the point, and actionable. Add additional value by promoting industry news, insightful articles, and other posts from third parties so that it's not always about your company. Also, make sure your tweets are short enough to be retweeted without being truncated.

If you are new to Twitter and are working on building a following, consider following:

- Prospects in your database

- Customers

- Key influencers

- Bloggers and authors

- Media

- Analysts

- Competitors

- Partners

- Employees

- People who use the hashtags your company uses

Set up searches in Twitter to alert you to when your brand is mentioned and ensure that you respond promptly to queries. Try to tweet once a day or more often by scheduling your posts in advance—and remember to look at your analytics to see which posts were most popular to influence future content ideas.

Facebook

Consider your corporate Facebook page a place to build thought leadership, connect and engage with your audiences, and build your reputation. You can leverage all sorts of content within Facebook, including text-based updates, photos, links, and videos, as well as creating events. The more variety, the better. After you have built the page and have populated it with helpful content, invite your employees, customers, prospects, and partners to like your page and content. It's also useful to advertise within Facebook to generate a wider following to your page.

YouTube

Because YouTube is the second-largest search engine after Google (and part of Google), having a presence on YouTube is important in getting found by your audience. Having said that, there are many elements to consider, including creating your channel, uploading and tagging videos, and analyzing and optimizing your channel. You'll want to pay attention to acceptable formats before you create any videos specifically for YouTube. Like other social media platforms, YouTube has community features such as commenting and the ability to like content. Think about how you can address buyer concerns with videos such as featuring interviews with contented customers, how-to's, best practices, and more.

The idea is to build a community of subscribers, and you can help do that by optimizing the assets on your YouTube channel with the correct keywords in your tags, title, and description, because this is an important source of information for Google search results. Other factors influencing your success include the quality of the video, as rated by watch time, recency, and relevance to the search query. Video is quite a different medium than other online content, and YouTube has created the following playbooks and training to help you maximize your results:

- Creator Playbook: www.YouTube.com/yt/playbook/index.html

- Creator Academy: www.YouTube.com/yt/creators/education.html

Google+

Another Google property is Google+, the company's social networking platform. Much as with other platforms, there's a newsfeed, the ability to communicate with others (called Hangouts), and the ability to manage connections (called Circles), among other features. It makes sense to have a corporate Google+ Page because the information posted there is used in Google search results.

Tips for Optimizing Your Social Media Presence

- Maintain a consistent brand presence across all channels via graphics and voice and tone.

- Use engaging content to attract followers and likes.

- Make sure you are not just promoting, but also listening and participating. Have a two-way conversation with followers.

- Be consistently active on each platform.

- Add social sharing icons to your website, blog, and newsletter to make it easy to share content.

- Link your corporate social profile pages back to your website so that visitors can easily find more information about your company.

- Add social profile links, such as Twitter handles and LinkedIn profile pages, to any bios on your website or author bylines.

- Use keywords in photos, corporate profiles, and posts so that your social media activities can boost your SEO.

- Use hashtags on Twitter, Facebook, Pinterest, or Google+, and tag other content in other platforms (for example, YouTube videos) in order to be more easily found.

- Search for new hashtags regularly, because they evolve over time.

- Consider using a social media management platform, such as Hootsuite, to help aggregate your social news feeds and manage your activity.

Measurement and Reporting of Brand Awareness Initiatives

Most people start reporting on the results of these initiatives by assessing volume, such as in these ways:

Public Relations:

- Number of articles, and what percentage appeared in relevant media for your audience

- Number of clicks in a news release

- Number of impressions from a news release

- Brand awareness score—the number of branded keyword searches to your site and year-over-year percent increase/decrease

- Percentage of web traffic from media outlets

- Number of media links to the site

Social Media:

- Number of social media tweets, retweets, posts, favorites, likes, followers, comments, and impressions

- Percentage of web traffic from social media channels

- Number of social media links to the site

It's a solid starting place, but go beyond that and use your corporate and marketing goals to measure your brand awareness activity. In other words, measure how these activities contributed value to the business.

For example, how did they help your company:

- **Make money**—By referring visitors who became leads who then purchased

- **Save money**—By using this channel versus another, more costly one

- **Create happier customers**—By enabling fast response times to queries on social media and alerting the company to these questions in the first place

Just as you will need to attribute your demand generation efforts, you also must do so with brand awareness activities. For example, how many leads did your brand awareness efforts bring in that contributed to revenue? What percentage of revenue was that?

If you are using a marketing automation tool, you'll be able to track clicks from your social media platforms with custom redirects. If you are using social media for brand awareness, you are likely leading your users to non-gated content on your website such as blog posts. Since they aren't registering for that (and if they haven't registered before), you won't know who they are. But if they have registered before, this activity will be tracked in your marketing automation platform so you can report on activity—did it make a difference in your pipeline or to your revenue goals?

Key Highlights

You have plenty of options when it comes to reaching your audience, from media and analyst relations to public relations programs and social media. Be sure to choose the right goals and programs, and to measure and report on your results. Creating a brand awareness program out of news pitching, analyst briefings, customer advocacy, speaking engagements, awards, and bylines, and through social media promotion, listening, and participation, takes a great deal of organization and oversight. You'll want to create policies about engagement with journalists and social media and communicate them to the company.

Recommended Reading

- *Full Frontal PR: Getting People Talking About You, Your Business, or Your Product*, Richard Laermer with Michael Prichinello, Bloomberg Press Books, 2004.

- *Guerilla P.R. Wired: Waging a Successful Publicity Campaign Online, Offline, and Everywhere in Between*, Michael Levine, McGraw-Hill, 2002.

- *In the Line of Fire: How to Handle Tough Questions...When It Counts*, Jerry Weissman, Pearson Education, Inc., 2005.

- *Social Marketing to the Business Customer: Listen to Your B2B Market, Generate Major Account Leads, and Build Client Relationships*, Paul Gillin and Eric Schwartzman, John Wiley and Sons, Inc., 2011.

- *Social Media Metrics: How to Measure and Optimize Your Marketing Investment*, Jim Sterne, John Wiley and Sons, Inc., 2010.

- *The B2B Social Media Handbook: Become a Marketing Superstar by Generating Leads with Blogging, LinkedIn, Twitter, Facebook, Email, and More*, Kipp Bodnar and Jeffrey L. Cohen, John Wiley and Sons, Inc., 2012.

- *The New Rules of Marketing and PR: How to Use Social Media, Online Video, Mobile Applications, Blogs, News Releases, and Viral Marketing to Reach Buyers Directly*, David Meerman Scott, Wiley, 2013.

Online Resources

- MediaPost's Social Media Daily, www.mediapost.com/publications/social-media-marketing-daily/

- Public Relations Society of America, www.prsa.org

- Social Media Examiner, www.socialmediaexaminer.com

Endnotes

1. "B2B Content Marketing: 2014 Benchmarks, Budgets, and Trends—North America," http://contentmarketinginstitute.com/wp-content/uploads/2013/10/B2B_Research_2014_CMI.pdf.

2. Ibid.

9

Programming, Part 2:
Demand Generation

Demand generation is all about acquiring, converting, and engaging prospects. In doing so, you are creating buyer preference and becoming the vendor of choice in order to meet your company's quarterly sales forecast and annual revenue goals. Out of all the tasks that B2B marketers undertake, generating leads and creating demand are by far the most important because they are so integrally tied to revenue.

A good demand generation program will help you create sustainable, predictable revenue by giving sales enough of the high-quality leads they need in order to close business. Demand generation programs require the same kind of planning that brand awareness does: identifying goals, strategies, tactics, and metrics.

These steps will help you ask the right questions related to what you are trying to accomplish:

- What goals do I need to achieve in order to support the business?

- Have I profiled my prospective customer? Is that buyer profile still valid?

- What are the key questions my buyers are asking at each stage of the sales cycle?

- Are my key messages relevant and actionable?

- What content do I need to develop to generate pipeline and close deals that lead to actual revenue?

- In which channels should this content be promoted?

- Do I have alignment with sales on what a qualified lead means, and when to pass leads to sales?

- How did we do? How can we do better?

Demand Generation Goals

Your demand generation program (as well as each campaign) should always have objectives associated with them. You should understand not only what kind of quantity and quality of leads it will take to support the business, but also how you want to operate; in other words, should you maximize response at any cost or minimize cost per lead? Your demand generation goals could include these:

- Generating top-of-the-funnel leads (acquisition and conversion)

- Nurturing middle-of-the-funnel prospects (engagement)

- Closing bottom-of-the-funnel opportunities (close)

- Accelerating pipeline velocity

- Winning back lost customers

- Up-selling current customers

- Optimizing the lead-to-close ratio

Managing Leads

One of the top challenges will be garnering enough quality leads to satisfy your sales team. That results in two very important questions:

1. How many qualified leads are enough to meet quota?

2. What is considered a qualified lead?

Generate too many low-quality leads and your sales team will stop paying attention to them. Generate too few high-quality leads and they'll scream for more. To derive an appropriate lead quantity, you'll need to know this information:

- Your corporate revenue goal

- What your revenue base already is

- What the difference between the goal and the base is; for example, how much additional revenue your company needs to generate this year to make its goal

- What marketing's contribution toward that additional revenue is expected to be

- Average deal size

- Lead-to-close ratio

For example, let's say your annual revenue goal is $10 million. You have a base of $6 million in recurring revenue, so your company needs $4 million in net new revenue. Marketing is on the hook for half of that—$2 million in net new revenue. If you know that your average deal size is, say, $100,000, you know you'll need to create 20 new customers on top of your current base, not accounting for any attrition. Let's say that for your company, you close every 2% of leads. That means you'll need at least 1,000 leads to close 20 customers. What's important about this model is when deals are expected to close and revenue is expected to be generated. For example, if all the new deals come in the fourth quarter of your fiscal year, you will meet your deal goal, but not your revenue goal. That's why it's important to pay attention to how long deals take to close, what's already in the pipeline, and your lead-to-close ratio in order to perform accurate forecasting of what is really needed to meet your annual revenue goals, not just your lead volume goals.

For those who don't already have a process in place to manage leads, Figure 9.1 shows a straightforward lead management process.

Figure 9.1 Lead-to-Close Process.

This process was first described by SiriusDecisions, a well-known B2B advisory firm, and is now in common use in most B2B companies. If you haven't yet adopted a lead management process, consider talking to your sales team about how to incorporate this lead management continuum into your workflow:

1. You'll run a number of demand generation programs, including advertising, content marketing, events, and other programs to generate leads.

2. The total number of leads you garner will be put through some sort of qualification process, typically scoring and grading. Those leads that meet the minimum criteria set in conjunction with your sales team are deemed "marketing-qualified leads," or MQLs.

3. These MQLs then get passed to sales, where they are further vetted, usually by business development reps or an inside sales team. Whichever MQLs don't make the cut get tossed back to marketing for nurturing. The ones that remain in sales are known as "sales-accepted leads," or SALs.

4. These SALs are then further vetted, at which point one of three things can happen: (1) They lead nowhere and get tossed back to marketing, (2) they turn into sales-qualified leads (SQLs) that stay in sales to be worked, or, even better, (3) they turn into sales-qualified opportunities (SQOs), which then lead to closed business.

This is just one example of a lead management model, and there are many others. For example, you could segment your funnel by probability of closing (5–100%), or what stage they are at in the buyer journey (Awareness, Research, Evaluation, Decision), or whether they are top of the funnel, middle of the funnel, or bottom of the funnel. It does not matter how you describe your sales cycle as long as you have developed relevant criteria for each stage and a process for moving leads toward close.

How do you know how many leads will convert? It depends on your lead-to-close rate. Typically, a quarter of all B2B leads are not even qualified and never will be—for example, companies that don't fit your buyer profile and will never purchase your product, even if they are interested in it. You'll have a lot of inquiries, but not a lot of MQLs—in my experience, only about 3% to 10% of leads/inquiries are ever qualified enough (via score and grade) to pass to sales; how many of those turn into actual new business depends on your close rate. Based on SiriusDecisions' research, a B2B company needs to generate 351 inquiries to acquire *one* new customer. If you don't know your own company's lead-to-close rate, use that as an assumption for the first year and see how well you perform against it as a benchmark.

I recently sat down with Keith Cooper, Executive Chairman of SiteSpect's Board of Directors, who explained the fine art of revenue forecasting. Typically your company's bookings are described as total contract value (the monetary value of a deal over time) and annual contract value (the monetary value of the deal in this fiscal year). Revenue, on the other hand, is the actual money you've received in-house. So, if you book ten two-year deals worth $500,000 each, you have brought in a total of $5 million in total contract value and $2.5 million in annual contract value. Deals closed earlier in the year are more likely to deliver revenue in that year; however, if none of your new deals pays an invoice this year, that's zero dollars in revenue received. See how complicated this can get?

So that's lead quantity and how it relates to revenue forecasting. Let's talk about lead quality. The process for answering the question of what is a qualified lead requires an active and ongoing conversation and alignment with your sales team. You will need to establish what kind of score (level of activity) and grade (company fit) the lead has. As we read in Chapter 5, "Marketing Automation," you'll want to pass leads only to sales that show a high level of interest (high score) and a good fit (high grades).

If you find that you just aren't getting the quality of leads you need, there are several areas to investigate for immediate improvement:

1. **Process**—As noted previously, don't turn all leads over to sales; automate their qualification with scoring and grading, and then pass them when they meet the minimum criteria. With the rest, you could segment and then nurture, giving them valuable information to further them along the purchase path.

2. **Dissonance**—If your initial marketing copy (ads, social posts, e-mails, for example), doesn't align with your landing page visually and verbally, your audience will be thrown off the path. Keep them on track with consistent messages and graphics.

3. **Messages**—You might not have identified the key pain points your buyers are experiencing and therefore your programs are not driving them to take action. Check your messages with current clients to ensure that they're relevant.

4. **Subject Lines/Ad Copy/Offer Names**—Even if you have identified the right messages, you might not be describing them as effectively as you could. I have found that when you focus on how to solve a problem with enumerated benefits that resonate with an actual problem the buyer is trying to solve, you'll have the most success.

5. **Offer**—Perhaps the problem lies in your offer. Top-of-the-funnel offers such as whitepapers and e-books will generate lots of leads, but of lower quality (at least less serious leads if they're just starting

their research). Bottom-of-the-funnel offers, such as free trials or evaluation guides, will have lower responses rates that are typically better qualified.

6. **Channels**—You might get more leads from certain channels (content syndication, for example) that are of lower quality than other channels, such as e-mail. Examine the lead-to-close ratio in each channel to understand which ones are optimal for your company.

Consider creating a standard set of definitions and defined process between sales and marketing. What is the process for lead grading and scoring? What is the minimum threshold for a marketing-qualified lead? How do you pass leads to sales? How do they pass leads back that aren't qualified? Another process you want to define is around follow-up times. What can you expect in terms of sales turnaround times on various types of inquiries, such as demo requests, sales inquiries, pricing inquiries, general inquiries, content downloads, and webinar registrations?

Understanding the Buyer Journey

Understanding the buyer journey is one of the most important undertakings for successful demand generation. Without being able to get into the mind of your prospective customers, you won't understand the challenges they are facing, the context of their problem, how your solutions map to their needs, or what content offers they're most likely to respond to.

Mapping the journey becomes much easier when you have a handle on who your buyer is, and that's why segmenting and developing a buyer profile is so important. You should know buyers' characteristics, decision-making process, evaluation and decision criteria, budget, and timeline.

One thing to note is that your buyer might not be the same person as your user, and there are likely other influencers and decision makers involved. If you are not sure which is the role most responsible for purchase, consider testing campaigns to different audience segments to find out which one is most influential in the purchasing process.

Also, the reason to respond to a demand generation campaign can be very different from the reason to purchase your product. That's important because if someone responds to your offer and they look qualified and get passed to sales, their intent might be very different than buying—and sales follow-up will seem intrusive and irrelevant. Ideally, you are using demand gen campaigns to identify who is experiencing the pain you solve so that you can further influence those people as they research options.

Engage your sales team in reviewing the buyer journey so that you can be sure it aligns with the reality they encounter every day. In other words, make sure you understand the problem your buyers are trying to solve and the activities they are undertaking in each phase of their journey so that you are not communicating benefits or differentiators that don't actually map to their problems or help them in any real way.

A Little Nomenclature

You might be wondering what the differences are in the buyer journey, the conversion funnel, and the sales cycle. The good news is that these phrases all describe the same process, just from different perspectives:

- **The buyer journey** describes the steps prospects take in becoming aware of a problem, researching solutions, evaluating vendors, and making a decision.

- **The conversion funnel** is how the marketers map that journey toward a purchase decision of their own products and services, from reach, acquisition, conversion, engagement, close, and retention.

- **The sales cycle** describes how those steps are managed by the sales team for the purposes of forecasting, from leads to sales-accepted leads to sales-qualified opportunities to close.

The Buyer Journey

Figure 9.2 shows the general steps in a typical B2B buying process; these are also the steps you likely took when looking for analytics, experimentation, automation, or targeting solutions.

Figure 9.2 A Typical B2B Buyer Journey.

Step 1: Awareness of a Problem

Usually, something happens on the buyer side to make the buyer aware of a problem. It could be something within the buyer's department, organization, or marketplace in which they operate.

Regardless of where the problem originates, it triggers a search for information, and when I say search, I mean Search. As in Google. The majority of B2B buyers turn to search engines as well as the wisdom of the crowd (for example, social media such as LinkedIn) to discover and understand how other companies solved similar problems. Remember, a lot of prospects doing research will not be a good fit for your company, regardless of how interested they are.

Step 2: Researching Solutions

Fairly quickly, those searches become more specific and turn into researching options for solving the problem. Buyers will visit multiple vendor websites, download content, subscribe for more information, and sign up for webinars. As soon as prospective buyers register for something or raise their hand in some way (filling out a contact form, for example), they should go into a lead nurture program. Approximately one-third of all leads that register will be actively researching solutions but not yet ready to buy and need to be nurtured to both further them along the journey and better evaluate their interest and fit.

Step 3: Evaluation of Vendors

At this stage, buyers are actively comparing your features, functionality, differentiators, ease of use, and price against those of your competitors and figuring out which is the best match. These are the sales-qualified leads and opportunities you learned about earlier in this chapter. This is the part of the buyer journey in which you want to make sure you give the buyer head-to-head comparison checklists as well as case studies and testimonials.

Step 4: Decision to Purchase

At this point, you've pretty much done everything you can to facilitate the buyer journey, and you want to make sure your sales team has everything they need—client referrals, ROI calculators, documentation, and third-party validation such as analyst research.

But it doesn't stop there. Think about how the buyer journey continues past the decision to purchase, and the opportunities you have to retain the business, up-sell, cross-sell, and create customer loyalty. I think of clients as a segment of my database to which I must continually market and communicate. Granted, creating a satisfied client is not the task of just marketing—customer operations, professional services, product management, and other client-facing departments are all key to a holistic customer experience.

Developing Content to Support the Buyer Journey

You need to be very strategic in developing content that will help your prospective client move through the buying process. One of the delicate balances in B2B marketing is figuring out how to incorporate what the buyer needs to hear with what you as a vendor have to say, depending on where the buyer is in the process. In other words, the content needs to appeal to your audience and also be in line with your goals. You'll want to have content for every step of the way—the beginning, middle, and end of the process.

By the end of the process, you want to have addressed three questions that buyers sometimes don't even know they are asking:

1. **Why this?** Why should I change what I am doing? (Sometimes it's easier not to do anything different.)

2. **Why now?** Why should I do that now? (Why is it critical to act right away?)

3. **Why you?** Why should I choose you over the competition? (This is your unique selling proposition you learned about in Chapter 7, "Planning.")

You want to accompany your buyer on the journey in a systematic, programmatic way with content that is planned out, mapped to your buyer's needs, and delivered through channels with which they engage. The more you can be found by your buyer with the information the buyer needs, the more you will influence the purchasing decision. For each campaign, make sure you know your:

1. **Goals**—Goals could include, for example, net new leads, new customer acquisition, customer up-sell, competitive displacement, cross-sell, renewal, referrals, and so on. As we noted in Chapter 7, these goals should always be aligned with your corporate strategy and sales objectives, such as building out a partner program, launching new products, gaining ground in new industries or geographic territories, increasing the number of closed deals, increasing the dollar amount of revenue, and accelerating deals.

2. **Messages**—Messages should focus on what's in it for the buyer, why they should care, why you, and why now. Focus on how you can help, how you are better, and why you are a better fit than the competition. Remember that this needs to be conveyed through content that might not directly reflect your solution set, but should nevertheless position you as the leading authority.

3. **Channels**—Channels used for your marketing programs; for example, social media, PR, display advertising, retargeting, e-mail marketing, direct mail, etc.

Those three key elements (goals, messages, and channels) will drive what format your messages will take. These content formats include but are not limited to the following:

- Webinars

- E-books

- Whitepapers

- E-mail

- Case studies

- Product literature

- Ads

- Web content

- Videos and podcasts

- Blog posts

- Social posts

As you start to map out the buyer journey, your marketing mix will start to look like this:

- **Not in the Funnel: Create Awareness (Reach)**

  - *Tactics*—Media and analyst relations, social media, and public relations programs

  - *Content*—Press releases, bylines, analyst reports, social and blog posts, and RSS feeds

- **Top of the Funnel: Generate Leads (Acquisition and Conversion)**

  - *Tactics*—Advertising (PPC, targeted display, retargeting, social advertising), trade shows, and content marketing

  - *Content*—Whitepapers, e-books, guides, videos, and webinars

- **Middle of the Funnel: Nurture Leads (Engagement)**

  - *Tactics*—Lead nurture via e-mail drip marketing, advertising, and field events

  - *Content*—Product webinars, case studies, FAQs, and product literature

- **Bottom of the Funnel: Close Leads**

  - *Tactics*—Lead nurture via drip marketing, advertising, and field events

  - *Content*—Social proof such as testimonials, case studies, buyers guides, ROI calculator, checklists, and sample RFPs

- **Out of the Funnel: Retain Customers (Retention)**

  - *Tactics*—User events, ongoing communication, and support

  - *Content*—Documentation, newsletters, and product updates

As you continue to map your messages, content, and channels, you will create a content map that will start to look something like what's shown in Table 9.1.

Table 9.1 Content Marketing Map for the Buyer Journey

Buyer Phase	Awareness of Problem	Researching Options	Evaluating Vendors	Purchase
Content Nature:	Topical	Product/ Corporate	Technical/ Reference	Legal
They're Looking For:	Topical, educational content, and thought leadership pieces	Competitive differentiators and vendor comparisons	Business credentials and social proof	Contracts, term sheets, SLAs, and other legal documents
Your Goal at This Stage:	Be found	Be considered	Be preferred	Be chosen
Typical Messages:	Introduction to ABC	How our ABC solution solves the buyer's problem	Why Client A chose us	Pricing
	Why ABC method is a good idea	How our ABC solution compares to the competition	How Client B benefited from our ABC solution	Payment options

Buyer Phase	Awareness of Problem	Researching Options	Evaluating Vendors	Purchase
	What the benefits of ABC are	Why our ABC solution is better	Here's third-party validation on our ABC solution	Our ability to service the buyer's business needs
	Why ABC matters	The benefits of our ABC solution	Why you can't live without our ABC solution	Our ABC solution's typical ROI
	How ABC method helps solve XYZ problem	How to choose an ABC solution vendor	Customer references and testimonials	Our available training and support
	Why doing ABC is a good idea	Ten must-haves in an ABC solution		
	Who should care about ABC	Best practices in implementing an ABC solution		
	When ABC is a good idea	Where alternative ABC solutions fall short		
	Seven tips to solve XYZ problem			
	Three top best practices in ABC			
Typical Content:	Bylined articles	Bylined articles	Bylined articles	ROI data
	Presentations at industry shows	Presentations at industry shows	Presentations at industry shows	Trials
	Blog posts	Blog posts/website content	Blog posts/website content	Contracts
	Social media posts	Social media posts	Social media posts	
	Infographics	Infographics	Case studies	
	E-books	E-books	Analyst reports	
	Whitepapers	Whitepapers	Client reference calls	
	Information briefs	Product literature	Awards	
	Videos	Webinars	Webinars	

Buyer Phase	Awareness of Problem	Researching Options	Evaluating Vendors	Purchase
		RFIs	RFPs	
			Product demos	
Typical Channels:	Media	Media	In-person visits	In-person visits
	Trade shows	Trade shows	Field events	1-1 e-mail
	Content advertising	Product advertising	Retargeting	Conference calls
	Blog/website	Blog/website	Blog/website	
	Newsletters	E-mail marketing/lead nurturing	E-mail marketing/lead nurturing	
	Search	Search	Search	
	Social media	Social media		
		Direct mail		

How to Tell Your Story Through Content

There are at least two perspectives by which you can deliver your message:

1. From your perspective

2. From your visitor's perspective

For a more powerful story, consider featuring your prospects and customers as the hero of the story. What are the circumstances in which they embarked on the journey? What are the problems with which they were struggling? What did their search for answers look like? What was their breakthrough moment, and what were the results of that breakthrough (for example, the results they've seen now that they are using your product)? This is a great format for case studies, testimonial videos, and other narrative pieces that are powerful with prospects.

Everything should revolve around your buyers and where they are in the buying process. By creating campaigns that encompass messages, content, and channels, you can avoid the siloed approach wherein marketers create campaigns around content or channels. In other words, think top-down campaign creation to support sales goals rather than the fact that you just published a whitepaper and need to promote it over social media.

Campaigns should also involve sales; your inside sales/business development reps (BDRs)/telemarketing department are an important part of the lead generation process and need to be aware of what marketing is doing to help them and what they can do to help marketing. Working together will yield the best results. For example, let's say you are launching a new campaign around a product introduction to up-sell customers. In addition to e-mailing and targeting customers with advertising and social media, the BDRs can be following up with their own phone and e-mail outreach, so make sure your messages match.

Selecting the Right Marketing Channels

Let's talk more about the channels at your disposal in B2B marketing. The first thing to know is that they are proliferating rapidly—social media didn't exist ten years ago, and advertising has transformed from print advertising in trade publications into highly targeted auction-based or cost-per-impression pay-per-click (PPC) and retargeting models.

Before we dive into these channels, make sure you know the difference between what's known as paid, owned, and earned media. Paid media means the advertising you buy. Owned media are the outlets under your control (your website, landing pages, social media corporate profile pages), and earned media is typically anything written about you, such as social media posts and articles. Earned media and paid media drive traffic to owned media.

Regardless of which channels you select to support your goals and messages, they will drive the format of your content. When you are designing a campaign around a specific goal, think about surrounding your prospects with multi-touch, multi-offer campaigns delivered through multiple channels. Demand generation is definitely not a one-and-done activity.

The idea is that, for maximum effectiveness, you want to get in front of your prospect as often as possible with different content in different outlets. These include brand awareness programs, which we've already discussed, as well as these options:

- Websites

- Mobile

- E-mail marketing

- Content marketing

- Trade shows and events

- Direct mail

- Advertising

Let's take a deeper look into these channels.

Websites

Your website is obviously the foundation to all of your digital marketing efforts, effectively the digital front door to your business. What happens when you open your front door? You let a visitor in, engage him, make him feel good, and have a conversation. It should be the same way on your website. Your brand, key messages, and unique selling proposition should draw visitors in, make them feel good (recognizing the battles they're facing, assuring them their problems can be fixed, offering solutions, for example), and start a two-way dialogue. Your website should present a consistent brand image, create authority, explain your differentiators, provide valuable content, and capture leads.

You can assess your website based on how well it's doing meeting the goals of buyers in each stage of the conversion funnel. For example, your website should be able to do the following:

- Attract visitors to your website who are not in the funnel

- Acquire top-of-the-funnel inquiries by giving them valuable content in exchange for their contact information

- Nurture middle-of-the-funnel leads with additional resources, differentiators, and tools

- Qualify bottom-of-the-funnel prospects based on behavior, signaling a readiness to engage in a sales conversation

Buyers want to know you care about them and want to engage with you. What kinds of opportunities are you giving on your website for prospects to reach you and engage in a dialogue? Every site has landing pages and forms, but do you have live chat? Click to call? In other words, the more you can promote personal interaction, the more engaged your prospect will be. Your website should support buyer interaction with sales beyond a one-way form submission to marketing, because personal engagement is a key differentiator in its own right.

Giving buyers a voice also means giving them the ability to say something about your company outside of your website—for example, sharing your content on social networks. In turn, this underscores the value of your content (if people are sharing it, that's a good sign it's worthwhile). Be careful to measure the need for social amplification with the need for copyright protection; it's a delicate balance.

Visitors also want to know how you compare to the competition, and whether you are an authority. So in addition to giving them lots of resources about your key differentiators, you want to be sure you are establishing credibility with case studies, video testimonials, quotes, third-party validation such as analyst reports, your own thought leadership via bylined articles and blog posts, and a beefy About You page that highlights your company's accomplishments, awards, milestones, and expertise.

Also, you should have content based on your buyer profile, buyers' unique problem set, and where they are in the purchasing process. These resources should be in different formats (text, video, audio) so that visitors can consume the information in the format they prefer. If you have ever studied how people learn, you'll know that some people process information visually, some kinesthetically, and others through auditory means. So make sure you have content that communicates visually, is interactive, and also recorded to appeal to everyone in your audience.

Design Considerations

Just as you seek to maintain curb appeal for your own office, you must do so on your website—first impressions count. Ensure that the design of the site and the voice and tone of your copy reflect your corporate identity guidelines. Many websites today are built in WordPress or Drupal and are easy to create and maintain.

Your website should feature a well-designed corporate logo, clear and simple navigation, short-form and long-form content, supporting images to your key messages, a privacy policy and terms of use, and an easy way to contact your company as well as follow you on social media. Remember to highlight social proof in the form of client logos, testimonials, and case studies, and write your copy from the perspective of client benefits.

When you are developing or refreshing your website, look at your data to understand which content your visitors preferred (and which content they didn't). Take design guidelines from your best-performing pages to enhance the ones that aren't working. And think about designing for mobile first—whether through responsive design, mobile sites, or apps. To ensure optimal browsing, you should make sure that your website displays properly on any screen size (responsive design) or design websites optimized for devices, screens, and users (adaptive design). You might even try a combination of both approaches; it does not matter which one you use as long as mobile is in the mix.

Also think about where your visitors are coming from and what kind of content you have for them to consume. I've worked for a company that had a very high bounce rate on its key landing pages. As we delved into what was happening, we realized that the largest visitor segment was coming from Brazil, where the main language is Portuguese, but there were no content resources in that language anywhere on the website. After deciding this was a marketplace we wanted to go after, we developed pages and content in Portuguese that Brazilian IP addresses would be redirected to. As expected, bounces greatly diminished.

But how do you know what will appeal to your visitors? As you read in Chapter 4, "Experimentation and Optimization," it takes more than a gut feeling to create a compelling website; you must test all the elements— look and feel, content, user experience, features, and functionality. Most important, there will never be a time when your website is finished; it is a fungible channel that reflects your ever-evolving messaging and responses to a changing marketplace.

Blogging

As a key part of your website, blogging is a useful way for generating demand as well as creating brand awareness. It's helpful for SEO (which stands for Search Engine Optimization) in that it keeps your website content fresh, and it creates engagement with visitors. It's also one of the most difficult things to do on a regular basis unless you have a stable of writers on your staff. There are many ideas you can blog about; some of the more common ones include these:

- Posts on company and product news and new content

- Reflections on industry trends and news, key acquisitions, best practices

- Curated lists of people to follow, books to read, tools to use

- Case studies and success stories

- Product checklists and what to look for in a vendor

- Competitive comparisons

- Interviews with influencers and customers

Think about the format of your blog posts—they don't always have to be just text. You could create a video of a customer interview, record a podcast on best practices, or produce an infographic on recent industry growth statistics. In other words, the content you use in other areas of your website is perfectly bloggable.

Landing Pages

The key pages on which your visitors are likely to respond to your content offers are typically landing pages that include forms. Assuming you have marketing automation in place, after someone fills out a form on your site, it will add that activity to the person's lead record in your CRM if such a lead record already exists, or it will create a lead record for previously anonymous visitors and append all of their previous activity. Given the potential for capturing leads, you want to make sure that landing pages are not adding any friction to the process. You can do that by taking the following actions:

- Stripping out any peripheral navigation and extraneous links. (Having said that, Google AdWords has just started decreasing quality score in ads that lead to landing pages without navigation, so it might be worth it to test adding navigation back in.)

- Focusing solely on the content offer (rather than your products or company).

- Providing a singular call to action; for example, "Download Now" or "Register Today" or "Experience XYZ in Action."

- Keeping the form as short as possible by asking for only the most critical information.

Being Found

Search engine optimization is the art and science of having your website found by prospects via organic search queries. Your buyers are going online to research options, and you want to ensure you are at least on the first page of search results. Organic search is one of the most important ways B2B buyers find their vendors, which means you must perform search engine optimization on your website in order to be found and acquire traffic to your website. There are many ways to tackle this issue, and it starts with a structural assessment of your website and web pages. You'll want to make sure you have the right keywords in your page titles, descriptions, and tags.

On top of that, new content is favored by search engines, particularly Google, so keep your website content fresh and relevant to visitors. That's why blogging has become so popular, because it's an easy and effective way to generate new content. Don't overlook link building as an important way to acquire referral traffic and be seen as an authority in your field, which will also help with search results. For the best results, focus on high-quality backlinks instead of lots of low-quality links. One way to build links is through a vigorous social media program.

All told, Google looks at more than 200 factors in ranking your company in its search results, and it's impossible to optimize for all of them. Also, Google is constantly updating its search algorithm, so one technique that works one year won't necessarily be helpful the next. Stick to the basics:

1. First and foremost, the more you create a great user experience on your site by thoughtful navigation, functional information architecture, and clear copy and images, the better your chances of success at SEO. The search engines are basically looking for the same things your users are.

2. Your website is constantly being crawled by search engines, so:

    a. Keep it operational. Just as you don't want missing information for prospects, you also don't want it missing for Google, which looks for 404 errors that ding your ranking. Make sure your links work and make sense.

    b. Keep it structurally sound. For example, ensure that your meta-descriptions, metatags, alt-tags, and all other descriptive information are accurate, complete, current, and include your keywords.

    c. Keep it fresh. Not only will new content engage users, but original content also is valuable for SEO purposes. Just be sure not to duplicate content, which is frowned upon by search engines.

3. Write for your audience, not for search engines. The days of keyword stuffing are over; it just creates a poor user experience. Use your main keywords a couple of times on a page and don't worry about putting them in every sentence.

If you are not sure where to start with SEO, think about your primary keywords—these are the foundation of your organic search program. You should already have a good idea what your keywords are from the positioning and messaging exercises. If you don't know, Google's Webmaster Tools will also help—in there, as well as in your analytics, you will see search queries that drove traffic to your site. Also, look at what else has been written about your company and consider creating a tag cloud that will emphasize your most used keywords (try www.tagcrowd.com or www.wordle.net for this). Track your success by measuring the volume and percentage of traffic to your website from organic search versus other means; if you are doing SEO correctly, you should see your organic search traffic growing over time.

Minimizing Friction and Anxiety

As you read in Chapter 4, finding ways to minimize friction (anything that stands in the way of a conversion) and anxiety (the fear, uncertainty, and doubt of entering information) is important to test. Let's take a closer look at some of those sources of friction and anxiety:

- **Not Easy to Use**—Is information easy to find? How much clutter does someone need to wade through? The design of your website and the user experience can be a differentiator for your company— either good or bad.

- **Missing Information**—Does your website contain all the information your prospects are looking for?

- **Message Dissonance**—Does your website say something different than what your sales team or marketing initiatives are telling your prospects?

- **Slow Site Speed**—How fast is your website? Speed is important, because the longer your visitors have to wait, the more likely they are to go somewhere else. It also conveys a metamessage that you don't really care about their time.

- **Inability to Engage**—As we noted before, if you don't have ways to establish a dialogue with your prospect on your website, you're missing out on a key opportunity to differentiate yourself. Offer chat options in a non-intrusive way—you want visitors to engage with you, but you don't want it to look like you're stalking them.

- **High Pricing**—Not everyone who comes to your website is ready to buy, but it might make the buying process easier if you could give your prospect insight into your product at a reduced cost. You might not be able to offer freemiums, but perhaps there is a low-risk, low-cost evaluation or proof-of-concept trial version. This also addresses the following point.

- **Inherent Risk**—If it's a big purchase, the buying process will be more complex, and the decision to purchase riskier. The more resources you can offer to explain why choosing your company is not risky or at least less risky than the alternatives, the better.

Establishing Authority

Your website is where your content strategy is most evident, and providing accessible thought leadership content will underscore your domain expertise and industry authority. It's also a great way to engage prospects. We'll talk more about this in the later section titled "Content Marketing," but in terms of establishing authority in the minds of your prospects as they peruse your website, think about presenting them with industry research, buyers' guides, whitepapers, e-books, how-to's, curated reports, and interviews with customers, industry experts, and influencers.

It's important how you organize your resources section. One of the huge leaps forward I've taken is to list resources by topic and not by format. For years, I organized website content in the resources section by format in this way:

- Case studies

- Datasheets

- E-books

- Videos and podcasts

- Whitepapers

But prospective customers visit your website to find the answers to their questions, which are topic-related, not format-related, so re-organizing by topic will add a lot of value to your buyer's visit. Best of all, you get to use your keywords. What I've found is that prospects still like to consume case studies and videos as separate pieces of content, so I kept those in the new resources menu drop-down shown in Figure 9.3.

Figure 9.3 Resources Menu from SiteSpect.com.
Source: SiteSpect, Inc.

Mobile

Mobile is another important element of your digital marketing portfolio and is becoming ever more important in the B2B arena. The way to succeed in mobilizing your marketing is to understand what your prospects and customers are doing with mobile. They are likely using mobile devices to search on product solutions, compare features, read reviews, look at your website, read your e-mails, and follow you on social media.

When thinking about your mobile initiatives, start with your website. In doing so, you have plenty of options:

- Use a responsive design that adapts to screen size.

- Create mobile-specific sites, such as m.*site*.com.

- Target mobile visitors and specific devices using your experimentation tool and serve them only mobile-ready content, based on:

  - Device type, such as tablets versus smartphones

  - Specific mobile operating systems

  - Screen dimensions and ability to rotate

  - Browser capabilities

  - Network data speeds

  - Preferred markup language

  - Keyboard type

- Build your own mobile app, particularly if you have a transactional site.

Given that your buyers are searching using mobile, your advertising must be optimized for mobile; fortunately, Google AdWords gives you the ability to display several types of ads optimized for mobile devices. Since your ads will be shown on a small screen, you'll want a crisp message and call to action that leads to a landing page optimized for mobile; you can also create ad groups such that only your mobile ads appear on mobile devices.

And, when sending e-mail, be sure to test your e-mail on all mobile browsers; your marketing automation provider should have this built into its functionality.

E-mail Marketing

E-mail marketing is the bread and butter of your lead generation and lead nurturing efforts. It's much less expensive, much faster to implement, and much easier to implement than direct mail. There are typically several ways to accomplish e-mail marketing:

1. E-mail marketing in-house to your opt-in database

2. E-mail marketing to a rented list through a third-party e-mail service

3. E-mail marketing through a third party, such as a publisher, to their newsletter subscriber base

Let's look at each option.

1) In-House E-mail Marketing

Most often used to nurture leads, mailing to house lists gives you control over which messages your prospects see and the order in which they see them, and enables you to see how often they open and click through. Examples include monthly newsletters, e-mails from a drip program, webinar invites, and event invites, among others. Creating a reusable template for each of these use cases that reflects your brand will make creating new e-mail campaigns much easier. Think about sending these e-mails from the prospect's assigned sales rep or at least a real person so that it does not look like a corporate promotional blast.

One easy way to spruce up your e-mail marketing is to add distinction to your signature; for example, a company award, third-party validation, a new feature article, or a new case study. For example:

- Learn how customer XYZ increased revenue by 329% *<hyperlink>*.

- See why analyst firm ABC named us a leader *<hyperlink>*.

2) E-mail Marketing to a Rented List

If you are trying to gain net new leads, this form of direct response e-mail marketing can help. The success of this type of campaign will be determined by the following:

- The offer you are using to entice action (usually getting the recipient to register on a landing page).

- The relevancy, freshness, and accuracy of the list you are renting.

- The creative treatment of the e-mail. Your approach needs to cut through the clutter of the recipient's inbox.

- The brand consistency between the e-mail and the landing page. Just as consistent visual and verbal clues assure the recipient that they are in the right place, the opposite is also true: If your e-mail looks and reads one way and your landing page looks and reads completely differently, you will likely suffer from low conversion.

Having said that, make sure that list recipients are generally aware of you as a company—your lead generation efforts from cold lists will be much lower than from lists populated by recipients who know you. You can accomplish this by being active in social media and trade media (for example, groups on LinkedIn in which your list recipients might participate, publishing content on LinkedIn with information vital to those recipients, or writing bylines in the trade publications they read). There are two ways to e-mail to a rented list: through a third-party e-mail house and through a non-opt-in service such as Clickback.

3) E-mail Marketing Through a Third-Party Publisher

There are undoubtedly trade publications with websites that cater to your audience. These usually feature some sort of newsletter sign-up to garner e-mail addresses that the publisher then sells to vendors in the form of e-mail marketing services. You won't typically get your hands on the list itself, but you will be able to give the publisher an HTML and/or text e-mail to send to their list. This is known as a co-branded e-mail and will feature an offer and a call to action, typically a registration on a landing page to receive a whitepaper, sign up for a webinar, or download a free trial, for example. The landing page might be on your website, or hosted by the publisher, depending on the program. For example, many content syndication e-mails lead to the publisher's site to be captured there and then given back to you in the form of a list to be uploaded into your CRM. Either way, co-branded e-mails are a great way to broadcast to a targeted demographic and build your house list.

How to Build an E-mail List

One of the daunting tasks for B2B marketers is to build their house list, but over time, it becomes quite routine as long as you are mining all opportunities. For example, when someone registers on your website, have your marketing automation platform add the person to the e-mail list. As you go to trade shows and events, add scanned badges to the house list and any other prospect information you can get. If you engage in third-party content syndication, add those e-mails to the list. And make sure you have an easy way for visitors to sign up for the newsletter on the website if they don't want to register for something. You'll be surprised by how quickly your list grows.

E-mail Marketing Best Practices

It's easy to make mistakes in e-mail marketing. I once read an article claiming that putting RE: or FW: in the subject line would boost open rates because the recipient would think the e-mail is part of an active discussion and would therefore pay more attention to it. I decided to try it, and it absolutely worked, delivering the best e-mail open rates ever, but this technique also attracted the attention of my executive team, who suggested this looked like spam sent on behalf of the company. Here are some other dos and don'ts:

First off, pay attention to the law. The U.S. CAN-SPAM acts enables the sending of non-opted-in e-mail as long as there is an unsubscribe function, a physical mailing address, and a subject line that matches the e-mail content. You won't be so lucky in Canada, which recently adopted the Canadian Anti-Spam Law (CASL), which states that recipients must expressly opt-in in order to be e-mailed or contacted via social media. CASL makes clear that registering for something on your website by filling out a form does not express consent, so for these folks, you must have them double opt-in whereby after they register for something, you then send them e-mail confirming that it's okay to e-mail them (and they opt in).

Speaking of spam, don't. Don't be too promotional or use all capital letters. No one cares about your INCREDIBLE NEW VIDEO THAT WILL CHANGE THE WAY YOU DO BUSINESS except for your prospect's corporate e-mail spam filter.

Think about timing. Don't send too many or two few e-mails. Every two weeks is a good balance, particularly when it's a mix of promotional and non-promotional content, but there are many vendors that disagree because they are e-mailing me every couple of days.

Create compelling e-mails. They should feature an engaging subject line (and if you're not sure how engaging it is, test it), be personalized, feature one singular message with a supporting call to action, and be easy to read. Your prospects are busy, so keep your e-mail short, interesting, and valuable. Draw your recipients in with a question in the subject line, the promise of new content, or the expectation of benefits from reading the e-mail.

Make sure your e-mails are flawless. Check for spelling, punctuation, grammar, design consistency, proper branding, and functional links, and check that all information in the footer is up-to-date. I can't tell you how many times I've sent out newsletters that displayed last year's copyright date in the footer. Or the time we moved offices and I kept forgetting to update our address. Also, make sure if you are using variable tags that everyone on your list has that information filled out.

Test, test, and test again. Your e-mail marketing or marketing automation tool will give you an easy way to send e-mail to a seed list, and you'll want to make sure you are on that list to see what the e-mail looks like. You'll also want to run rendering tests to make sure your e-mail works in all desktop and mobile browsers.

Segment your list. Your prospects won't be interested in everything your company offers, so make sure you understand what their interests are. If you don't know, ask them, or look at where they've been on your website. It's simply not good enough to send the same content to your entire list. You can segment by demographic information such as geography, industry, company size, titles, or behavioral criteria such as product interest, whitepaper offer, or pages visited.

Clean it up. Every time you send out e-mail, some of those addresses will bounce, and some recipients will unsubscribe. Remove those addresses from your list to keep your deliverability rates high so that your e-mail sender reputation does not suffer.

Send both HTML and text e-mails. HTML e-mails tend to be perceived as spam more often than text e-mails, so it's a good option to have both in order to avoid the Junk folder. Also, the images in your HTML e-mail will likely be suppressed unless the recipient opts to display them—make sure you describe them appropriately.

Communicate internally. When you send out e-mail to your database, let your sales team know. Provide them with a copy of the e-mail that went out and some statistics. That way, they not only will be apprised of your efforts, but also might be able to reuse the e-mail with other prospects.

Content Marketing

According to the "B2B Content Marketing: 2014 Benchmarks, Budgets, and Trends—North America" report[1] sponsored by Content Marketing Institute and MarketingProfs, 93% of B2B marketers are engaging in content marketing. It's no surprise, because content marketing accomplishes so many things at the same time. Consider that providing relevant, valued content does the following:

- Establishes your authority in the marketplace
- Creates trust with your buyer
- Increases buyer engagement with your company
- Helps your SEO
- Generates brand awareness
- Garners net new leads
- Enables you to nurture those leads

I don't know of any other marketing activity that does all that, do you? An often-quoted statistic from the Corporate Executive Board states that a B2B buyer's journey is 57% complete by the time they engage with a sales rep. Along the way, you are educating prospective clients on the marketplace, issues, and problems you solve, and in doing so, you are aligning with the steps they are taking—from the time they are an anonymous visitor on your site to the time they sign the deal.

Today there are multiple channels at our disposal to communicate directly with buyers. For example, every time you produce a case study, an e-book, a whitepaper, or a webinar, you should publicize that information. Today, every B2B company must act as its own media/publishing company, combining the creation, distribution, and promotion of their own content with creating blogs, commenting on articles, syndicating content, and releasing your own news directly to the marketplace.

The challenges that content marketers face include producing enough content, producing enough kinds of content, and measuring its effectiveness, among other things. Not sure what to write about? Ask sales the kinds of questions their prospects asked in the past week; I guarantee you'll come up with at least a couple of ideas for articles and blog posts. You could also ask customers, prospects, or your executive team, or write a response to a current news item if you are completely stumped. The idea is to generate ideas and to be able to tie them into your corporate strategy, marketing goals, and buyer journey.

As Always, Strategy First

Develop a creative brief to ensure that each content piece you develop is strategic. The creative brief is an organizational tool that should at least cover these items:

- Objective

- Audience

- Topic

- Key messages and value proposition

- Format(s)

- Calls to action

- Keywords

- Deadline

- Necessary and optional reviewers

So Many Types of Content, So Little Time

Consider supplying your buyers with a steady stream of industry thought leadership, product news, and how-to's, and best practices on processes and strategies. You'll want to have content for every stage of the buyer journey, from identifying the problem to researching solutions to evaluating vendors. This kind of information can take the following forms:

- **Webinars** are live and on-demand presentations about particular topics, solutions, or best practices. They are an extremely effective content type in engaging buyers and, depending on the topic, can be very good for nurturing and identifying who is ready to buy. Having said that, there is no other demand generation activity that requires quite so much work, with so much inherent risk, as delivering a live webinar. These risks include connectivity problems, audio quality, and distractions in the live environment such as ringing phones and sirens. For that reason, I recommend that if you are going to make webinars part of your content marketing strategy, you consider pre-recording them.

- **E-books** are design-heavy documents, typically in landscape format, that present on specific or broad topics of interest lending themselves to a more graphical format than whitepapers. I am a big believer in e-books because their visual nature can communicate more information than other media—and busy buyers are more apt to skim the visually appealing content chunks/copy blocks of an e-book.

- **Whitepapers** are excellent vehicles for more heavy-duty technical subjects, in-depth thought leadership, or anything that simply requires more explanation. Although it's a bit of an investment up front identifying experts who can help you write them (unless you are lucky enough to have that expertise inside your company or are an expert yourself), consider whitepapers your evergreen content that will pull leads year after year.

- **Information briefs** and other types of collateral such as datasheets, technical briefs, and brochures are typically more product-related and present a quick overview of tips, solutions, or product features. You want to make sure that these pieces are the least promotional of your content marketing library, because they represent the nuts and bolts of your core offering. Keep them factual, informative, and educational.

- **Videos** are an engaging visual medium that will help bolster your messaging, your lead gen, and also your brand. I believe that the reason they are so popular is that people love watching other people. So don't make your videos just of presentations, but also of people interviewing each other, topic roundtables, client testimonials, and other people-centric storylines. Leave the PowerPoint for the webinars. Also, if you are hosting a video on Youtube and sharing it on your site, add the following parameter at the end of your video URL so that other unrelated videos do not cue up at the end of the video: /?rel=0

- **Podcasts** are the audio version of videos—think of them as your own personal radio show. You could either produce your own or be interviewed on someone else's podcast. One of the great benefits of podcasts is that they are fairly lightweight—it's easy to interview guests, or just speak on topics of interest. Keep them short; 20 to 30 minutes is always a good guideline for recorded content.

- **Blogging** is the holy grail of content marketing; if your company doesn't have a blog yet, you don't have a lot of company these days. Whether your posts are long or short, keep them interesting, salient, and frequent.

- **Case studies** are one of the best ways to demonstrate social proof, credibility, and industry authority by illustrating how your products have helped clients. For other potential buyers to see these results helps them justify their decision in choosing you. Summarize the challenges, solution, and results the clients have seen and then dive into the story of how they found your solution, what their problem was, why they chose you, how they use your solution, and more detail about the results. Any client quotes from case studies should also be sprinkled throughout your website such that regardless of what page your prospects visit, they will see client testimonials.

- **Infographics** work great when you have lots of statistics and metrics that can be displayed visually, such as Number of X that do Y or Percentage of A with B Problem.

Content Marketing Best Practices

As you develop content, *aim for visual consistency* across all channels (in other words, the same brand experience across all touchpoints—product interface, usage, corporate look and feel, website, marketing campaigns, e-mails, advertising, etc.).

Also, *ensure experiential consistency*. For example, is there a paper stock, weight, and gloss that you prefer for print collateral? Make sure it's always the same. This also extends to your buyers' interaction with your verbal brand such that your positioning, messaging, tone, and voice are consistent across these areas:

- Sales collateral

- Signage

- Advertising copy

- Website copy

- Marketing campaign copy

- Offer content

- Presentations

- RFPs

- E-mail templates

One of the most important things you can do in content marketing is to assess what content you have that maps to the buyer journey, determine where the gaps are, and *fill in those gaps.*

The next best practice is to brainstorm and keep a running tally on ideas and *create an editorial calendar* of how you will present these ideas to the marketplace. The buyer journey content map presented earlier in this chapter will give you a head start.

Learn how to brainstorm—in other words, how to come up with continuous ideas to keep your content fresh. What I've done is to subscribe to every newsletter I can find that covers my industry; they all get delivered to a single folder in my e-mail, which I peruse once a week to understand market shifts, competitive trends, evolving buyer needs, product news, and other information that I can write about.

Have everyone on your *staff on the hook for new content* around your top-level campaigns depending on their function; this is one way to keep from getting siloed. For example, your trade show manager should be thinking about how to communicate this quarter's theme during each show across the show assets and promotions.

Think short-form content. Although your long-form evergreen content lasts longer, you need a stable of short pieces (graphics, short posts, etc.) for air cover while you develop the bigger pieces of content.

Most important, *think about how your content fits together* not just by campaign or type but also where it falls along the buyer journey. Most content strategies start with informational, educational content in order to impart knowledge about a particular product or company. To be persuasive and move buyers through the purchase process, you will also need content that appeals to buyers' emotions (best done with more personal media such as videos), motivates them to take action (best done with evidence-based content such as case studies or third-party validation), and then inspires them by showing what is possible with your solution. This way, you get the buyer on your side and that's exactly what good demand generation programs do: They generate buyer preference. It's absolutely possible with content marketing.

Trade Shows and Events

For many B2B companies, exhibiting at trade shows is the best opportunity for meeting face-to-face with prospects, communicating your differentiators, and garnering net new leads. Although trade shows are a lot of work, and traditionally the most expensive channel for B2B leads, they can be crucial in generating new business, giving you valuable face time with buyers and current customers—as well an opportunity to understand how your competitors are presenting themselves. Trade shows are also an opportunity to scope out potential partners and find new hires.

Again, think of trade shows as part of a broader campaign with many programming parts; the show needs to be strategic to the goals, messages, and content of those campaigns. The key to success in trade shows is planning, planning, and more planning. You'll be successful if you have fully researched potential shows and chosen the ones that are aligned with your target markets, accounts, and buyer profile; have produced a booth that fits with your corporate identity; have well-trained booth staff; and run preshow, on-site, and post-show marketing campaigns.

But before you get to those campaigns, you have to figure out which shows you should go to and procure your booth space (spaces near food and entrances are always good spots). If budget is not an issue, it's best to exhibit at both horizontal and vertical shows—in other words, shows that target the titles of your buyers in any industry as well as shows that target the industries you market to but might have a broader mix of titles. Unless you can find the unicorn of shows that caters to both your buyer profile and your target industries, exhibiting at horizontal and vertical shows will likely be the best way to cover your marketplace. Find out what kinds of attendees the show is targeting and whether your competitors are exhibiting in order to choose the shows that are best for your company.

If you need to create a trade show booth, make sure it's consistent with your visual and verbal branding guidelines so that it aligns with your corporate identity. There are typically limits on how high your booth can be, so make sure you know what those regulations are before designing a booth. Trade show space is typically sold in 10' × 10' chunks, so that will likely be your minimum booth size. I've produced booths as large as 40' × 60' with a presentation theater, a second-floor meeting room, and multiple demo kiosks. Keep your design engaging and interactive to draw prospects in and give them something to do in the booth—grab literature, watch a presentation, interact with personnel, pick up novelties, or avail themselves of services such as beverages and snacks.

Before the Show

If you start planning your outreach several months ahead of time, you should have plenty of time to set up meetings with prospects, customers, trade media, and industry analysts who will be at the show. Make sure you are reaching out over several channels, such as social media, e-mail, website, and PR. In addition, you'll want to set up a goal for how many net new leads to garner at the show. Plan out your signage, giveaways, and content offer; arrange for shipping of booth assets; and let your sales team know the plans for the show. You can't overcommunicate goals, roles, and procedures when it comes to trade shows. What are your expectations of the booth staff? What's the pitch or specific campaign for the show? What should team members wear? Can they eat in the booth (depends on whether you've ordered cleaning)? What are the plans for before and after show hours—are you planning a huddle or a regroup off-hours? Is there a staff dinner planned? Whatever the answers are, let the team know.

During the Show

The day has arrived when you have traveled to the show, have set up the booth, and are now staffing the booth and meeting with attendees. Start with chitchat before selling products. Open-ended social questions such as "How is the show going for you?" or "What's been the best part of the show for you?" can get the ball rolling. Avoid yes/no questions that lead to dead ends in the conversation. Monitor your lead count against the quota you set during pre-show planning and figure out what you're going to do if you are low—get a second lead retrieval scanner and engage prospects in the aisle if you have to.

It's also good to meet with trade press and analysts at shows because these meetings will help you understand who you are pitching and often lead to other opportunities for interviews or bylines further down the road. Another possibility during the show is to capture client or partner testimonials on video. And, although it's becoming more difficult for vendors, speaking opportunities are a great way to drive traffic to the booth, gain visibility for your company, and add value to the conference.

After the Show

The number-one mistake exhibiting companies make is post-show follow-up—either neglecting to do so or hammering leads with multiple e-mails and phone calls. The better route is to send them a thank-you e-mail for visiting the booth with the content offer you promised them at the show. Suggest they connect to your company page on LinkedIn/Google+/Facebook. After that, you'll want to score and grade the lead and, if it meets the minimum requirements, pass it to sales. Those leads that don't get assigned to sales should go into a lead nurturing program.

Trade shows are an excellent source for new content—field notes, trend examples, impressions of the show, key takeaways from the conference, and activity on the exhibit floor all make great blog posts and e-mail newsletter articles.

Even with planning, trade shows can be fraught with unforeseen circumstances. Here are a few from my career:

- All the details in the world didn't make a difference to a sales rep who wasn't paying attention and showed up at the right hotel chain at the wrong address; turns out there were two Hyatts in town.

- The most rock-solid shipping arrangements came to nothing when faced with a massive landslide that wiped out the truck delivering my trade show assets (which meant potted plants and a measly skirted table for the sales reps).

- Even the most stringent planning can fall apart when you realize at the last minute you've forgotten something important. Very early in my career, two days before a big show, I realized I had failed to secure hotel rooms for myself and the booth staff. We ended up staying at a ridiculously expensive hotel far from the convention center.

If you've never sponsored a show or exhibited before, don't underestimate the amount of work it'll take to pull it off. At a minimum, you must take care of these details:

- Procure contracts.

- Process invoices.

- Select booth space.

- Provide company logo and description.

- Ensure you have a booth; if not, design and produce booth assets (back wall at a minimum).

- Arrange shipping of the booth and monitor.

- Select and ship reprints and novelties.

- Create and ship signage.

- Order lead retrieval, carpeting, furniture, electrical, Internet, and materials handling.

- Create a pre-show marketing campaign to prospects in the geographic area of the show, former attendees, or prospects with the same interest as the show subject.

- Promote your presence via your website, news releases, social media, and e-mail marketing.

- Coordinate with the sales team to staff the booth.

- Educate sales on goals, themes, procedures, and the show presentation.

- Book travel and hotels for reps if there is no one else to do it.

- Update the show presentation.

- Ensure that the booth arrives, is set up correctly, and then is broken down and packed properly.

- Ensure that booth personnel are on time and ready to engage.

- After the show, upload the lead list into your CRM, and assign leads to sales reps.

- Send out a post-show follow-up with your offer (typically a whitepaper or e-book).

- Add the leads to your nurture program or assign to sales.

- Track and report on show leads as they move through the pipeline.

Events

In addition to third-party-produced trade shows, another in-person option is producing your own *field events*, such as breakfast, lunch, or dinner meetings or educational workshops of any length in key cities. These are a terrific option for nurturing prospects who are at the opportunity stage with whom you'd like to further the relationship.

As with trade shows, you'll need to set goals, create a plan, undertake the marketing aspects (pre-event invites, landing page, content, logistics, and post-show follow-up), and you'll also need to program the event itself—booking speakers, creating presentations, agreeing on topics and content, and so forth.

Try to make field events as interactive and engaging as possible; even if you are delivering a presentation, you can have a two-way conversation. I recently attended a roundtable breakfast put on by DemandGen Report (www.demandgenreport.com); they were garnering ideas for their 2015 editorial calendar. The expertise of the participants in the room was inspiring, and the organizers did a fantastic job asking open-ended questions and then letting the audience exchange ideas.

Field events are also great for clients to network and trade tips (and from what I've seen, job opportunities). Don't underestimate your user conference's significance in retaining customers.

Another way to reach your prospective audience is through *virtual events* held online. Think about these as actual conferences or field events, but all the content is delivered online. Although this can be a technical challenge, it's an opportunity to reach a larger audience at a reduced cost.

In addition, the marketing department is likely to be asked to help arrange *company events* such as summer outings, holiday dinners, sales kick-offs, and other large meetings. Not only that, but unless there is a specific training department with its own logistics experts, the marketing department is usually required to organize customer meetings, conferences, and regional events (in addition to prospect trade shows and events).

Trade Show Best Practices

To start, make sure the right staff is in the booth. They'll need to be trained, adhere to the expected schedule, and be engaging with prospects.

Overcommunicate goals, roles, and procedures with your booth staff. As in, "We need to garner 125 leads from this show. We expect you to come to the booth ready to work and scan badges as you engage with attendees. At the end of the show, please go to Show Services and pick up and fill out the bill of lading and return it when you're done packing the booth."

Don't get gimmicky. Although dissonance generally creates discussion, you don't want to do something that isn't in keeping with your brand value. For example, if you are offering serious solutions, featuring a juggler, clown, or model in your booth does not send the right message.

But do use a drawing to attract traffic, giving prospects the opportunity to get their badge scanned not just for follow-up content offers, but also to be entered to win something (for example, an iPad, a Kindle, or some other valuable gadget).

Consider developing a survey to help qualify prospects. It can look like industry research, but it will also help you better understand their readiness to buy. And you might end up with some new content to market.

Get graphic—the fewer words in your trade show design, the better. Images are higher impact than a lot of copy. If you do have copy, don't display it below table height—no one will see it.

Follow up on leads as soon as possible after the show; response times matter in keeping conversations fresh in buyers' minds.

Procure exhibit space for next year's show before you leave the current show. The show producer will stop by your booth and tell you when you'll be able to pick space.

Think of a snappy giveaway that fits in with your campaign. For example, at a recent trade show, SiteSpect gave away foam puzzle pieces that fit together to form a square, printed with our messaging. The signage promoting the giveaway was about "Helping you solve the puzzle of optimization," and it was a big hit with attendees.

By the way, given how crowded shows have become, I would caution against launching anything at a show these days—a better formula is to launch the week before so that you are not competing with anyone else's news, and then continue the buzz at the show. This approach also provides a great opener with prospects.

Direct Mail

There are a lot of great reasons to undertake direct mail to help you achieve your demand generation goals. With the overload of e-mail, a personal letter can really stand out. Also, you'll generally find that physical mailing lists are more accurate than rented e-mail lists, and also offer more ability to slice and dice the data (using filters known as selects; for example, geography or title).

I am a big fan of keeping direct mail very simple; the only thing you are looking for in direct mail is a response, and in doing so, relevance matters. I've been the unfortunate recipient of some irrelevant (and offensive) campaigns:

- A letter from a web development agency promoting their services, signed by a female sales rep with a photo of her wearing a strapless dress

- A package from another web development company introducing themselves and suggesting I clear away the stink of past website projects with the enclosed Poo-Pourri toilet spritzer

No one wants to do business with companies that exhibit questionable judgment. Don't let that be you. To maximize your response rate, you'll need to plan out every element:

- Offer

- Packaging

- Creative treatment and production

- List

Offer

Forget about selling your product or service in a direct mail campaign; remember, the only thing you are looking for is a response to your offer— so make sure it's good enough for people to want to respond. Of course, your offer relates to the problem that your product solves, so that should be enough to entice list recipients to act. Still, it depends on the following three things as well.

Packaging

You are looking to create as personal an experience as you can. How would you package something you sent to a treasured friend? Don't do anything less for your prospects. Use the best packaging you can find: heavy-weight envelopes that are addressed to a person, not a title; that are stamped, not metered; and that contain gorgeous, watermarked stationery that's laser printed, not ink-jet printed.

Creative Treatment and Production

Of course, your offer and packaging should reflect the corporate identity of your company, reflecting the color palette, typography, iconography, and brand voice that you use in other channels, to create a consistent experience with your company.

Lists

There are two ways to go here: You can rent lists from credible list brokers (usually representing publisher, show, or association membership lists), and you can also use your in-house list (assuming it's up-to-date). If it's not, get it appended and cleansed. I'd advise that you do not use list brokers trying to sell you the installed base of your competitors; these are generally bogus.

Test Your Direct Mail

Just as you optimize your e-mail marketing, website, and advertising, you should also test your direct mail. This is how I first got started with experimentation—in the physical world. Testing will incur an additional cost through the mail house, but provides a helpful way to understand which audience segments responded to your offer.

For example, let's say you want to figure out which job titles that you target are the least expensive to acquire. You'd segment the titles into separate lists and track the results of the mailing. For example, in a segmented mailing of 10,000 titles each, we might get the following hypothetical results:

	Control	Title A	Title B
Cost of direct mail campaign	$10,000	$10,000	$10,000
Response rate	3%	2.50%	4%
Lead volume	300	250	400
Cost per lead	$33.33	$40	$25

In this scenario, we find that Title B had the highest response rate and the lowest cost per lead.

In any event, be sure to:

- **Segment your list** and personalize the content and the offer; this means you will have separate mailings to separate audience segments to drive relevancy and, ultimately, response rates.

- **Lead with enumerated benefits** to get the recipient's attention. For example: "Fill out this survey and learn 7 ways to optimize your website."

- **Be accessible.** Just as you would have your physical address on your e-mails, you should do the reverse on your physical mail—include a URL, an e-mail address, and a phone number.

Advertising

Advertising offers you many opportunities to get in front of your prospects, and it's in the artful combination of these approaches that you will see the best performance. As with other channels, you'll need to decide what it is that you are promoting: your company, its products and services, or a content offer. The good news is that you have many opportunities to get this mix right. Like most marketing channels, advertising is proliferating rapidly and now includes the following:

- Paid search

- Targeted display

- Retargeting/remarketing

- Social advertising

- Content syndication

- Print display

You might start by advertising a content offer that lists best practices for your industry. After prospects register, they are added to a lead nurturing list, where they are e-mailed increasingly valuable pieces of content and are retargeted across the web with the similar high-value content via display retargeting. Whichever approach you take, be sure you are using your positioning and messaging matrix to drive creative concepts and copy. At a minimum, you'll need to create online display and text ads that include the following:

Display Ad:

Headline

Imagery

Copy

Call to Action

Text Ad:

Headline (25 characters)

Copy (35 characters each on two lines)

URL

Paid Search (Google AdWords)

Paid search comprises pay-per-click networks such as Google and Bing, enabling you to target your audience and generate leads fairly quickly and much more inexpensively than other channels such as trade shows. Because PPC is so targeted, search volumes for keywords typically are fairly low and costs per click can be high. Research keywords for each phase of the buyer journey and make them as specific as they need to be for your market. Pay attention to match types, which also affect search volume.

The home page of your Google AdWords accounts will give you a quick overview of clicks, impressions, click-through rate (CTR), average cost per click (CPC), converted clicks, cost per converted click, and cost. You can view this for any time period and also compare two time periods against each other. This page also shows you more:

- Good-quality but low-traffic keywords

- Keywords below first-page bid

- All enabled keywords

- All non-active keywords

- All enabled campaigns

- All non-active campaigns

- All non-active ad groups

From the home page, the Campaigns tab leads you into a deep dive of your AdWords account, which includes additional tabs for campaigns, ad groups, settings, ads, keywords, audiences, ad extensions, dimensions, and Display Network.

Think of your campaigns as containers for related ad groups that are holders for different variations of ads. For example, you might have a white-paper campaign with two ad groups for two different whitepapers. Each of these ad groups should contain several ads with different headlines and copy to see which one performs best.

To figure out how much you should spend, consider a top-down approach. For example, if you know you have $30,000 to spend per month, you know you can spend $1,000 per day across your campaigns. If you are running five campaigns, that's $200 per campaign per day.

Regardless of how much you spend, the success of your Google AdWords pivots on keywords. Do your keywords receive traffic, are they appropriate for your ad, and are they plentiful in the ad headline, copy, and landing page (or whatever page the ad points to)? This kind of keyword density and consistency will lead to a higher quality score, enabling your ad to be shown more often over time.

Quality score is an important metric that is generated when your keyword matches a search query. The higher your quality score (1–10/10), the higher your ad will be listed. Google does this so that they show the best-matching, most relevant ads that get the most clicks; that way, the advertiser can get traffic and Google can make money. Many factors go into a quality score, including click-through rate, keyword relevance within an ad group and ad copy relevance, landing page quality, and site speed, among other things.

The Opportunities tab will tell you how raising your budget, creating new ad groups from existing keywords, adding new keywords, or optimizing your ad rotation will help you get more clicks. Analyze each one and choose wisely; just because Google is suggesting a new keyword does not mean you have to use it.

On the Tools tab is a Keyword Planner that will help you search for new keywords, understand their search volume and forecasted traffic, and brainstorm new keywords to plan your next search campaign. The Display Planner tool will help you get ideas for and information about where to place your display ads, based on keywords and landing pages. You should also use the Ad Preview and Diagnosis tool in order to test the efficacy of your ads based on their keywords; this gives you an easy and free way to search for your ads to see how they are displayed without incurring actual impressions or click-throughs.

With Google AdWords, you can report by keyword, ad group, campaign, and search queries; consider setting up these reports so that they run automatically on a regular basis, such as weekly or monthly. If you are just starting out, consider hiring a PPC agency or using a tool such as WordStream (www.wordstream.com) to help get your account and campaigns off the ground and maintained on a regular basis. WordStream has an excellent online education center located at www.wordstream.com/learn. For an in-depth look at Google AdWords, visit their help center at https://support.google.com/adwords/. There you will find everything you need to know about setting up an account, managing ads, measuring results, invoicing, and training resources.

Paid Search Best Practices

- Understand the keywords your competitors are bidding on and compare them to your own to see if there are any you are missing that are critical to your success. Tools like SpyFu can help do this by showing you your company's average ad position relative to your competitors as well as the number of clickthroughs of your ads versus your competitors' ads.

- Set up search query reports and check them weekly. Your search terms will evolve over time as your business changes and the market evolves—make sure you keep your keywords up-to-date in your paid search.

- Ensure that your content for each phase of the buyer journey is separated into campaigns:

  - **Being aware of the problem**—Offer educational topical content.

  - **Researching options**—Offer differentiated, benefits-oriented product content.

  - **Evaluating vendors**—Offer buyers guides, third-party validation, sample RFPs, and other vendor comparison content. Make sure you are using the right keywords to describe how your buyer thinks of you; in other words, are they searching on companies, products, solutions, tools, suppliers, vendors, platforms, or what? If you don't know, check your site search queries from your analytics.

  - **Deciding on a solution**—Bid on phrases that your prospects will be using during this phase in their journey, such as these:

    o   Vendor *A* versus Vendor *B* comparison

    o   *(Your industry)* vendor comparison

    o   *(Company name)* reviews

- Use your brand keywords. Although you might be concerned that this will eat into your organic search, I've found that a search query that returns both organic and paid results often get better click-through rates. Also, since only your company can use your trade-marks in paid search copy, you'll have a higher quality score.

- Know what kind of matching option is best suited to your needs. These include the following:

  - **Exact Match** enables your ad to appear only when the search is exactly the word(s) you've specified. You create exact matches in Google AdWords by putting brackets around them; for example: [site optimization tools]. If someone searched for "free site optimization tools," your ad would not appear. If you offer something very specific, exact match is your best bet.

  - **Broad Match and Expanded Broad Match** enables your ad to appear when searches include your broad match keywords as indicated by plus signs. For example, a search for "free site personalization and optimization tools" will trigger your ad if you have "+site +optimization +tools" specified as broad match.

- **Phrase Match** enables your ad to appear when the search keywords contain the phrase in the same order as you specify; for example: "free site optimization tools" will trigger your ad if you have "site optimization tools" specified as phrase match.

■ Review keywords with low search volume, and consider pausing or deleting them—they're just not worth the time, money, and effort. At the same time, increase the bids of important keywords that fall off the first page.

■ Sprinkle your keywords through the ad and the landing page in order to increase quality score, increase conversions, and create a better overall experience.

■ Combine your keywords with vertical information to match very specific queries; for example, site optimization for e-commerce.

■ Think about your negative keywords and be sure to review them frequently. Along with a hundred other words, I used "free" as a negative keyword and then promptly forgot about it until I realized why a new ad group for a free whitepaper wasn't yielding conversions.

■ Be as precise as possible in your ad copy. You'll have to because you don't have a lot of characters to use.

■ Think about ad delivery timing (day-parting)—a lot of B2B buyers do their research during business hours, but if you check your web analytics, you might find that many potential buyers are actually researching on Sunday nights as they gear up for the work week. If you don't know, check. You might decide to run ads all week at all times or keep them limited to business hours.

■ Don't forget to set up conversion tracking on your website so that you can track, in either Google AdWords or Google Analytics, which campaigns yielded the most conversions (and then track those leads through your marketing automation system to see whether they lead to closed deals).

■ In Chapter 4, we talked about the importance of testing your site—and you should also do that with your ad copy. Pit headlines against each other and test alternative offers and calls to action to find the combination that converts best for your audience.

Targeted Display

Targeted display advertising can be an effective adjunct to your paid search strategy. Although many marketers complain of "banner blindness," display ads can still be powerful aids in moving your buyer through the purchase process. Options include Google Display Network, Bizo, and third-party websites (such as trade media publishers), among other outlets.

For example, if you do an e-mail blast with a third-party publisher, also consider advertising on the site for maximum effect. These site ads generally have lower click-through rates than e-mail blasts, but are a useful addition to your e-mail marketing strategy.

Ad networks such as Bizo enable you to target display advertising to the prospects you care about, using criteria such as company name, job function, industry, and more. Also, you can use their tracking pixel in your lead nurturing efforts so that the prospects in your drip programs receive display ads from your company on the websites they visit.

The Google Display Network will display your ads on sites that use keywords that match yours. You can also target specific sites, pages, and demographic segments. According to the Google website, more than a million websites, videos, and apps are currently available. It's fairly straightforward to advertise within the Display Network as an option within Google AdWords.

For all of your display advertising, think about the range of sizes available when creating your campaign. Universally supported display ad sizes include the following dimensions (width × height in pixels):

- Medium Rectangle, 300 × 250

- Rectangle, 180 × 150

- Wide Skyscraper, 160 × 600

- Half Page, 300 × 600

- Leaderboard, 728 × 90

- Button, 120 × 60

- Micro Bar, 88 × 31

In addition, there are other display ad sizes that have been used in the past and are still featured on some sites, including these:

- Square Pop-Up, 250 × 250

- Vertical Rectangle, 240 × 400

- Large Rectangle, 336 × 280

- 3:1 Rectangle, 300 × 100

- Pop-Under, 720 × 300

- Full Banner, 468 × 60

- Half Banner, 234 × 60

- Button, 120 × 90

- Vertical Banner, 120 × 240

- Square, 125 × 125

- Skyscraper, 120 × 600

For a full set of online advertising guidelines, I encourage you to read the Guidelines, Standards, & Best Practices page on the Interactive Advertising Bureau website at www.iab.net/guidelines.

But don't stop there; consider mobile and video advertising as well if that's appropriate to your company and industry. For example, if you find you have a high (or growing) percentage of website visitors from mobile devices, it's likely they are using mobile search, and you'll want to make sure you are using corresponding mobile ad units to meet their needs.

Retargeting/Remarketing

As discussed in Chapter 6, "Targeting and Personalization," retargeting services such as Bizo, AdRoll, AdBrite, ReTargeter, and Google remarketing show relevant ads to previous site visitors. Also, with some of these services you can target ads to prospects in your CRM or marketing automation database as well as on social networks. This keeps your brand fresh in the minds of potential buyers as they are served ads based on their interests around the web. You want to be careful to serve relevant ads and not be creepy. Retargeting can feel a little bit like stalking if you don't take a light touch or serve helpful content.

Social Advertising

Just as LinkedIn is an important social medium, it has also become an important advertising medium. LinkedIn offers you the choice of a self-service cost-per-click advertising platform, as well as premium display advertising (the latter for a minimum of $25,000 per quarter). LinkedIn enables you to target by sector, job function, skills, location, and more.

You can also sponsor your social updates, effectively paying to promote them just as you can on Twitter and Facebook (this is known as native advertising).

Although advertising on Facebook can be somewhat lacking in ROI for B2B companies, they have introduced targeting that can help. For example, Facebook Custom Audiences is an ad-targeting option that lets you find your existing audiences among Facebook members, using e-mail addresses and phone numbers, among other things. In this way, you can target the prospects who are already in your database if you don't want to go through a retargeting service.

Twitter advertising enables you to promote tweets, accounts, and trends. They currently have an ad tool in beta with which you can create campaigns by objective, such as engagement, website clicks, lead conversions, app installs, and followers.

You can advertise on each platform or use a service such as Bizo to combine your social advertising efforts.

Content Syndication

Another popular advertising tactic is paid content syndication, whereby you advertise content offers through third-party sites and their external landing pages. These are typically known as guaranteed cost-per-lead programs. Given that prospects register on third-party websites, it's not the best opportunity for creating a consistent brand experience, but the cost per lead is typically quite low, between $25 and $60, and can be effective for top-of-the-funnel campaigns. Content syndication leads typically go straight into lead scoring and grading, and then lead nurturing, before being handed over to sales.

Popular B2B content syndication networks include these, among others:

- Madison Logic, www.madisonlogic.com

- emedia, www.emedia.com

- NetLine, www.netline.com

- TradePub, www.tradepub.com

One thing to note is that when you cancel a content syndication service, you should search for the content titles previously advertised in the program and notify the service if they are still available. There will typically be some sites where your content is still offered, which means your brand is creating leads for the service, not for you. Make sure they take down all your content.

Print Display

You might find that participating in regular print ads in relevant trade publications is a good way to reach your audience. Typically, there are two kinds of display ads (this is true for both print and online):

- **Brand**—Educating the marketing on who you are, what you offer, why you are better.

- **Response**—Offering content in response for a registration, typically via a corporate landing page.

Working in the Internet industry, I have not had great lead generation results with print ads. Consider starting small, with directory ads in trade publications, to minimize risk.

Lead Nurturing

Now that you know your goals, have figured out your messages, and have turned them into campaigns across multiple channels, the results are pouring in. But what are you going to do with all those leads? Not too long ago, they just went straight into the CRM to languish. Not anymore. With the advent of marketing automation technology, we can continue engaging with prospects and sharing their journey with them.

Think about all the different audiences you can nurture:

- Anonymous visitors (the majority of visitors who don't fill out a form but who can be retargeted)

- Known prospects, segmented by demographics or behavioral criteria

- Customers

- Lost customers

- Partners and potential partners

- Influencers

Nurture them through multiple channels to surround your buyer with relevant messaging in order to create buyer preference:

- **Drip marketing programs** delivered through marketing automation featuring new content designed for each step of the funnel in a variety of engaging formats including webinars, infographics, and whitepapers. Consider nurturing your prospects not more than once a week but not less than every six weeks for maximum effect. You can create any number of lead nurturing programs:

- *Welcome campaigns*—Thank prospects for signing up for a news-letter or downloading content. You can also automate welcome campaigns for new client onboarding.

- *Deal acceleration*—To help sales gain more velocity in the pipe-line, consider segmenting opportunity-stage deals and offering them social proof content (use cases, case studies, client testi-monials, or articles on client usage) and third-party validation (analyst reports and buyers guides, etc.).

- *Winbacks*—Even the best of companies lose customers, but there is always an opportunity to get them back if you stay top of mind and provide salient offers.

- *Up-sells*—Work with your sales team to identify which customers could benefit from additional products and services from your company.

- *Cross-sells*—Perhaps you have a great customer with many divi-sions that are not using your products or services; consider send-ing cross-selling campaigns into those other divisions that might not be aware that their company already uses you.

- *Thought leadership*—For those very top-of-the-funnel leads, you don't want to hard-sell; you want to educate and inform. Send them topical content, links to articles, and helpful blog posts.

- *Inactive prospects*—Every database has captured leads who then don't come back to the site; you can activate interest by sending targeted, relevant offers with a time- or supply-based urgency. For example: "We're giving away five hours of consulting for every new customer who comes onboard before the end of the year."

- *Competitive displacement*—You should know what sets you apart from the competition; use that information in every part of your funnel to differentiate your offerings.

- **Display retargeting** that will keep your brand in front of prospects wherever they are on the web. Create thought leadership campaigns for each audience segment.

- **Social advertising** will further your reach and visibility with poten-tial buyers.

Ongoing Funnel Optimization

In general, there are four areas of the conversion funnel where potential opportunities get lost:

- **Not in the Funnel**—The number of prospects who were served an ad and did not click through to a landing page. Address this through continual optimization of keywords, bids, budgets, and ad copy.

- **Top of the Funnel**—The number of prospects who came to the site and then left without filling out a form. Address this through testing and optimization of your site (see Chapter 4).

- **Middle of the Funnel**—Prospective customers who filled out a form on the site, visited you at a show, or downloaded a whitepaper through a third party, but did not become customers. Address this with automated lead nurturing and retargeting.

- **Bottom of the Funnel**—Clients who did not renew or who canceled. Research shows that two-thirds of B2B clients who cancel do so out of indifference, and the opportunity here is to engage and remind them of your value. This is where regular communication, client events, forums and online communities, and account management typically comes in.

Key Highlights

Demand generation is all about creating buyer preference. It starts with defining goals, understanding the buyer journey, creating content for each phase of that journey, and choosing the right marketing channels. You have plenty of choices in acquiring, converting, and engaging prospects, starting with your website and mobile channels, e-mail and content marketing, trade shows, direct mail, and all forms of advertising. Make sure you are nurturing leads as well as optimizing every part of the conversion funnel.

Recommended Reading

- *Balancing the Demand Equation: The Elements of a Successful Modern B2B Demand Generation Model*, Adam B. Needles, New Year Publishing, 2012.

- *The Marketing Performance Blueprint: Strategies and Technologies to Build and Measure Business Success*, Paul Roetzer, Wiley, 2014.

- *Maximizing Lead Generation: The Complete Guide for B2B Market-ers*, Ruth P. Stevens, Pearson Education Inc., 2012.

- *Predictable Revenue: Turn Your Business into a Sales Machine with the $100 Million Best Practices of Salesforce.com*, Aaron Ross and Marylou Tyler, PebbleStorm, 2012.

- *The Truth About Leads*, Dan McDade, Onsei, 2011.

- *Think Outside the Inbox*, David Cummings and Adam Blitzer, Leigh Walker Books, 2010.

Online Resources

- Buyer Persona Institute, www.buyerpersona.com

- Content Marketing Institute, http://contentmarketinginstitute. com

Endnote

1. "B2B Content Marketing: 2014 Benchmarks, Budgets, and Trends—North America," http://contentmarketinginstitute.com/wp-content/uploads/2013/10/B2B_Research_2014_CMI.pdf.

10

Programming, Part 3: Organizational Enablement

Although brand awareness and demand generation programs are important in generating visibility, credibility, leads, and buyer preference, marketing is also in a position to help sales close deals through sales enablement activities, to retain customers through loyalty programs, and to support the entire organization through creative and editorial services.

Sales Enablement

Enabling your sales team is all about getting the right sales content into the hands of the right sellers at the right time through the right channel to move the right sales opportunity forward. The place to start is with two-way communication—not just presenting what you are doing, but also listening to feedback, fielding requests, and asking questions to get further insight. This leads to better alignment between sales and marketing and fewer surprises. Here are just a few of the things you can do to enable your sales team.

Work Together

Meet regularly with the sales leader to plan, share status updates, and create road maps. Work together to create the buyer profile and understand what actions are important in scoring leads. Map out the buyer journey with sales and share any insights you know about the buyer's pain points, company, or industry.

Give Them Useful Information

Give sales plenty of content to handle objections, raise key questions, and add value to the conversation. Share the competitive analysis for your industry. Make sure your sales team knows about all the great marketing content available, where to find it, and what offers are best for what sales stage; you'll want to share the content map with them at the very least. In particular, make sure they are armed with bottom-of-the-funnel material, such as buyer's guides, as well as social proof, such as testimonials, case studies, competitive checklists, value or ROI calculators, and sample RFPs, and let the team know when new content is available.

Follow Key Accounts

Follow your company's top prospect and customer accounts on Twitter, Facebook, LinkedIn, and Google+; respond to their corporate posts and retweet salient posts. You could even set up Google Alerts for your top accounts and use news, new blog posts, and new content as a reason for marketing or sales outreach. To research the top potential buyer contacts, join their groups on LinkedIn, and respond to their posts. Don't forget to target key accounts with display advertising and set up separate account lists in your marketing automation system for personalized campaigns.

Provide Training and Support

Communicate product launch plans and ensure that the sales team is ready to sell new features and functionality by training them on the key messages and differentiators. If your positioning or messaging changes, and it usually will over time, communicate that to sales and consider a special update meeting/training. Present your annual marketing plan at the earliest convenient time in the new year, usually during the annual sales kickoff event.

Offer Services

Consider running customized campaigns for your sales reps in their territories, particularly if you aren't already running segmented lead nurturing campaigns. You could also offer to write and edit requests for proposals with the appropriate competitive positioning and key messages.

Partner on Technology

Make sure the sales team understands the tools you are using, such as marketing automation, and how they should use those tools and the benefits those tools convey. For example, with marketing automation, you'll want to make sure your sales team knows about the following:

- New leads

- Real-time visitor activity

- Insight into prospect behavior

- Where to find and how to use reports

- Where to find and how to use e-mail templates

- How to interpret e-mailed reports of visitor and prospect activity

Two additional ways in which marketing enables sales that are specific to technology companies are product marketing and channel marketing.

Product marketing is usually responsible for the product positioning and messaging, and turning that into scripts, competitive comparisons, objection handling, e-mail content, and other tools for the sales team. Product marketing is the keeper and advocate of product knowledge within a company, and as such, team members must have a thorough understanding of and hands-on experience with how the products function, what the key features are and their benefits, what the product roadmap looks like, and an in-depth view of the buyer's needs, wants, and aspirations. This is the team that will generate product datasheets and whitepapers, webinars, and sales enablement tools such as product demos, value/ROI calculators, sales presentations, and go-to-market strategies. In smaller companies, product marketing is also the group responsible for competitive analysis. For competitive vendors, you should be tracking their activity (and it's quite likely they are tracking yours). One way to do this is to aggregate their public-facing activity. For example:

- What news releases did they distribute?

- What are the topics of their latest blog posts?

- At which upcoming industry trade shows are they exhibiting?

- What are their latest tweets and posts?

Aggregating this information will give you an easy way to identify trends over time for each vendor—are competitors stepping on your messaging?

Do you need to differentiate even more? Are they headed in a completely different direction? You'll want to know, so keep an eye on it.

Channel marketing is a group that exists only if your company has a channel sales function; it serves to both market the partner program and serve the marketing needs of the channel partners, such as integrated technology partners, marketing or referral partners, and resellers. In this way, the channel marketing team will build out the partner program pages and sign-up process on the website, create program collateral, and do anything that channel sales needs in order to recruit new partners. In support of the marketing needs of the partner, they'll usually create a partner program portal on the website for the partner to log in and see all the resources available, with a quarterly communication about new and updated materials. If you have a partner program, consider partners as a segment to target and personalize—they should have their own e-mail list, advertising program, shows, and collateral. In other words, everything corporate marketing does to market the company and its products is fair game for channel marketing to use in marketing the partner program.

Customer Retention and Loyalty

Now that you've attracted visitors, converted them into leads, and helped turn prospects into customers, you need to think about how to help the organization keep those customers. Obviously, delivering on your company's brand promise is the most important way to keep the trust and loyalty of your clients. Does your product perform as advertised? Assuming there's no misalignment between customer expectations and reality, marketing is in a good position to facilitate retention in a number of ways.

After new customer deals are closed and onboarded, consider them as a new segment to which to market and communicate. Just because they are now a customer doesn't mean it's the time to stop putting the company's best foot forward. This is where regular communication, client events, forums and online communities, and account management typically come into play. Just as with prospects and partners, you can use almost every marketing channel to engage with customers and create a vibrant customer community.

For example, send *regular e-mails* featuring:

- Snippets from news releases, bylined articles, recent speeches, and awards

- Blog posts

- Links to new website content

- New customer case studies

- Product how-to's and other usage tips

- Product road map updates

Mention customers in your social media outreach; *recognize their good work* publicly. Work with customers on news releases and case studies featuring why they chose you and their experiences with your products and services; publicize, promote, and socialize these pieces.

Consider creating a *gated online community* (invite only) for customers so that they can share knowledge, ask questions, and collaborate with other members. Communities are a great way to gauge sentiment about your brand and help clients maximize their investment in your company. Use forums, Yahoo! Groups, and LinkedIn Groups. These communities could be organized around products, customer industries, or even events.

Form a Customer Advisory Board as well as a Beta Testers Group to *gain customer feedback* on the product road map and future features, as well as to keep key customers informed and engaged.

Assign members of your executive team to your key customers for the highest-level insight into accounts; if you have an account management function, these people would be the executive sponsors of such a program.

Ensure that your customers are following you on social media by inviting them to like your Facebook page, invite them to LinkedIn Groups, follow them on Twitter, and make sure you display your social media network links on all client communications.

Regularly meet internally to *discuss client viability* and assess any critical clients that need immediate intervention; this can have a dramatically positive impact on revenue by mitigating retention issues. It takes so much money to win every client; why not do everything possible to retain them? In addition, *hold regular check-in meetings with clients*, on the phone, via Skype, and in-person. *Invite clients to any nearby field events* in which they can learn something new about what you are doing, and also add their vote of confidence to the other audience members (particularly important if you are running prospect field events). Speaking of events, consider *creating an annual user conference* to discuss the product road map and keep your clients up-to-date on your product and company plans. Nothing beats in-person events for creating and maintaining relationships.

Creative and Editorial Services

Part of marketing's job is to act as a service bureau for the creation of marketing materials. It's helpful if you've developed a couple of tools to facilitate this responsibility. At the very least, consider developing these materials:

- **Creative Briefs**

  A creative brief is a form that you or your colleagues requesting a new project fill out to agree on goals, end results, and deadlines. What is needed? Why? What is the deadline? What should it look like, what should it include, what is the format, and are copy and imagery available? Sometimes, just the act of asking the questions can change the direction of a project. The more details you've gathered through a creative brief, the more aligned you'll be on shared projects.

- **Templates**

  Consider developing templates for presentations, collateral, documentation, stationery, and other shared items that colleagues can use to start from scratch while more easily following corporate identity and editorial style guidelines. Don't expect your colleagues to be able to create a presentation that conforms to guidelines if you don't give them a template.

- **Corporate Identity and Editorial Style Guidelines**

  One of the things you will do when you finish the positioning and messaging is to ensure that your branding guidelines are communicated. These include corporate identity and editorial style guidelines. Your company's Corporate Identity Guide comprises visual guidelines and includes usage tips on how to use the logo, the corporate and product color palette, specific imagery, typography, logotypes, templates for collateral, e-mail signatures, presentations, and stationery. For example, if you have a color logo, do you have black-and-white versions? Under what conditions should each version be used? Is it okay to mix the black-and-white logo with parts of the color logo? What is the aspect ratio such that the logo will always be consistently proportioned?

The Editorial Style Guide functions as the go-to resource for how to write for your company. For example, if you have a deep preference for things like hyphenated compound modifiers, serial commas, and standardized capitalization, you should consider creating an Editorial Style Guide. This is helpful for your writing staff, guest bloggers, and partners. Such guides typically cover these details:

- Your preferred external style guide, such as *The Associated Press Stylebook* or *The Chicago Manual of Style*

- Your preferred dictionary

- Your specific company and product terms

- Guidelines on capitalization, punctuation, numbers, and attribution

- Commonly misspelled words in your industry

- Voice and tone

- Trademarked/service-marked terms

- Product descriptions

- Brand promise and personality

- Corporate boilerplate

- Contact information for additional help from marketing

Key Highlights

While you are able to reach your audience through brand awareness activities and create buyer preference and create leads through demand generation programs, you can also work on enablement activities that create greater alignment between sales and marketing. In addition, marketing helps with client retention through loyalty programs and initiatives, and adds value to the rest of the organization through creative and editorial services.

11

Budgeting

Unless you've been doing budgeting for a long time, it can seem pretty complicated, but it doesn't have to be. There are some basic guidelines for B2B marketing spending that can help shape your annual planned marketing spend.

Approaches to Budgeting

Here's what I've seen from 30 years in the field: Most B2B organizations budget for marketing as a *percentage of sales,* and in doing so generally spend somewhere between 2% and 11% of their revenue on marketing. As a guideline, the larger companies tend to spend less, and the smaller companies tend to spend more.

From my experience, I've seen most B2B companies fall in the 5% to 10% range (which covers all marketing expenses—programs and staff). So for a company with annual revenue of $100 million, a median of $7.5 million will be reinvested into marketing.

As a broad guideline, in many B2B companies, marketing is now responsible for 25% to 50% of revenue,[1] so the budget has to support the brand awareness, demand generation, and organizational enablement programs that drive the quantity and quality of leads that result in the number of deals to support whatever dollar figure is stipulated, as well as the staff to run those programs.

In the case of the hypothetical $100 million company with the $7.5 million marketing budget, let's say that their base revenue is $60 million, and they need to generate $40 million in additional revenue to make their number. In this hypothetical example, let's say marketing is responsible for 50% of the revenue, which means they have to bring in $20 million in net new revenue. Let's say the average deal size is $400,000, which means marketing has to bring in 50 deals, and that their lead-to-close rate is 1%, which means they must generate at least 5,000 leads.

If 30%, or $2.25 million, is spent on staff, that leaves $5.25 million in the programs' budget. Typically, up to 75% of the programs' budget is spent on lead gen, which would mean spending $3,937,500 on lead gen, or up to $787.50 for each lead ($3,937,500/5,000). This is a high cost per lead, but because of the high deal price, it works. A company such as this is likely to be engaging in costly high-touch, in-person field events and custom programs that support large deal sizes and result in a higher cost per lead.

So using a percentage of revenue is one way to budget, but there are other ways to think about budgeting for marketing—and they all lead to pretty much the same answer.

You could budget by *campaign ROI*. The idea is to keep the campaign spend between 5% and 10% of the amount of net revenue expected to be generated. So if your campaign goal is to net $500,000 in revenue, try not to spend more than $50,000 on the campaign. If you use this method, you'll want to have experience and history with this method in order to hone your forecasts.

And if you are going to budget by campaign, you'll want to know what your campaign ROI number is so that you can do a *break-even analysis*. In other words, how much revenue do we need to net in order to pay for the campaign? Anything over that is ROI.

Another way to arrive at a budget number is to understand the maximum *cost per acquisition* your company is willing to pay. This could either be the cost per lead or the cost per customer as a percentage of margin of revenue. If you have a low profit margin, your cost per acquisition has to be pretty small.

So those are three ways to determine your overall marketing budget—a top-down approach as a percentage of revenue, a bottom-up approach by campaign, and cost per acquisition.

Another way I know of to set marketing budget is by *marketing costs per unit of sales*, in which you know historically how much it has cost to market each unit. So if you need to make $10 million, which means selling 20,000 units, and it costs marketing $30 to sell a unit, you will need a marketing budget of $600,000.

Regardless of how much budget you set, the big question becomes this: How do you figure out where to spend the budget? It all depends on your goals, and that's another reason why having solid (and the right) marketing goals makes such a big difference in success. If your marketing goal is to create thought leadership for your company, but your corporate strategy is to double sales, neither your marketing goals nor your budget will be aligned with what the company is trying to achieve, and all your planning efforts will be wasted.

After that, the place to start is to think about the balance between the cost of your people and the cost of your programs. You don't want to spend everything on programs and have no one to run them, and conversely, you don't want to spend everything on people and have no budget left over for marketing programs. A general rule of thumb is to allocate 30% to 40% for staff and the remaining 60% to 70% on programs—but your budget could be vastly different, depending on whether outsourced staff is considered in the programs' budget, in which case that percentage will be larger.

Then you figure out how to split the programs' budget between the various brand awareness, demand generation, and organizational enablement activities. Companies that are in customer acquisition mode (and do you know any that aren't?) typically spend up to 75% of the program's budget on demand-generation activities, with the remaining 25% split between brand awareness and organizational enablement.

Deciding how much to spend can also be a factor of market conditions. If the marketplace is crowded with competitors, you'll need to spend more in order to rise above the clutter. That same is true if you are a new company with no established brand—you'll have to spend more to get noticed first before you can make sales. If you are just trying to grow like crazy, you'll also spend more.

Key Highlights

Budgeting can be difficult if you've never done it before, but industry benchmarks and approaches exist to help guide the amount and percentages of marketing spend. Consider what approach is best for your company, the amount of budget you'll need to meet your goals, and how that budget will be proportioned between staff and programs.

Endnote

1. In one company where I worked, the CFO demanded that marketing be accountable for 100% of lead generation, and I think that's a big mistake. Both sales and marketing should work together to figure out how much of the quota each department owns, and come up with individually aligned plans to support those numbers. Not holding sales accountable for any prospecting at all defeats their purpose, unless you have a purely transactional e-commerce model (in which case you aren't likely to have reps at all).

12

Staffing

In the current competitive hiring environment, finding the right marketing resources and building an effective team are more difficult than ever. As we've reviewed the trends, technologies, and tactics required for stellar B2B marketing, perhaps none is more important than having the right DNA in place. But the right people are difficult to find, because today's B2B marketers must have an almost impossible pantheon of skills and talent. They must:

- Be able to turn goals into strategies

- Be able to differentiate their products

- Be able to understand the buyer journey

- Understand the mind-boggling proliferation of channels and devices

- Know how to develop engaging, well-written content

- Be able to execute programs and tactics on multiple levels

- Be comfortable not just with words, but also with math and analysis

- Be an excellent problem solver

- Have the emotional maturity and intelligence for dealing internally with colleagues, managers, executives, and the board of directors, as well as dealing externally with prospects, customers, vendors, agencies, and freelancers

That means B2B marketing managers must look for a new breed of talent, one skilled in both traditional and digital expertise. This unique combination, though difficult to find, is what will bridge the marketing talent gap.

Where to Start

The first thing to do is to assess how each functional area is staffed, based on the needs of the business. Think about the skill set you have in-house, what areas you can outsource (such as writing and design), and what gaps you need to cover with new hires or training. What kind of seniority do you need on the team, and where would the company be fine with a more junior person who could be coached along the way?

Basic Skills Needed in Today's Marketing Profession

Regardless of who you need on the team (whether or not you are leading a team), there are some critical hard and soft skills that make up a competent B2B marketer. So whether you are new to marketing or an old hand, you and your team must come equipped with the following skills:

- **Writing and editing skills**—It does not matter what your position is, what your function is, or what level you are at—if you cannot write, you should not work in marketing.

- **Clear communication skills**—You need the ability to express yourself clearly not just in writing, but also in speaking. You'll be expected to present your ideas, speak at conferences, run meetings, and keep everyone on track.

- **Organizational/project management skills**—You'll be juggling a million balls and will be expected to keep them in the air at all times. Professionals who can come up with ideas; get buy-in and budget; create content, events, campaigns, and results; get consensus; and implement, evaluate, and do that again and again are valuable to the organization.

- **Proactive thinking skills**—If you can think a couple of steps ahead and debate the pros and cons of different paths, you're ahead of your competition.

- **An eye for design**—Having a solid sense of what looks good and is consistent with brand standards (and what isn't) is helpful.

- **Proficiency in math and analysis**—You'll need to be able to figure out the budget, the conversion rates at each step of the conversion funnel, and the statistical significance of a website test, as well as analyzing referral sources to key content. So from mining digital analytics and customer data to ROI reporting, you need to be comfortable with numbers and analytical thinking.

But That's Not All

In fact, modern B2B marketers are expected to be able to do it all, whether or not they are specialists. The smaller the company, the more you will take on as a generalist (which will make the preceding list look like the starter course to a much longer menu of required skills). For example, these skills and abilities might well be required:

- Being knowledgeable and comfortable with new and evolving marketing technology

- Adapting to new tactics such as mobile marketing, social media marketing, and content marketing

- Understanding how to optimize the buyer journey, from leads that are not-in-the-funnel, to top-of-the funnel, middle-of-the-funnel, and bottom-of-the funnel to close

- Knowing what content to deliver at the right time in the buyer journey in the right channels

- Being able to segment and target buyers

Aptitude and Attitude

Even if you do not have all the previously listed skills, there are certain outlooks that will help you add value to the company as you gain the requisite experience. These include but are not limited to the following:

- **A willingness to learn beyond your comfort zone.** Marketing professionals who can keep their skills fresh by continually pushing beyond what they know will keep up-to-date with a quickly evolving profession.

- **A willingness to continually improve processes.** Just as you improve *what* you do, you should think about improving *how* you do it. How can you provide value to the business better, faster, and cheaper?

- **An ability to relate/high emotional quotient.** Maybe you aren't the best writer in the world, but if you can capture the emotional heart of a story and relate it to a professional who can write it for you, that's the next best thing. If you can listen to prospects and clients and communicate what they need, great. Paying attention, listening, and relating are key interpersonal skills.

- **Comfort with change.** It's important that you have an agility in adapting to change of all kinds, such as changes in the following:

  - Goals

  - Strategies

  - Competitors

  - Messaging

  - Colleagues

  - Leaders

  - Customers

  - Processes

  - Daily Routine

  - Responsibilities

- **Ease around technology.** As marketing becomes more automated, more complicated, and more technical, a comfort level with technology of all types is required. This could range from some coding to competency using software programs to quick hacks outside your functional area (even writers should know basic design hacks such as cropping an image in Paint or Photoshop and dropping it into a file, for example).

- **Bias for action.** When in doubt, work it out! Do something! Even if it's the wrong thing, it's better than sitting on your hands, over-thinking the next move. You will at least learn something.

Managing the Marketing Team: Six Key Ingredients

As you plan and execute marketing campaigns, ensure that you have complete agreement and understanding on six key ingredients for success with your team. Discussing them and agreeing ahead of time will facilitate a maximally functioning team (and save you some grief in the long term):

1. **Goals**—The team needs to agree on what they are trying to achieve, both strategically and tactically. In other words, they agree to and understand the overarching marketing goals, the goals of their functional area, and campaign goals.

2. **Roles**—The team needs to agree on who is doing what, both within the team and within the larger organization, particularly overlapping teams such as corporate marketing and product marketing. Not clearly defining roles is one of the biggest areas of personal conflict within a company, so agreeing up front can reduce aggravation.

3. **Procedures**—The manager and direct reports need to agree on how things get done ahead of time so that there are no surprises (such as something taking longer than expected). It's also helpful to communicate procedures to other teams. For example, the sales team is always interested in how the marketing team is doing things, and the more you can inform them and answer their questions, the better aligned you will be.

4. **Standards**—The leader needs to set the standards by which the department will operate. It's helpful to think about what your standards are for yourself and whether you have communicated them. Sometimes you might think everyone knows your standards when in reality they are not expressly communicated and therefore cannot be divined by mere mortals who aren't mind readers. Inform your staff of the standards and policies in place in the department and the company. Ensure that they know about the corporate identity guidelines, editorial guidelines, social media policy, and media policy.

5. **Expectations**—Along with the conversation about standards, you should communicate your expectations about everything related to marketing, such as adherence to deadlines, treatment of audiences (for example, are you formal or informal with clients?), and expected reporting, among other things.

6. **Consequences**—What happens if your team misses the goal, steps on some other team's role, doesn't follow procedure, doesn't meet standards, and/or disappoints your expectations? What will happen? Make sure your team knows the answer and make sure you follow through on those consequences.

A Day in the Life

B2B marketing is a lot of things—interesting, creative, challenging, analytical, and strategic—but it's not glamorous. The payoff of well-planned goals and strategies is content and campaigns that lead to new customers and additional revenue, and the road to get there is paved with quite a bit of hands-on hard work, including these tasks:

- **Communicating**—You'll be communicating from the time you wake up to the time you go to sleep—phone calls, conference calls, Skype, and water-cooler chat.

- **Writing**—From memos to e-mails, project directions, creative briefs, policies, implementation plans, marketing plans, and content, you'll likely be writing all day long.

- **Editing**—At the same time, you'll be reviewing other writers' work, editing and shaping editorial content, blog posts, and marketing materials to conform with corporate voice, tone, messaging, and positioning.

- **Planning**—You'll be planning annually and chunking those plans into quarterly programs and campaigns that will need to be created, executed, evaluated, and reported regularly.

- **Managing Content**—You'll be moving files virtually among your staff, writers, designers, and agency. Even well-seasoned staff can have problems juggling multiple revisions to multiple pieces with multiple owners and multiple deadlines while trying to do the rest of their job. I once distributed a news release on *BusinessWire* that was the next-to-final version because I had saved the final to my desktop, and the next-to-final version in my documents folder, but then mistakenly uploaded the wrong version. It happens.

- **Managing Conflict**—As in the rest of life, you'll be managing differing expectations, disappointment, interpersonal squabbles, misunderstandings, intrusions, and poor performance.

- **Influencing**—You likely have a point of view about something that you may or may not be in a position to implement (or don't want implemented), and you'll need to be able to influence your manager as to your position.

- **Meeting**—You'll be attending or running several or many meetings each week, such as status updates, planning meetings, brainstorming meetings, and vendor meetings.

- **Meeting Deadlines**—You'll be meeting (or not) daily, weekly, monthly, quarterly, and annual deadlines in order to deliver on your goals.

- **Creating**—You'll be brainstorming ideas, seeing which ones stick, and bringing the best ones to life.

- **Destroying**—At the same time, you'll be stamping out the bad ideas before they can take hold.

- **Making Progress**—You'll be making a little bit of progress on your plans, programs, and tactics every day. Sometimes you'll feel as though you've lost ground, but you will make it up the next day, week, or month.

- **Measuring and Reporting**—You'll be checking on campaigns, understanding how they've contributed to pipeline and deal flow, and reporting and/or presenting regularly on key metrics to your executives and board members.

- **Presenting**—You'll likely be participating on panels or presenting sessions at trade shows, customer conferences, prospect meetings, or webinars, contributing your expertise as an industry expert. If you are not comfortable with public speaking, get training; experience helps. Toastmasters, Dale Carnegie, local adult education classes, and professional associations such as the American Marketing Association and American Management Association, as well as national franchise trainers, all teach presentation skills.

- **Managing**—You'll be managing the following:
  - **People**—You'll be managing staff, dealing with executives, board members, freelancers, and agencies. Mostly you will be providing guidance and keeping projects on track while managing expectations. You'll be hiring, firing, managing, coaching, and facilitating workflow.

  - **Process**—You'll be creating standard operating procedures, approval flows, review cycles, and other means of creating productivity within the team.

  - **Technology**—You'll be on your own buyer journey, sourcing vendors, evaluating and implementing technology, learning new tools, and teaching others. Whether using, implementing, or integrating dozens of software-as-a-service tools, there is a minimum level of technical proficiency required to succeed in marketing, and the bar proceeds to rise ever higher.

- **Procuring**—You'll be garnering contracts for shows, services, projects, retained freelancers, and cloud-based technology.

- **Reviewing**—You'll manage review cycles not only within the team, but also with other departments. For example, if you are a public company, likely you are required to have all public communications, such as news releases, reviewed and approved by the legal department.

- **Budgeting**—You'll be budgeting, signing off on invoices, and asking accounting about the status of a check when a vendor inquires. You'll be making sure that the invoices you are signing are in line with the budget and that you have all the requisite permissions, such as P.O. numbers before starting projects with vendors.

Training as a Competitive Advantage

If you find that your skills or your team's skills are lacking, invest in training. There are any number of online courses, local classes, adult education workshops, vendor-provided seminars (paid and free), and industry conferences that can provide insight into the big picture as well as skills development in specific areas. Assess where your team needs help and have them come up with their own customized training plan. It's quite likely that your competitors are not doing this, given how little is spent on marketing training—so this can be a big differentiator as well as a competitive advantage.

Key Highlights

Technology has raised the bar in marketing, and higher-level skills and approaches are needed now more than ever. Professionals who invest in their training, have the right combination of aptitude and attitude, and can juggle all the elements of a typical day in the life of a modern B2B marketer will be the ones who bridge the ongoing transition to data-centric, technology-driven marketing.

Recommended Reading

- *Drive: The Surprising Truth about What Motivates Us*, Daniel Pink, Penguin Group, 2009.

- *Immunity to Change: How to Overcome It and Unlock the Potential in Yourself and Your Organization*, Robert Kegan and Lisa Laskow Lahey, Harvard Business Review Press, 2009.

- *Leading So People Will Follow*, Erika Anderson, Jossey-Bass, 2012.

- *The Acorn Principle: Know Yourself, Grow Yourself*, Jim Cathcart, St. Martin's Press, 1998.

- *Why Managing Sucks and How to Fix It: A Results-Only Guide to Taking Control of Work, Not People*, Cali Ressler and Jody Thompson, John Wiley and Sons, 2013.

13

Measuring

How do we measure success in marketing? Times were we would measure engagement metrics such as percentage of opens in e-mail and their click-through rates. But those days are over. No one really cares about clicks and impressions these days. With marketing being held more accountable for business goals, we have to measure in bottom-line business metrics. For example:

- Number of marketing-sourced deals in the pipeline (opportunities)

- Percentage of marketing-sourced pipeline

- Dollar amount of marketing-sourced pipeline

- Number of closed marketing-sourced deals

- Percentage of marketing-sourced revenue

- Dollar amount of marketing-sourced revenue

- Number of marketing-influenced deals

- Percentage of marketing-influenced revenue

- Dollar amount of marketing-influenced revenue

The best way to ensure that you are on track for what you've agreed to deliver is to continually monitor your funnel dynamics—what is happening versus what you want to happen—every step of the way. One way to do that is by sales-stage ratio analysis, which I've mentioned before; for example, the number of leads to marketing-qualified leads. The closer you can get to 1:1, the better lead quality you are delivering. But that's impossible, and you'll be lucky if 5% to 10% of your leads make it to the marketing-qualified lead stage. Focus on continually improving the lead flow through the pipeline as well as measuring the velocity—the speed at which you can move leads through the pipeline to close is also a measure of their quality.

Program Metrics

In terms of measuring your programs, let me suggest the following as a guideline:

- **Not-in-the-Funnel/Reach Initiatives**

  Typically focused on impressions, number of likes, and percentage growth:

  - Number of likes on your Facebook company page increased by X% year-over-year

  - Brand keyword searches to the website increased by X%

  - Social shares of your blog posts increased by X%

  - Views of content on SlideShare increased by X%

  - Views of videos on YouTube increased by X%

- **Top and Middle of the Funnel/Acquisition, Conversion, and Engagement Metrics**

  Typically focused on lead generation, scoring, grading, and pipeline velocity:

  - ABC campaign (webinar, e-mail blast, etc.) generated X# net new leads

  - Lead score increased X%; lead grade jumped a grade higher

  - Lead-to-close velocity increased by X% (leads are moving through the pipeline faster)

- **Bottom-of-the-Funnel/Close and Retention Metrics**

  Typically focused on ROI and revenue generated:

  - Percentage of deals sourced by marketing

  - Dollar amount of revenue sourced by marketing

  - Best sources of leads that turned into customers

  - Cost per acquisition, cost per lead

  - Increased customer retention by X% (conversely, decreased customer churn by X%)

  - Number of RFPs generated; net new revenue amount

The place to look for this information usually starts in your CRM; if you have integrated your marketing automation system with your CRM, it should be easy to generate reports on campaigns. Your marketing automation system will also help you with life cycle reporting and lead velocity, as well as your most important keywords search engines and referral sources (which should also be available through your web analytics tool).

Measuring Total Return on Investment

We talked a little about this topic as it relates to campaign ROI in Chapter 11, "Budgeting," but let's go into it more deeply here as it pertains to overall marketing ROI. There is a specific formula you can use to understand your overall value to the business, and it goes like this:

> Total number of impressions across all marketing vehicles × average response rate = number of leads generated × lead-to-close ratio = number of net new customers × annual customer value = revenue – total marketing expenses = your return on investment.

You'll need a lot of information to be able to use that formula, but it's an interesting exercise to perform quarterly or year-end when you have results that you can plug into the formula. It basically boils down to "marketing-sourced revenue minus marketing expenses = marketing ROI."

Also consider reporting on the customer ROI and ROI ratio; in other words:

- The customer lifetime value of marketing-sourced deals minus their acquisition cost = customer ROI.

- The customer lifetime value of marketing-sourced deals divided by the customer acquisition cost = customer ROI ratio. For example, if you spent \$150,000 to generate \$3 million in revenue, that's a 19 times return after your initial investment.

A Word About Marketing Attribution

You'll want to track whether marketing either sourced or influenced revenue. For example, did leads that turned into new customers click on an ad or a social post, visit the website, request a demo, download a whitepaper, view a webinar, read a newsletter, click on a lead nurture e-mail, or visit your trade show, among other things? If one of those things was the first touch, you'd consider it a marketing-sourced lead. But marketing does not source 100% of the net new customers; if we did, we wouldn't need the sales team. So it's important to know what influenced the buyer journey, and whether marketing sourced that buyer.

And that's where the simplicity ends, because accurately attributing the full buyer journey can be difficult without advanced modeling capabilities, but looking at marketing performance across channels will give you a better idea of how to assign value to your campaigns. If you take the examples in the previous paragraph, how would you know which activities were more influential than others?

The two important things to know are:

1. The lead source (paid search, trade shows, for example)

2. All the touch points that convert a prospect into a customer (retargeting, social, e-mail, sales outreach, etc.)

If you look at the buyer journey for prospects who converted versus those who did not, you will be able to see some key trends. For example, you might garner lots of leads from content syndication programs with third-party publishers but not see any of those leads in the closed deals for the year. Or, as you look at closed deals, you see that a significant percentage came from a specific trade show. That's a great start. If you use programmatic advertising, you'll definitely want to look into attribution solutions such as Convertro, MarketShare, and Visual IQ. In the meantime, there are some attribution models that can help:

First click/first touch attributes the conversion to the first click or marketing touch the buyer encountered.

Last click/last touch attributes the conversion to the very last click or marketing touch the buyer encountered.

Both of these are pretty simple, but they don't model reality if you have a long sales cycle with many touches along the way. That's where the *multi-touch model* comes in, which assigns equal attribution to multiple touches. This assumes, however, that all touches are equally influential.

Because that's often not the case, companies typically design a *custom model* that approximates their actual buyer journey whereby the greatest attribution is given to the touch points that have the most impact. You'll know what those are only if you can deep-dive into your analytics.

If you are going to perform marketing attribution, you must have a way to record the source of leads as they move through the sales cycle—be sure that the lead fields you have created in your CRM are also mapped to the contact records so that when a lead is converted to a contact, the lead source field (and all other fields) map appropriately. Also, make sure you associate contacts with account records so that the lead source will be captured on the account level and more easily measured and reported. In the end, you should be able to report which customers came from which sources without too much digging.

Key Highlights

There are many things you can measure and report on across brand awareness, demand generation, and organizational enablement programs—and none is more important than those that contributed to the bottom line. Find a way to attribute your efforts to company revenue.

14

Conversations with B2B Marketing Experts

Because this book has been written from my own perspective, I thought it would be helpful to bring in a few other expert voices to round out the picture of what it means to be a B2B marketing practitioner today. I've worked with these executives in various capacities over the years and value their opinions on all things marketing. These are our experts:

- Jane Buck, Director of Customer Acquisition, Dyn

- Stefanie Lightman, Senior Vice President of Global Marketing/ Corporate Strategy, Sitrion

- Alex MacAaron, Creative Director and Queen B, B Direct Marketing Communications

- John Matera, Vice President of Marketing, RedTail Solutions

- Hans Riemer, Founder and President of Market Vantage

- Heidi Unruh, Vice President of Marketing, PaperThin

Jane Buck

Jane Buck serves as the Director of Customer Acquisition at Dyn, where she drives customer acquisition and lead generation efforts. Jane, a 20-year veteran, brings a dynamic mix of business development through strong relationships, creative tactical process implementation, and portfolio analytics to drive growth. When not at Dyn, Jane is an acclaimed teenager wrangler, a high-volume crafter, a skier, and a political junkie. She served as the VP of Marketing at QualitySmith, responsible for lead generation and driving growth through partnerships with vendors such as Google, Yahoo!, Coremetrics, and SiteSpect. Previously, she was the Director of Customer Acquisition at Custom Direct, responsible for garnering 4.5 billion impressions in print and managing an online annual budget of $30 million. Jane started her career in Circulation, which she says is one of the best places to learn the math of marketing.

What does your typical day look like?

I have a typical week. I review my reports and "numbers" on Monday. On Tuesday, I make strategic tweaks and adjustments to programs to improve or optimize. Wednesday, I like to plan ahead for the next month or quarter by checking in on the budget or new content to invigorate programs. Thursday, I like to look into next week and meet with my boss and peers to align. Friday is a deep-dive numbers project with pivot tables! Analysis heaven.

What is the scope of your responsibilities?

As the role of "The Experienced One" on the marketing team, I have built my responsibilities to include coaching and mentoring the team to use analysis to make decisions, not gut or intuition, unless the numbers are not there to guide you. In a well-funded, immature start-up, I feel like I protect my company from making mistakes that will be costly and unproductive. In my role, I develop process, guide the conversation, and honor the ROI.

How do you measure success?

The success measure is always the same but reviewed from many angles: return on investment. I review the total portfolio, the channel, the offer, the segments, and the creative within each line of business.

Out of everything you do today, what is your most important responsibility?

Mentoring and elevating the experience of my staff and those that report to my peers. I help my team learn by doing...sometimes that means by making mistakes. My role is to minimize the risk and appreciate and share the learning.

What are the things you have to do to support/achieve that?

Even though I can do everything that needs to be done, I don't. I have to delegate, monitor, and build check-ins and safety nets. I hire inquisitive, smart, and eager-to-grow people.

What do you enjoy most about your job?

In my current role, I enjoy the diversity and opportunity in my day. I feel I can contribute on many levels, and when I am in the strategic conversations, my day is a win.

What's your biggest challenge and how are you solving it?

My biggest challenge today is sorting through the new applications that are trying to get us to buy/try them. We can get so distracted by the possibility of a big win that we don't vet them thoroughly in our complex environment. These applications do something, or do something better than our marketing automation or CRM components. The integration using an API always involves a developer and their time is overallocated. I often pine for the days of a simple Excel spreadsheet, ruler, and highlighter—that was easy integration!

How has technology changed how you work/what you do in the past ten years?

I live on the Internet, in the cloud. I can now work any time of the day or night. I can work from my car. I like the flexibility and that I am not bound to a desk.

Is there a worst/strangest moment you'd care to share?

I keep track of every mistake I have made...and in that I'm 30 years in, that's quite a few. I wear the small ones as a badge of learning and the large ones as a badge of shame never to be repeated. Of course, many of them were not even noticed by anyone but me. Thankfully, the ones that were noticed were not critical to the success or failure of the business.

What are your favorite tools you use to get the job done? How have they helped you?

Now my tool of choice is the *big* whiteboard that is omnipresent in meetings. I am able to outline the problem, review accountability and actions, and take a picture and send it to the attendees. My team finds the whiteboard activity very supportive—we stand together in front of the board to learn, optimize, and set a plan for the immediate and distant future. I rarely leave a whiteboard without inserting my "dream" for three or six months from now.

Sites you like to visit for professional advice?

I have little to no time to troll for ideas. I religiously read *Website Magazine* only because it is easily digested and typically a reminder to me that I need to learn or incorporate a new concept or revisit an old strategy. I like the print version as I can rip out pages for my team!

How else do you stay up-to-date?

LinkedIn. I like to tap my media vendors for ideas and always participate in their roundtables to discuss with other peers. I reach out to a handful of people on Twitter, and sometimes I go old-school and pick up the phone!

If you were to give advice to someone considering a career in B2B marketing, what would you tell them?

Do not overestimate the power in the data. In my experience and opinion, B2C is more forgiving and a volume play. B2B is about the data. You should make an effort for one prospect when necessary and don't overlook the demographics and potential in scoring/modeling.

What's the most exciting opportunity in B2B marketing today?

Marketing automation—many are implementing and few are implementing it right, but if you have e-mail campaign experience, jump on this train and enjoy the creativity of segmentation, messaging, and the power of the tool.

Stefanie Lightman

Stefanie Lightman brings 20 years of technology marketing and strategy experience to her role as Senior Vice President of Global Marketing/Corporate Strategy at Sitrion, where she is responsible for driving Sitrion's vision and strategy along with key marketing initiatives to drive customer acquisition and retention. Stefanie is a long-time marketing professional, passionate about turning great ideas into real revenues—the advantages that a clearly defined strategy and strong alignment between sales and marketing can bring to an organization. As co-founder of ifridge & Company, she has helped many technology companies successfully align their strategic direction. Previously, Stefanie held executive roles for several technology and software companies, including Open Text, RedDot Solutions, Akamai Technologies, and Sun Microsystems.

What does your typical day look like?

At Sitrion, I am responsible for all the teams that contribute to "go-to-market," which means corporate marketing, demand generation, sales, and product marketing, so my day can be quite varied. I spend a lot of time working through our messaging and how to translate what we do from a technology perspective into what makes people buy. We sell to both IT and LOB (line of business) so our messages need to hold value for the different audiences. I look at real-time activities/metrics to help make decisions and also try to be on prospect sales calls as often as possible to hear from the people who buy what they really need. The other side of my role is to care about the consistency of message and our analyst relations/public relations (AR/PR) approach. When it comes to our messaging, it's important that everyone from a developer to a salesperson understands our vision and mission and can translate that to their individual job. On the AR/PR side, it's about keeping in touch with the industry, what's being said, what's the perception of Sitrion in the market, and continuing to evolve our position globally.

What is the scope of your responsibilities?

- Team leadership/direction setting for sales, demand generation, corporate marketing, and product marketing

- Interactions with product development, support, and services to keep alignment

- Speaking at industry events

- Meeting customers

- Analyst and media relations

How do you measure success?

We are a very metrics-driven organization. We set goals along the entire lead-to-close process. How many marketing-qualified leads did we generate (by product and by buyer; i.e., IT versus LOB)? How many of those turned into appointments (a first qualified meeting)? Of the appointments, how many moved to real opportunities and then how much business did we close?

We have targets and percentages we try to hit, but it's really about assessing every step of the funnel and maximizing for results. I am a big believer in everyone caring about the entire funnel, which is why we've pulled all the "go-to-market" roles under one team. Demand generation needs to look at not only the volume of leads, but also how that impacts revenue. Product marketing needs to understand what is selling and what's missing the mark on their products to continually tweak. Sales needs to augment what they get from marketing with their own business development practices to ensure that each region stays healthy. If everyone can align and care for the same metrics, you will find better success.

Out of everything you do today, what is your most important responsibility?

Consistency of message—Sitrion has evolved a lot over the last year. We changed our approach to the market, added new products, and changed up the teams. This can be chaos to even our small organization. I want everyone to know our elevator pitch and feel aligned with our overall mission and vision. From there, it's about working with the teams on how this translates into their areas. What sales tools are needed? Does our website reflect our story? Are our product road maps aligned? Seems like a perfect synergy but it's a lot of work and repetitiveness, and at the end of the day, it's the most important role I have.

What are the things you have to do to support/achieve that?

I try to create materials that people can refer to, but I also try to make it fun. We rolled out our elevator pitch and then had a contest where I randomly called people and had them tell me the pitch. You need to get the people to believe it, not just repeat it, and that takes time and creativity.

What do you enjoy most about your job?

I love translating technology to the business. It is so easy to get caught up in the tech terminology but how does this really impact the organization? Talking to customers and learning how they are finding success makes the entire story come together.

What's your biggest challenge and how are you solving it?

We can always use more budget, resources, etc., but the reality is, that's not really attainable. So what can you do? Prioritize—this is where metrics come into play. Look at what's working and focus there; don't waste cycles. Leverage the fact that we live in such an open world. Social media, for example, is a huge outlet that didn't exist before. It's challenging because although there are more channels you need to feed, if done right, it can be very rewarding.

How has technology changed how you work/what you do in the past ten years?

Marketing is fundamentally different due to technology. The buyer can be completely self-sufficient—researching options and gathering reviews—and you now need to compete fully with that process. This seems daunting, but I think it's actually exciting. You can think about how you really talk to people during the buying cycle and understand that there are many factors contributing to the process.

On the flip side, our access to who's buying is so much better. I know who comes to my company website and how I can target specific buyers. The ability to stay focused becomes obtainable.

Best moment ever in your B2B marketing career?

Akamai was by far my best experience. I learned a lot about B2B marketing there and living through that entire roller coaster was such an amazing experience in general.

Is it the thing you are most proud of in your career? If not, please describe.

I am definitely proud of the work we did at Akamai. But on a personal level, I am also quite proud of my time at RedDot, which was a B2B content management solution that came along in a fairly crowded space. We quickly found our niche (I think clear differentiation was key) as a mid-market solution, and by the time we were acquired, the marketing team was responsible for 65% of the revenue from demand generation activity.

Did technology play a role in that?

One thing RedDot did well was invest in the right marketing tools even when budget was an issue. We invested heavily in marketing early and implemented salesforce.com and other tools from the start, making it easier to get very focused on our marketing efforts and track and readjust based on metrics.

Is there a worst/strangest moment you'd care to share?

Not really a worst/strange moment but one that I laugh at all the time. At Akamai, we had a budget of $40 million (or at least that is what I remembered) and then things got a bit tough. I remember my manager calling me in her office and saying we need to work with $11 million for the following year. I was devastated...how would we get it all done? Fast-forward just another year or two and I've operated budgets of less than a million dollars for companies with $50 million-plus in revenue. So, it can be done and done well. I guess I didn't know how lucky I had it!

What are your favorite tools you use to get the job done? How have they helped you?

I am a big believer in investing in tools that help with marketing automation. I've used Eloqua and Marketo. Regardless of which one you use, being able to effectively market to prospects and bring them through the funnel requires smart technology, so I rely on this heavily. The other tools include analytics and social monitoring. Knowing what the market is saying and how they are talking about the solutions you sell allows you to craft the message in the language of the buyer. While this can be done more manually, the tools help to get a clearer picture and make faster course corrections.

Sites you like to visit for professional advice?

- www.marketingprofs.com
- www.cmocouncil.org
- https://econsultancy.com

How else do you stay up-to-date?

I like to network with other marketing professionals. Living in New York City, there are a bunch of Meetup opportunities that I try to take advantage of. For me, I can read everything, but talking through success stories with others is most valuable.

If you were to give advice to someone considering a career in B2B marketing, what would you tell them?

Go for it. People may think that consumer-based marketing is "cooler," but don't underestimate B2B. We sell solutions that help businesses run, and the buyer is still a person who appreciates a clear and "cool" message.

What's the most exciting opportunity in B2B marketing today?

I may be biased here, but I think technology B2B marketing is where it's at. Companies need to make intelligent technology decisions to stay ahead. Taking something that can often seem overwhelming and filled with technical terminology and turning it into a compelling must-have product is a ton of fun.

Alex MacAaron

Alex is the Creative Director and Queen B of B Direct Marketing Communications, to which she brings more than two decades of experience in direct marketing, advertising, and new media communications in Boston and New York.

Her agency positions have included Chief Operations Officer and Executive Creative Director for Direct Results Group/SourceLink; and Vice President/Creative Director positions for Berenson, Isham and Partners; Cuneo Sullivan Dolabany; and Redgate Communications.

Over the years, she has developed and implemented integrated marketing campaigns for B2B clients such as IBM, GTE Internetworking, Forrester Research, Polaroid, Quaero, Avocent, Ahura Scientific, and Bit9.

Alex is the recipient of dozens of advertising industry awards, including numerous regional awards as well as national/international honors such as multiple DMA Gold ECHO Awards, the BPME Gold Award for Broadcast Promotion, and the "Best of Show" Silver Microphone award for a jingle package. She has judged the Echo Awards, the Caples, and several regional shows, and was a featured speaker at the DMA's Annual Conventions in New Orleans and Atlanta. She has also taught at local universities and frequently lectures for various New England associations.

Alex is the past President of the New England Direct Marketing Association, and the author of an acclaimed business book, *The New Marketing Conversation*, published by Southwestern Thomson. In 2008, she was recognized as New England's Direct Marketer of the Year.

When not working on advertising copy, she's a frequent contributor to the online magazine *Women's Voices for Change,* to which she contributes movie, theater, and television reviews, as well as lifestyle pieces. Alex is also the author of *Lovin' the Alien*, a popular blog and book on parenting "tweens."

What does your typical day look like?

I founded B Direct (originally as Plan B Marketing Communications) 11 years ago. At the time, "virtual agencies" were still somewhat of a novelty. Today, they are more common, and I enjoy many intrinsic benefits. My schedule (thanks to always being able to connect through technology) is quite flexible. Typically, I go to my office early to put the day's activities in order. However, I take breaks to drop off my daughter at her high school, midday to go to the gym, and sometimes to watch my daughter's equestrian training or events. The flip side of all this flexibility, of course, is that I'm often found working during weekends or after hours.

What is the scope of your responsibilities?

I'm responsible for B Direct's agency operations, client relationships and ongoing satisfaction, business development, operations, creative and communications strategy, concepts, and copywriting.

How do you measure success?

We're a direct marketing agency first and foremost, so we measure the success of our work by results. We are careful to articulate goals and expectations at the start of each campaign, and we work with the client to track and analyze response.

Out of everything you do today, what is your most important responsibility?

Helping my clients succeed.

What are the things you have to do to support/achieve that?

Listen, clarify, and then offer my best guidance and work hard on their behalf.

What do you enjoy most about your job?

The creative process and finding new ways to persuade prospects to engage with my clients' companies.

What's your biggest challenge and how are you solving it?

Because we are such a small team, we often have challenges where scalability is concerned. (See the above comment about working weekends at times.) Staying lean and nimble is, however, a conscious choice. We work with a limited number of valued clients and do our best for each.

How has technology changed how you work/what you do in the past ten years?

Wow, this is a great question! There is simply no way that we could have started (and thrived) as B Direct without the recent advances in digital and mobile technology. It has enabled us to serve clients without the capital expenses of brick-and-mortar office space, IT, or support staff.

In terms of the work we do on behalf of clients, we began as mostly a direct mail shop. Today, I would estimate that our projects break down to approximately one-third digital (web, e-mail, online video), one-third design and events, and one-third direct marketing (direct mail print advertising and direct mail).

Best moment ever in your B2B marketing career?

Winning a DMA Echo Award as well as NEDMA's Best of Show for a 3D cereal box for InterSystems.

Is it the thing you are most proud of in your career? If not, please describe.

I think what I am proudest of is not a particular project, but a body of effective work and my role in leading, training, and encouraging dozens of exceptionally creative people over the years.

Did technology play a role in that?

Yes! I am still helping creative people understand how to embrace technology. For example, later this week, I'll be leading a workshop for a team of writers and designers, where we'll cover how traditional copy and art direction skills can be evolved to work in new media, such as search and social sharing.

Is there a worst/strangest moment you'd care to share?

Too many! (This is tough.) There was the time we spent weeks (literally weeks) fine-tuning the color palette for a particularly challenging client. Late one night, going over yet another draw down at the printer, the client turned to us and said, "I don't know why I'm even here. I'm color-blind."

What are your favorite tools you use to get the job done? How have they helped you?

Again, we really couldn't operate without digital technology. At any given time, I'm on my laptop, my iPad, my iPhone, or some combination of all three! We use conference technology and document-sharing technology. We encourage our clients to embrace social and viral media.

But, somewhere deep down, I'm still an analog girl at heart. My absolutely favorite tool is my New Yorker Desk Diary.

Sites you like to visit for professional advice?

I'm a dedicated Googler. I don't have particular sites, but I search any and all topics related to my clients' products and solutions, their competition, and the tactics we're developing.

How else do you stay up-to-date?

I have been and remain active in the New England Direct Marketing Association. I attend their events (and often I help plan them).

If you were to give advice to someone considering a career in B2B marketing, what would you tell them?

That they shouldn't think of B2B as anything other than B2P (business-to-people). The best way to connect with an individual businessperson is to tap into the "person" part. For more than a decade, our most creative—and in many cases, wildly effective—campaigns have been the ones that resonated with the audience's inner vision rather than their job description...whether they saw themselves as a superhero, an innovator, or a rock star.

What's the most exciting opportunity in B2B marketing today?

New ways to engage with customers that recognize—and reward—individual preferences and interests. Successful communications strategies are driven by this focus on relevance and individualization.

Is there anything I haven't asked that you'd like to share?

I think a big distinction between B2B and B2C is that B2B marketing is often concerned with selling extremely high-ticket solutions that require an integrated cycle of acquisition and nurture. Compared to, say, a one-shot B2C magazine subscription mailing, this allows us to think through and fine-tune strategy. Budgets are often more liberal, and we can flex our creative muscles by developing sequential campaigns, 3D clutter-busters, etc.

John Matera

John Matera is Vice President of Marketing for RedTail Solutions, a Westborough, Massachusetts, supplier of managed cloud services. Before that, John was President of Qitera, Inc., a subsidiary of the German social media company. His 30-plus years of experience include leadership positions in general management, marketing, and sales for high-technology firms. He is a magna cum laude graduate of the University of Pittsburgh and attended the Columbia University Graduate School of Business Marketing Management Executive Program.

What does your typical day look like?

I use CRM and marketing automation tools to execute and monitor the success of inbound and outbound programs. Depending on requirements, this may involve content creation (we used to call that "writing," didn't we?), program automation setup, reporting, or website work. Communication with the sales team is a given, and those interactions are both informal and automated (for leads generated).

What is the scope of your responsibilities?

I am responsible for all of marketing, including communications, branding, advertising, sales tools, and operations.

How do you measure success?

Metrics on opportunities generated and closed, by source, are our most important indicators of success. I follow the numbers and adjust programs to improve performance and meet or exceed goals. Our close rates are quite consistent over the last five years, so if we get the opportunities, we make our numbers.

Out of everything you do today, what is your most important responsibility?

Lead generation. We have a well-honed sales process and quick sales cycle. Daily, I have to evaluate whether we are optimizing lead generation, including new conversions, nurtured prospects, and referrals from partners.

What are the things you have to do to support/achieve that?

The marketing automation/CRM system/website CMS trio is where I live. There are lots of other tools such as document creation and video hosting that are important to use effectively, but it is the setup and automation of process that are most critical. I cannot imagine doing marketing without integrated MA/CRM/CMS.

What do you enjoy most about your job?

Marketing is the best profession if you are a "people person" who likes diversity, as I do. I deal not only with creativity in words, sounds, and pictures, but also with innovation in systems, media, and processes. All of this is focused on interactions with real individuals. What could be more challenging and stimulating than that?

What's your biggest challenge and how are you solving it?

Administrative help is a big limiter. No matter how automated you get, there is always a need to clean and tune databases, enter information, and write reports. With more productivity, there would be free time for other important work.

How has technology changed how you work/what you do in the past ten years?

Systems used to control how you work; now we control them to do our work. The ease of implementing and accessing cloud systems, combined with flexibility to adapt them to our needs, has matured enormously in those ten years. I do much more marketing with vastly less systems overhead than ever before. It keeps getting better.

Best moment ever in your B2B marketing career?

When I got a standing ovation from sales at the annual kick-off meeting for implementing a new marketing automation system that increased the number of qualified leads dramatically.

Is it the thing you are most proud of in your career? If not, please describe.

The recognition from sales was an unexpected thrill, which made it my first thought for "best moment." I am most proud, though, of an animated video that I wrote, produced, and directed. I used outside talent for the art, animation, and voice-over, but the whole thing was mine from concept to completion. It was the first time I had done something like that. The result was very well received, and it came in on time and within budget—a very small budget. Making something wholly new is always stimulating.

Did technology play a role in that?

Technology was certainly involved in its production, but technology's biggest role was in the video's dissemination. Being able to host the video on our website easily with full-text SEO, send links to it in e-mail and social media, and see who watches and for how long is really amazing. All of this is tied into MA/CRM, so sales can see viewers instantly. I would only be guessing about the success of the video without that ability to distribute, measure, monitor, and react.

Is there a worst/strangest moment you'd care to share?

I sent an e-mail targeted for a specific set of partners to my entire database. The thought of all those "Why did they send me this?" impressions was awful. That sickening feeling when you realize what you did—and that it is too late to stop it—is memorable enough to make you very careful afterwards.

What are your favorite tools you use to get the job done? How have they helped you?

My three most important tools are marketing automation, CRM, and website CMS. I use Pardot, salesforce.com, and WordPress. They are simple to use, well integrated, and flexible enough to do whatever I need. Since becoming facile with them, I think about marketing and not about the tools. Of this trio, marketing automation is my favorite because it has been the most transformative. Setting up automatic alerts based on prospect behavior and/or grade has alone shortened sales cycle, increased sales, and cut marketing overhead.

Sites you like to visit for professional advice?

I pay attention to popular culture and what other marketers are doing. The spectrum from great ideas to utter garbage on radio/TV, in print, digital media, or retail displays is a constant source of inspiration and challenge for me. It is important for me to watch and listen to all those channels of information.

AdAge and Quartz are my favorite websites, and LinkedIn Groups are valuable for specifics on the particular systems I use.

How else do you stay up-to-date?

I stay in touch with colleagues through e-mail, social media, and in-person events. Every interaction is a learning experience in this field that is so full of bright, energetic people.

If you were to give advice to someone considering a career in B2B marketing, what would you tell them?

Learn to write. Read. Everything you do in marketing is language. You cannot express ideas in text or images or music effectively without knowing how to articulate them in concise, evocative prose. Everything else about B2B marketing is easy to learn. If you cannot write or do not like writing, pick a different career.

What's the most exciting opportunity in B2B marketing today?

Targeting of audiences through multiple media channels is now very sophisticated, but not all of what can be done should be done. Devising print, desktop, mobile, social, and broadcast media programs to interact most appropriately with prospects and influencers is very exciting. Those who know to use all this data *about* people to interact *as* people will succeed.

Is there anything I haven't asked that you'd like to share?

Never before have so many powerful tools been so easy to use at so low a cost. Any size company can do things formerly restricted to giants. You are free to use your imagination and hard work to accomplish formerly impossible marketing goals. This is a great time to be in marketing.

Hans Riemer

Hans Riemer is founder and president of Market Vantage,[1] a company that has helped hundreds of organizations increase their website traffic and convert more visitors into sales leads since 2002. Before Market Vantage, Hans worked in corporate marketing and sales for technology companies for over 25 years, including 4 years in Europe. He has led marketing communications and product management programs for Apollo Computer, Hewlett-Packard, Hitachi Software, Groupe Bull, and Novell, among others.

Hans started leveraging the Internet for marketing in 1996, when he designed and built an e-commerce website that supported secure online ordering for a company he co-founded. Intrigued by the ways in which the Internet could change the way businesses and customers connected, he noticed that it was very hard to find experts in this specialized area of marketing, hence the impetus to start Market Vantage. Since then, his company has developed, implemented, and managed hundreds of successful Internet marketing and lead generation programs for a wide variety of organizations.

Hans holds a B.A. degree from the University of Massachusetts in Amherst, where he studied architectural design as an undergraduate followed by a graduate program in computer science.

What does your typical day look like?

It varies. Occasionally I work on the business itself, which includes our IT platforms, HR policies, or dealing with administrative tasks. For example, we are in the process of migrating from a server-based environment to one where our data and applications reside in the "cloud." I am also responsible for most of our own content development, which includes our website copy and our blog. Most days I have some direct involvement with client deliverables, and I manage to fit in some learning every day. This includes reading articles and blogs, participating in forums, and attending webinars. There's so much happening in the online marketing space, you need to stay plugged in to keep up. You have to enjoy dealing with constant change if you are going to be an online marketing expert!

What is the scope of your responsibilities?

I have three main areas of responsibility. First, I bring in new business and make sure projects stay on track. Second, I hire and manage the best people I can find. Third, I manage cash flow so that the bills and payroll are covered. I spend a fair amount of my time making sure everyone is working at the best of their ability and our clients are getting our best work. I chair a weekly all-hands meeting in which we review how each client project is going. Each member of the team has unique experiences and abilities. Putting our heads together helps us come up with great strategies that produce significant, measurable improvements for our clients. This is also a time when we discuss our internal processes to make them more effective.

How do you measure success?

When I started this business 14 years ago, I decided that our strategy for growth would be to do our utmost to exceed the expectations of our clients. By doing great work for them, not only would they remain our clients for a long time, but they would also tell others about us. As it turns out, most of our business comes through referrals. Most of our clients have been with us for more than three years, with some quite a few years longer. We help them set realistic expectations and tell them the truth. Sometimes that's not easy, particularly when we need to tell them something they don't want to hear. For example, we are often approached about working on bringing traffic to a poor-quality website. In this case, we recommend that the client undertakes an overhaul of the site first, with or without our help. It may cost us in the short term, but it engenders trust. Our clients seek our counsel and treat us as an extension of their team. They may not always follow every recommendation we give them, for financial or other reasons, but I feel that our advice is always appreciated and carefully considered.

Out of everything you do today, what is your most important responsibility?

My most important responsibility is creating a culture of excellence in our company. I expect our people to stretch, to learn new skills, and grow. I am passionate about what we do and expect everyone on the team to be passionate as well.

What are the things you have to do to support/achieve that?

I spend one-on-one time with each individual on our team almost every week. We talk about their goals and aspirations, both professional and personal. We talk about what is going well and what seems to be more challenging, and what can be done about it. I reward initiative and hard work, both financially and with increased responsibilities. We hold each other accountable. When something isn't going as well as it should, we talk openly about what is happening and what can be done to improve it. Our work requires incredible attention to detail, and while mistakes do occasionally happen, we're not in the business of assigning blame.

What do you enjoy most about your job?

I love watching people grow in their abilities and confidence. We have hired young people right out of college, as well as older people who have been bumped around in the corporate world. The young and inexperienced usually need more coaching and supervision. Those who have already worked in several different companies may have been dragged into internal politics—I try to create a culture in which one is encouraged to learn new things and think beyond one's immediate job. It's amazing what people can come up with in such an environment.

What's your biggest challenge and how are you solving it?

It's difficult to balance resources against projects. Sometimes the team feels overwhelmed by the amount of work we have to complete. At the same time, I tend to be financially conservative and don't want to overhire and put employees or the company at risk. So we have a few carefully vetted virtual employees who extend our labor force. In addition, we have outsourced our bookkeeping for about five years.

How has technology changed how you work/what you do in the past ten years?

Our work started out being a blend of technical and creative, and that hasn't changed much. On the other hand, search engines have evolved enormously. SEO has gotten much more nuanced and complex, which is actually a good thing because it means that search rankings are not as easily manipulated. Online advertising has certainly gotten much more expensive. In B2B markets, we often see clicks for $20 and rarely see them for under $4, whereas ten years ago, clicks averaged about $1 to $2. There's less room for error, the stakes are higher, and the overall skill level of the participants has improved, so it's gotten more difficult to produce profitable results. That's been good for us because it means that our expertise is more necessary than ever.

Best moment ever in your B2B marketing career?

Easy: starting my own company and having the stamina and the good fortune to follow through to a successful outcome. It was a bit scary at first, but it's incredibly rewarding to earn your living with your wits—plus a laptop and Internet connection, of course!

Is it the thing you are most proud of in your career? If not, please describe.

It is certainly at the top of my list. I am also proud of an accomplishment at Apollo Computer, where I worked in the mid-to-late 1980s. This was a company full of exceptionally bright people. When they hired new salespeople, they'd put them through a rigorous training class that ran for several days. Marketing people from a wide variety of roles came in and gave the training, so each salesperson got exposed to about 30 to 40 individuals and they rated them. I remember winning the "Top Dog" award for best trainer several times. It was a great feeling because I knew the other marketers were really smart and engaging, so it definitely wasn't an easy win!

Did technology play a role in that?

You'll laugh. We printed our material on acetate sheets using an early laser printer (we had the latest technology) and presented them by laying them on the glass of an overhead projector. You could send out your files and get them done on 35mm color slides, but that was very expensive, so we used that more for sales presentations, not in-house work.

Is there a worst/strangest moment you'd care to share?

Overall, I must say my recollection over the course of my 25-year corporate career is pleasant. I got to meet many, many wonderful people, help lots of professionals and companies succeed, and I got to travel, which I like because I enjoy discovering new places.

That said, here's an episode of my life that was definitely challenging.

Shortly after I got married, I was recruited for a position as VP of Marketing of a public company in the Midwest. It was a technology business that was restarting after having filed Chapter 11 and obtaining a substantial injection of new funding.

I knew going in that the software technology the company sold was obsolete—this was the main cause of their Chapter 11 episode. But they had assembled a team that was developing the next-generation product from scratch and it sounded like a game changer for the industry.

The business and technical folks were first-rate and there was a strong sense of camaraderie, plus the key investor was an organization that seemed financially astute and had deep pockets. So my wife and I quit our jobs in New England, packed our household, and headed west.

About six months into my new job, I started having misgivings. The software development project timeline kept expanding and the Engineering VP kept advocating for additional prototyping and dry runs. A few more months went by and it started looking like we might be out of runway before we could possibly start generating any revenue from the new product.

A candid chat with our CFO brought more bad news. When pressed, he confirmed my suspicion that at our current burn rate, we had less than six months of cash left. I knew the product wouldn't be demonstrable until long after that time, and what with a lengthy sales cycle, there was no way to generate orders soon enough to keep the doors open.

I asked whether our investor might decide to put in more money, but the CFO had already asked and been turned down. It seemed they preferred to write off the loss rather than risk throwing good money after bad.

Meanwhile, my wife and I were 1,000 miles from home. To make matters even more interesting, we'd had our first child and hadn't wasted any time conceiving our second. We had gone from two incomes with no dependents to one income with three dependents.

In the end, I was able to find a new job back East, and we were able to come back to a fresh start.

Lessons learned:

Anytime you are offered a job, you should treat it like an investment decision. Don't skimp on the due diligence. I had been blinded by the opportunity to play a key role in a turnaround. The generous stock options sealed the deal. There were questions I could have asked during the interview process that could have spared me, and my wife, a lot of missed sleep.

Don't underestimate the amount of slippage possible in software development projects. Best-case scenarios rarely play out that way in reality.

What are your favorite tools you use to get the job done? How have they helped you?

Google AdWords has revolutionized B2B marketing. People think of it as a way to pay to get traffic to your website, but it's really so much more.

It allows people to test various bits of marketing copy to see what resonates better with their audience. It creates a controlled environment where you can test landing-page copy and offers. You can experiment with geography as well as different platforms like tablets and smartphones to see how they affect your outreach.

AdWords is an incredibly feature-rich platform for getting the right message to the right person at the right time. We are constantly discovering new ways to find prospects and outsmart the competition.

Having said all of this, Google is a public company whose job it is to make money for its owners and investors. AdWords is a highly complex environment. For example, the formula by which your cost per click is calculated is rather complicated. Keyword Quality Score, which affects cost per click and ad placement, is a bit of a black box as well. Some of the ways in which AdWords is configured seem slanted more toward maximizing Google's profits rather than making advertisers successful.

Sites you like to visit for professional advice?

- www.MOZ.com
- www.searchenginewatch.com
- www.websitemagazine.com
- www.webpronews.com

How else do you stay up-to-date?

We belong to SEMNE, Search Engine Marketers of New England, and attend their monthly meetings. We read a lot of online articles and attend webinars as well as regional events focused around Internet marketing.

If you were to give advice to someone considering a career in B2B marketing, what would you tell them?

Don't just take marketing courses in college. You need to bring along a second set of skills. I call them "intersections." For example, if you want to be a marketer for a company in the mechanical engineering industry, you should have a basic understanding of mechanical engineering.

I studied architecture, computer-aided design, and computer science before embarking on my marketing career. It really helps to be able to carry on a technical conversation with people in the B2B space. I recall my first 100% sales job where I sold CAD systems to architects. I could not have gotten that job without understanding both the business and technical sides of the problem.

Being educated in multiple areas gives you credibility. For example, if you do search marketing where keyword choices often come down to nuances around technical terms, it can make or break your success.

What's the most exciting opportunity in B2B marketing today?

There's so much technology available that helps target specific messages to specific people. Almost everything is trackable. I've seen CRM start out as an interesting opportunity back when we ran individual copies of ACT or Goldmine on our Windows PCs. Now it's a complete necessity with companies like Salesforce.com experiencing incredible year-over-year growth. I see the same thing happening in the world of marketing automation. A few years ago, almost nobody had it. Now, many companies have it, but are still figuring out how to use it. In a few years, companies will either master these platforms or find themselves struggling.

Heidi Unruh

As Vice President of Marketing at PaperThin, Inc., Heidi Unruh brings 20-plus years of experience marketing and driving business for B2B software and professional services companies. She has worked with Art Technology Group, SunGard, BurntSand, and MarchFirst. Heidi spent her early career promoting companies such as Firefly and Barnes and Noble with top high-tech public relations firm Cunningham Communications.

What does your typical day look like?

I begin each day with a team meeting to review progress, discuss issues/ barriers to success, brainstorm ideas, prioritize projects, analyze results, and make course corrections where necessary. From that point on, my day usually includes one or two meetings, always includes writing some type of content to be leveraged in demand-generation efforts, always includes planning for the next best campaign, and reading and researching where necessary.

What is the scope of your responsibilities?

Since PaperThin is a small company, I am responsible for the strategic direction as well as the tactical execution of marketing programs.

Out of everything you do today, what is your most important responsibility?

Owning and driving results.

What are the things you have to do to support/achieve that?

Content marketing is at the core of what drives results for my organization. I spend a great deal of time thinking about content, creating content, fine-tuning content, repurposing content, leveraging content across multiple channels, and measuring the results.

What do you enjoy most about your job?

Marketing is a spectacularly fun profession. There is so much to learn and understand. Things change on a regular basis as new technology emerges, which keeps it challenging and interesting. Crafting strategic messages, creating content, and getting to the heart of what motivates people is particularly fun for me. But when it comes down to it, the most satisfying part of each day is watching every hard-earned conversion and deal come in. It's all about the numbers.

What's your biggest challenge and how are you solving it?

I don't have enough people, don't have enough resources, don't have all of the tools I need, don't have enough hours in the day. If only...every once in a while, the thought "what if?" creeps into my brain and I have to shove it back down into the recesses of my mind. What if I had enough budget to hire enough people and acquire the right tools to do the job the way it should be done? Wouldn't that be something? I guess part of the challenge of the job is being able to do more with less.

How has technology changed how you work/what you do in the past ten years?

What a fundamental shift! The amount of data we have at our fingertips now is both astonishing and dizzying. Without question, data gives me more insight—more real-time insight—into what works and doesn't, which allows me to pivot faster. Prior to the onset of modern marketing technology (CRM, marketing automation, CMS, analytics, etc.), I had to wait until a campaign ran its course to gain real insight into how well it performed. Today I can gain insights almost immediately and reposition quickly, which helps me ensure a more successful result in whatever I do.

Best moment ever in your B2B marketing career?

There was one particular campaign that was at once a complete success and a complete failure. Even so, I am very proud of the results. While working at a professional services firm, I was marketing a custom portal solution to the insurance industry. This was prior to the introduction of portal software. We conducted a good deal of research and targeted 100 insurance companies for the campaign. We got 98 meetings out of the 100 companies targeted, which is extraordinary from a marketing perspective. Where we failed was in driving actual business. Every single company wanted our solution, but none bought because the organizational change required to make it successful was too great.

Is it the thing you are most proud of in your career? If not, please describe.

While working at SunGard, I was brought on as Marketing Director responsible for marketing five software products, each of which suffered from poor product perception. Within six months, I had repositioned all five products, plus another two that were acquired along the way. I created new websites for each, new brochures and collateral, new trade show booths, and new sales materials. I also conducted an extensive press and analyst tour, all of which resulted in a complete turnaround in market perception. The sheer amount of work that was done, and the outcome, are what I am most proud of in my career. When a manager gives you the resources and the rope you need to do a job well, and doesn't look at the mountain of work and shudder and say it can't be done, but rather says, "Go do it!"...that is the sweetest that marketing gets. I find that, more often than not, management puts the brakes on great ideas with hurdles to overcome because they worry that these ideas can't be accomplished. The real magic happens when you give marketers with energy and vision enough rope and the tools to do what they were born to do.

Did technology play a role in that?

At that time (ten years ago), the only tool available that played a role was a rudimentary content management system that allowed me to quickly create new websites for each of the products. None of the tools that I regularly use today (analytics, search engines, marketing automation, etc.) existed back then. We've come a long way!

Is there a worst/strangest moment you'd care to share?

Strangest moment...I work for a web content management software company. So, as you might imagine, we use the words "web content" in pretty much everything that we do. A few years back, some delightfully twisted person created a social media tool called the "sausage bot," which automatically retweeted any tweet that had the words "web content" in it, but replaced those words with the word "sausage." The results were sometimes pretty darn funny. It did skew my results, though.

What are your favorite tools you use to get the job done? How have they helped you?

So many favorite tools! The web content management system is one of my favorite tools (which I also market). It is so much more than simply publishing content. I use the social media tool within it to publish and share content with any social media channel right from within the user interface. I can tailor messages, monitor performance in real time, schedule posts for the entire day, see instant feedback as people share and comment, and respond to comments, etc. The insights I get from these social interactions help me understand what my brand means to people and how it makes them feel. This helps me craft a better story with clearer messages that break through all of the noise, and create more valuable content. Create content, gain instant feedback, hone your message, rinse and repeat.

Sites you like to visit for professional advice?

I really respect Mike Troiano, CMO of Actifio. He is a former boss and has had several blogs over the years that I read religiously: https://medium.com/@miketrap.

How else do you stay up-to-date?

I read blogs and books feverishly. Too many blogs to list, really. I watch Ted Talks, read the annual Wave and Soda reports, watch online videos of industry thought leaders routinely, read Gartner analyst reports as they come out, and meet with analysts.

If you were to give advice to someone considering a career in B2B marketing, what would you tell them?

Be a sponge. Technology is your friend. Watch for technology trends, but focus on what drives value for your customer/brand/organization. Follow the results.

What's the most exciting opportunity in B2B marketing today?

I would have to say the near-constant onset of new digital technologies. It's what makes our jobs as marketers exciting, and also a bit nightmarish. It can be difficult to balance the excitement that comes with a newly introduced tool, which we must master, with the need to determine how it fits into the overall picture for our organization—especially when tools are being introduced at a feverish pace, and existing ones are evolving with equal speed. You must continuously ask the question "What does this mean for my brand?" so as not to get distracted.

Endnote

1. I have worked with Market Vantage at several companies, including my current employer, SiteSpect.

15

Summary

We've come to the end of a long and interesting journey. Along the way, you've learned about the key trends affecting B2B marketers today, including a rapidly changing buyer and a concomitant growth in data. Today, you have more channels and platforms at your fingertips but also a growing responsibility for revenue. With new tools and technologies, you're expected to do everything more quickly for less cost and consistently produce results.

As you choose these tools, take care to put strategy first and thoroughly evaluate which solution is the best fit for your needs. You'll want to be able to derive actionable insights from your web, marketing, and customer analytics and think about using predictive analytics to take those insights to new levels. Taken as a whole, this information will give you a clearer picture of your website visitors, converted prospects, customers, and the untold riches stored in your database. Use this information to understand what's working and not working on your website and in your marketing mix and to help you mine for new opportunities among prospects and customers.

After you have a handle on your analytics, you can also use that data to inform your testing program, along with other sources. To build that program, you need the right people on the team, the right testing tool, and defined goals, strategies, and tactics. You'll create bulletproof test plans, which will help you with all the steps in the experimentation process. Continuous experimentation will improve usability and increase conversion rates. You can test anything, and you should, because experimentation is a proven technique to improve the user experience across many channels. Use the principles of conversion psychology to create an ongoing, scalable experimentation program that optimizes your website, e-mails, ads, and anything else that can be tested.

Then, use your marketing automation platform to programmatically deliver campaigns and track buyer behavior. Make sure you inventory your company's needs and look for the platform that offers the functionality that best meets your needs, from campaign management, e-mail marketing, landing-page creation, anonymous visitor ID, and more. Don't overlook the importance of education in getting up to speed on this (or any) new platform and setting expectations with other departments on its usage. Think through what you want to accomplish and why before setting out to automate.

Via your experimentation, automation, and advertising platforms, you'll be able to perform targeting and personalization to deliver relevant content to visitors, prospects, and customers across all channels, platforms, and devices. The amount of personalization you can undertake is limited only by the data you have—the more information you have and the more accurate it is, the more personalized an experience can be. But before you can personalize, you must target; before you target, you must segment; and before you segment, you must have data. Use what you know, append what you don't, and clean when you can to have the right data to create a relevant experience.

Having a strong marketing technology foundation will help you carry out the programs specified in your marketing plan after you've defined your goals, target markets, accounts, and buyers, your positioning and messaging, and your strategies in order to decide which kinds of messages, content, and channels will fuel your programs.

To reach your audience, you'll carry out brand awareness initiatives such as media and analyst relations, public relations programs, and social media listening, participation, and promotion. Next, you'll focus on building a solid demand generation program that will help you create sustainable, predictable revenue by giving sales enough of the high-quality leads they need in order to close business. Demand generation programs require the same kind of planning that all good marketing requires: identifying goals, strategies, tactics, and metrics. You'll create buyer preference by understanding the buyer journey and mapping out content and programs for each phase, defining your lead management and nurturing processes, and selecting the appropriate channels to acquire, convert, and engage prospects. These channels include web and mobile sites (and possibly apps), e-mail marketing, content marketing, trade shows, and direct mail, as well as all kinds of advertising, including retargeting. Along the way, you'll create standards, policies, and guides to enable the organization to put its best foot forward, and you'll help to enable the sales team close deals and retain customers through loyalty initiatives.

Your marketing plan will also define who is employed within the marketing organization; what the marketing budget is expected to total; what percentage of the budget will be spent on brand awareness, demand generation, and organizational enablement activities; and how you will measure success for each of those areas. More than anything, find a way to attribute your efforts to company revenue.

Final Words

You now know every part of a B2B marketing plan and planning cycle, and you've benefited from reading the experiences of other marketers; take this knowledge into your workspace to inspire new ideas, ways of working, and solutions to problems. Put strategy first and know there are lots of tools, tactics, techniques, online resources, books, associations, and people to help you—even more than what was covered in this book. Take a step back and survey your situation with this new perspective and do something different, something unexpected. Most of all, have fun; marketing is an incredible profession, and I am thrilled to have been able to share the journey with you. Thank you.

For More Information

I encourage you to visit the following online publications for more information about marketing and the concepts discussed in this book. These are just some of the sites I follow to stay up-to-date. Although these aren't all B2B sites, they are great for keeping up with trends, so subscribe to their newsletters or blog posts. Also consider subscribing to your vendors' newsletters and blog posts; those are a terrific source of information as well.

Publications and Blogs

AdAge, http://adage.com/section/btob/976

Chief Marketer, www.chiefmarketer.com/b2b

Chief Marketing Technologist Blog, www.chiefmartec.com

ClickZ, www.clickz.com

CMSWire, www.cmswire.com

Customer Experience Matrix, http://customerexperiencematrix.blogspot.com/

DemandGen Report, www.demandgenreport.com

Direct Marketing News, www.dmnews.com/b2b-marketing/section/1623/

FierceCMO, www.fiercecmo.com

iMedia Connection, www.imediaconnection.com

MarketingExperiments, www.marketingexperiments.com

MarketingProfs, www.marketingprofs.com

MarketingSherpa, www.marketingsherpa.com

MediaPost, www.mediapost.com

Search Engine Land, www.searchengineland.com

Search Engine Watch, http://searchenginewatch.com

Social Media Examiner, www.socialmediaexaminer.com

Target Marketing Magazine, www.targetmarketingmag.com

Visibility Magazine, www.visibilitymagazine.com

Website Magazine, www.websitemagazine.com

Advisory and Research Firms

Econsultancy, www.econsultancy.com

eMarketer, www.emarketer.com

Forrester Research, www.forrester.com

Gartner, www.gartner.com

SiriusDecisions, www.siriusdecisions.com

PART IV

Appendices

Here you find a solid outline of a corporate marketing plan that serves as a mirror to the chapters in this book; use it to organize your planning, and you'll find yourself rewarded with a full-funnel marketing plan that will help you achieve your goals. In addition, I've included a case study on my time as Marketing Programs Manager at Akamai Technologies, helping to manage the company's sponsorship of NetAid. It's a powerful story of how cause marketing can help a B2B company communicate its most important messages.

A

Marketing Plan Outline

Here is a sample outline of a corporate marketing plan that is helpful in structuring the contents of your annual marketing plan. There is no one right way to create a marketing plan, but there are plenty of wrong ways if you don't consult the data, past results, and feedback from other people. Make sure your plan is based on what you learned from the previous year's results so that your data is driving solid decisions for future activities. This marketing plan outline should look familiar, because it covers everything you've learned in this book:

1. Executive Summary

2. Situation Analysis

   a. Corporate Goals

   b. Company SWOT Analysis

   c. Competitive SWOT Analyses

   d. Target Markets and Accounts

   e. Target Buyers, Users, and Influencers

   f. Company Positioning and Messaging

   g. Product Description, Pricing, Go-to-Market Strategy

   h. Product Positioning and Messaging: Features, Advantages, Benefits, Differentiators, and Unique Selling Proposition

3. Previous Year's Marketing Analysis

   a. Overview (number of new leads, customers, cancellations, total customers, and revenue)

   b. Leads by Source

    c. Customers by Source

    d. Website and Marketing Channel Analysis and Recommendations

4. Previous Year's Key Initiatives

5. This Year's Marketing Goals

6. This Year's Marketing Strategy

7. This Year's Programs

    a. Brand Awareness
        i. Overview—Goals, Key Activities
        ii. Media and Analyst Relations
        iii. Social Media
        iv. Public Relations Programs

    b. Demand Generation
        i. Overview—Goals, Number of Expected Leads, and Lead Management Process
        ii. Website and Mobile
        iii. E-mail Marketing
        iv. Content Marketing
        v. Trade Shows and Events
        vi. Direct Mail
        vii. Advertising and Retargeting/Remarketing
        viii. Lead Nurturing

    c. Organizational Enablement
        i. Sales Enablement
        ii. Customer Retention and Loyalty
        iii. Creative Services
        iv. Editorial Services

8. Technology

9. Staffing

10. Budget

11. Appendices: Media and Analyst Lists, Graphic Design Standards/ Corporate Identity, Editorial Standards Guide, Launch Plans, and Media Relations and Social Media Policies

B

An Examination of the Marketing Communications Tools and Techniques Used by Akamai Technologies During Its Sponsorship of NetAid

In July of 1999, I joined Akamai Technologies as the Marketing Programs Manager to help market Akamai's sponsorship of NetAid. What follows is my experience of that endeavor and a powerful story of how a B2B company can use cause marketing to serve its objectives. "Cause marketing" refers to for-profit businesses and non-profit organizations teaming up for a common cause. I specifically wanted to share this case study not only because it was one of the most exciting projects I've ever worked on, but also because NetAid was an excellent example of how cause marketing can help both companies and their non-profit partners meet their individual goals.

NetAid was created as a public-private partnership between Cisco Systems and the United Nations Development Programme (UNDP), with a mission of raising public awareness and action in the UN's fight against extreme poverty, characterized as living on less than a dollar a day. According to its organizers, NetAid marked the first time that the Internet, television, radio, and world-class artists joined globally to fight poverty.

The scope of the project included creating the NetAid website, www.netaid. org, and producing three overlapping concerts in October of 1999, which would be simulcast around the world on the web, TV, and radio. The website was critical in terms of streaming concert footage and securing donations and volunteer commitments from viewers.

Akamai leveraged NetAid as a way to build out its Internet content delivery server network to carry the content of what was expected to be the biggest Internet multimedia event to date, helping to create the business case for its ensuing IPO, also slated for October. The company's slogan for the project was appropriately "Akamai: Now Serving a Higher Cause."

NetAid's goal was to generate millions of hits and actions to fight poverty—from donations of time and money, to the contribution of ideas and involvement with leading anti-poverty organizations. NetAid followed in the footsteps of other high-profile cause marketing-related concerts, such as LiveAid and Farm Aid, but with the addition of an important communications channel—the World Wide Web—and featured several concerts in different venues rather than just one concert, which increased the complexity of its planning and production.

Akamai had begun as a company dedicated to ending the "World Wide Wait" through intelligent Internet content delivery. That means its services were designed to speed up the download of rich media, such as video, photos, Flash demos, and other graphic-intensive files. The company officially launched commercial service in April of 1999 with the announcement of Yahoo! as a charter customer. Now the company wanted to find a way to rise above the thundering noise of the dot-com boom to increase its visibility and cement its reputation.

For Akamai, one of the opportunities to do so came in the form of NetAid, when the company was approached in the Spring of 1999 by Cisco Systems, which had recently created the NetAid initiative with the UNDP.[1]

ZDNet.com (Ziff Davis) reported: "NetAid is expected to be the biggest event ever to hit the web. The NetAid.org site, built by corporate sponsor KPMG, expects to receive 60 million hits an hour on Saturday. Akamai Technologies and RealNetworks, which will manage serving the content and streaming video, are prepared to handle 125,000 simultaneous streams. Kim King, Akamai's NetAid program manager, estimates her company has donated time and equipment worth millions of dollars. 'High-tech companies get a bad rap for not caring about social issues,' King said. 'This is something the industry is really standing up for. It's something worthy, something precedent-setting.'"[2]

NetAid represented a global opportunity to team up with huge industry players and increase Akamai's profile in the marketplace. Thus, Akamai and KPMG signed onto this innovative fund-raising initiative as co-sponsors in April of 1999. I joined Akamai as the NetAid Program Manager in July of 1999. I had been busy with another start-up that had gone out of business when I called my former manager, Wendy Ziner, asking her for guidance on next steps. I had previously worked for her at Open Market, an e-commerce provider. She went on to describe the NetAid project, the opportunity to combine high-tech marketing with doing some good in the world, and I jumped onboard as quickly as I could.

In this capacity, I was responsible for promoting and coordinating Akamai's involvement in NetAid via all of our various marketing communications activities, including public relations, advertising, collateral, events, online marketing, and initiatives. There were several people on Akamai's NetAid marketing team, and my job was to make sure everything was coordinated, accurate, effective, on time, and on budget.

Strategic Communications Planning

The first communications planning meeting had already happened in May of 1999 at the Executive Briefing Center at Cisco headquarters in California, shortly after Akamai had publicly launched itself in April. The teams from each sponsor were introduced to each other and agendas were set for the follow-on meetings. From there, there were weekly conference calls and rafts of e-mails to facilitate the coordination of every single event detail—musicians, technology, marketing, logistics, and so on.

The Akamai team (now including me) went back to Cisco's offices in July to hash out the communications details, including the timing of news releases, press conferences, the creation of collateral, and advertising. Most important among these details was the public relations strategy and execution.

Cisco took the communications lead on the event. The planning included in-person and conference call meetings with communications representatives from Cisco, KPMG, and Akamai. There were several phases leading up to the actual concerts in which PR strategy was required, including these:

- Drafting initial releases announcing the events

- Holding two press conferences in New York City that included celebrity appearances from musicians and politicians

- The concerts themselves, which included on-site press briefings

- Follow-on news about how much money was raised

By the end of the strategic communications planning process, each sponsor had crafted their key messages to be promoted by their spokespeople to the media.

Timeline

NetAid was announced to the world in August of 1999 with a news conference in New York, attended by not only all the corporate co-sponsors and music media, but also the performing artists signed up to date.

Then, a month later, NetAid convened another news conference at the UN to launch the website.

In October of 1999, the NetAid concerts featuring dozens of performing artists were held at Giants Stadium in New York, Wembley Stadium in London, and the UN's Palais des Nations headquarters in Geneva, and simulcast live on MTV, VH1, BBC1, and www.netaid.org.

Here is an overview of the quick-moving timeline:

- **April**—Akamai publicly launches as a company. Cisco Systems approaches the company with the NetAid sponsorship opportunity.

- **May**—Kick-off meeting at Cisco headquarters; communications planning underway.

- **June/July**—Communications planning continues with weekly conference calls and a second visit to Cisco.

- **August**—The first of two news conferences is held, introducing the initiative and initial lineup of musicians and locales.

- **September**—The second news conference is held, unveiling the NetAid website and updating the world press on recent additions to the musical roster.

- **October**—Concerts are held; Akamai successfully IPOs several weeks later.

Marketing Communications Tools and Tactics

Press Releases

Akamai's PR team wrote and issued two news releases (September 21 and October 14) and participated in three others (two on August 12 and one on September 8). These news releases gave Akamai the ability to tell its side of the story and promote its participation in the NetAid initiative.

The news releases built the story of Akamai's involvement. They first introduced the concept of NetAid; subsequently announced the sponsors, the performers, the website, and the Internet service provider (ISP) partners; and then shared the results. Here are the headlines from each of the news releases:

- **August 12**—Akamai, KPMG Join Cisco Systems, UNDP in Building NetAid Technology[3]

- **August 12**—Top Performers Join Cisco Systems and UNDP to Help End Extreme Poverty

- **September 8**—Clinton, Mandela, and Blair Make First Hits on NetAid Web Site

- **September 21**—Akamai Taps Network Providers in Support of NetAid[4]

- **October 14**—Akamai Delivers for NetAid[5]

Akamai and the NetAid sponsors targeted top-tier press such as *Reuters*, *Businessweek*, *Washington Post*, *USA Today*, *Forbes*, and *US News and World Report*, and local dailies such as *The Boston Globe*, as well as technology publishers such as Ziff Davis and CMP publications. The resulting press coverage was both extensive—the NetAid story was picked up in newspapers, magazines, radio, and TV worldwide—and on message.

Press Conferences

Two news conferences were held: one on August 12 announcing the initiative, the sponsors, and the musicians, and the other on September 8 unveiling the website. The news releases were timed to coincide with the news conferences. Both news conferences were held in New York, given that the location is the headquarters not only of the UN, but also of music journalists worldwide.

The first press conference featured the likes of Quincy Jones, Bono, David Bowie, Puff Daddy (Sean Combs, now known as Diddy), Wyclef Jean, and Stereophonics, as well as the corporate sponsors. The second press conference to launch the website was held on September 8 at the UN, presided over by Kofi Annan, then Secretary-General of the United Nations, who officially unveiled the NetAid website with streamed, live participation from Bill Clinton, President of the United States; Tony Blair, Prime Minister of Great Britain; and Nelson Mandela, President of South Africa, who were the first visitors to click on the NetAid website. This press conference also featured the release of a new single by Bono and Wyclef Jean called "New Day," which received rotation on video music cable channels VH1 and MTV.

Online Marketing

Akamai's online marketing efforts for NetAid were both broad and deep. Akamai was featured on the NetAid website and also built a microsite, as well as a send-to-a-friend screensaver. The microsite featured information on NetAid and Akamai's involvement in the initiative. The screensaver was an animated version of one page of the microsite with the message "The Power to Alleviate Extreme Poverty Is Now Online" and was eventually downloaded by thousands of visitors. The look and feel of the microsite as well as the screensaver matched that of the collateral and advertising, underscoring Akamai's visual brand consistency.

Partner Marketing

As part of the massive server deployment required to stream the NetAid webcasts, Akamai needed to sign up as many ISP partners as possible. This was a strategic initiative in introducing Akamai to the ISP community and boosting the Akamai Accelerated Network Program (AANP), Akamai's ISP partner program.

Stefanie Lightman, one of the B2B marketing experts featured in this book, came onboard to direct the marketing aspects of the ISP recruitment program. For NetAid, those efforts included a news release and a two-page "thank-you" ad, which ran in the December 1999 issue of *BoardWatch* magazine and highlighted 33 ISPs. It was designed according to Akamai's graphics standards, using the look and feel of Akamai's NetAid collateral and microsite. This ad served three purposes: to thank the ISPs, to continue the promotion of NetAid, and to provide information on how to join the AANP.

Akamai also produced a direct response piece targeted toward partners who would be attending Internet World, which was held October 6–8, 1999, in New York, right before the NetAid concerts on October 9. The company used a drawing for free NetAid tickets to entice potential partners to the booth.

Collateral

Akamai created an 11×17-inch single-fold brochure with a semicircular full-page die cut on the front, with the message "Now Serving a Higher Cause." This slogan was meant as a double entendre given that Akamai serves content over the Internet. The brochure was included in all of Akamai's information kits promoting the event, which were distributed at the news conferences and also given to prospective customers.

Special Events

At the NetAid concerts at Giants Stadium in New Jersey and Wembley Stadium in London, Akamai hosted special events for its prospects, customers, partners, investors, and employees. These events, which were coordinated with the other sponsors, were held in the entertaining area at each stadium. For Wembley, Akamai's European salespeople invited prospects, customers, and partners directly. The Geneva concert at the Palais des Nations at the UN was the premier invitation-only concert locale.

Each of the concerts featured a press tent, and within the one at Giants Stadium, Akamai played a live image of the globe lighting up with all the online traffic from the concert, linking Akamai with its ability to effortlessly carry huge amounts of Internet traffic. This image was also featured in video news releases created and distributed during the press conferences.

Results

According to a news release issued by Cisco Systems over BusinessWire on October 15, 1999, "Powered by three concerts and television and radio broadcasts, netaid.org has registered 40,289,689 hits from people in 160 countries....These hits include over 2,000 registrations by non-governmental organizations and UN agencies, representing the front lines in the war on poverty, which have signed up to participate on the website. These numbers make www.netaid.org one of the most successful launches ever of a non-commercial website."

According to Keynote Systems, an independent Internet performance measurement company, Akamai enabled the NetAid.org home page to be delivered 32% faster than the average download speed of the top websites evaluated in the Keynote Business 40 Internet Performance Index for the week before the event. And Akamai signed up dozens of Internet service provider partners to build out its server network to 1,200 servers deployed across 40 carrier networks in 24 countries at the time. Today, Akamai has deployed the most pervasive, highly distributed cloud optimization platform with more than 160,000 servers in 95 countries within more than 1,200 networks, according to its website—and NetAid was a significant start to that growth. Today, Akamai carries approximately 15% to 30% of all Internet traffic.

The NetAid website raised tens of millions of dollars in a single evening from corporate sponsors and online donations. Due to its involvement, Akamai netted hundreds, if not thousands, of news articles published on the web, on radio, on TV, and in print. Three weeks later, Akamai went on to complete one of the most successful IPOs on NASDAQ in 1999—in a year that featured extremely successful IPOs.[6]

Postscript

Looking back on what was one of the highlights of my career, I am struck by how much marketing has changed in the past 15 years and how different it would be to market the NetAid cause today. For example, consider the plethora of initiatives that did not take place because they weren't invented yet:

- There was no pre-event, event, or post-event promotion over social media networks such as Twitter, Facebook, LinkedIn, Google+, Pinterest, and Instagram. Had NetAid happened today, I am sure there would have been coordinated, individualized outreach social promotion campaigns for each network.

- Although there was a website and microsite, there was no allowance for mobile because no one was looking at Internet content on mobile phones. Today, there would likely have been a responsive site *and* a mobile app.

- Although we did e-mail marketing, I am sure it would be much easier today with marketing automation to build the microsite, capture data, personalize the experience, and nurture these contacts.

- We likely would have run online advertising campaigns through Google, Bing, Facebook, LinkedIn, Bizo, ReTargeter, or AdRoll, and others.

- The analytics we gathered from the website were fairly basic compared to today's number-crunching approach in which we would surely analyze visitor flow through the website and experiment with various elements until the site was optimized for visitors to make donations.

Key Highlights

I wanted to share this case study because it was the best project I've ever worked on. A great deal of effort went into getting the messages right, telling Akamai's story through its support of the cause, and connecting that story with its intended audiences of prospects, customers, partners, investors, employees, analysts, and the general public. In the end, we were able to do some good in the world as well as promote our own cause, both toward successful ends. What could be better than that?

Endnotes

1. "An Unlikely Net Alliance Cisco, U.N. Plan Site to Fight Third World Poverty," *Washington Post*, August 12, 1999, www.cisco.com/netaid/wp.html.

2. "NetAid: The Net Fights World Hunger," ZDNet.com, October 8, 1999, www.zdnet.com/news/netaid-the-net-fights-world-hunger/103458.

3. "Akamai, KPMG Join Cisco Systems, UNDP in Building NetAid Technology," Akamai Technologies, August 15, 1999, www.akamai.com/html/about/press/releases/1999/press_081599a.html.

4. "Akamai Taps Network Providers in Support of NetAid," Akamai Technologies, September 21, 1999, www.akamai.com/html/about/press/releases/1999/press_092199.html.

5. "Akamai Delivers for NetAid," Akamai Technologies, October 14, 1999, www.akamai.com/html/about/press/releases/1999/press_101499.html.

6. "Akamai Shares Ride a Wave on Wall Street," Cnet.com, November 1, 1999, http://news.cnet.com/Akamai-shares-ride-a-wave-on-Wall-Street/2100-1033_3-232226.html.

Index

B